THE ERNEST BECKER READER

THE ERNEST BECKER READER

Selected, Edited, and Introduced by

Daniel Liechty

The Ernest Becker Foundation
in association with
The University of Washington Press
Seattle and London

© 2005 by the Ernest Becker Foundation
Printed in the United States of America
Design and composition by Marna Jeanne Lee,
  Illinois State University
12 11 10 09 08 07 06 05 04   5 4 3 2 1

University of Washington Press
PO Box 50096, Seattle, WA 98145
www.washington.edu/uwpress

Library of Congress Cataloging-in-Publication Data
Becker, Ernest.
[Selections. 2004]
The Ernest Becker reader / selected, edited,
  and introduced by DanielLiechty.
p. cm.
Includes bibliographical references and indexes.
ISBN 0-295-98470-8 (pbk. : alk. paper)
1. Psychology. 2. Psychology, Pathological.
3. Philosophical anthropology.
I. Liechty, Daniel, 1954– II. Title.
BF109.B43A25 2004 128–dc22 2004017743

The paper used in this publication is acid-free and recycled
from 20 percent post-consumer and at least 50 percent pre-
consumer waste. It meets the minimum requirements of
American National Standard for Information Sciences—
Permanence of Paper for Printed Library Materials,
ANSI Z39.48-1984. ♾ ♻

This book is dedicated to
Neil Elgee, MD
public mentor and intellectual midwife
of contemporary Ernest Becker scholarship.

Also dedicated to
Sheldon Solomon, Jeff Greenberg, and Tom Pyszczynski
three who refused to believe it when told
these ideas could never be tested scientifically.

Acknowledgments

There were a number of people who gave me their input as to what material should be included in this Reader. Of those people, I would specifically like to thank William DuBois, Jerry S. Piven, Sheldon Solomon, James B. McCarthy, Kirk J. Schneider, C. Fred Alford, Jeffrey Kauffman, Neil Elgee, Jeff Greenberg, Thomas Duncanson, David R. Loy, and Merlyn Mowrey. Jacqueline Ettinger, our editor at University of Washington Press, and Jeanne Lee, of Illinois State University, were both invaluable to this project. Thanks to Sam Keen for making the full, unedited text of his interview with Ernest Becker available. Four of my graduate students, Laura Jennings Mitchell, Michelle Conrady-Brown, Janelle Sumner, and Leesa Reed, all struggled valiantly through parts of the early manuscript. Much of the work was supported in many ways by The Ernest Becker Foundation. The Ernest Becker Foundation, in turn, was given a substantial anonymous donation specifically for the support of this project, for which I am very grateful.

Special and particular thanks and acknowledgement are due to Robert Pos and Marie Becker-Pos. Without their support of this project, it would never have been completed.

Contents

ERNEST BECKER IS MAINLY KNOWN FOR his last two books, *The Denial of Death* (1973) and *Escape from Evil* (1975). It is in these two books that Becker laid out his astonishingly synthetic thesis concerning the psychological, sociological, and cultural consequences of the human awareness of mortality and the implications this awareness carries in human affairs as both a positive and negative motivational factor. For many readers these books, though recognized as profound, were simply too dark and pessimistic about the human condition. To many readers, Becker seemed to offer no way forward, no human project for dealing positively with our death awareness and the repressed anxiety it produces, no programs for taking this into account and yet moving ahead to build liberal, democratic society. Many readers even went so far as to conclude that Becker's vision was anti-humanistic and anti-democratic, or certainly far outside the parameters of any social analysis on which democratic humanists could fruitfully draw.

What is not always recognized or understood in such criticism of Becker's later works is that these works themselves were building on more than a decade of previous studies. In these works, Becker tried in every way he could to support the democratic, humanistic project of our species (what he called the Enlightenment Vision) and to diagnose, criticize, and reanimate that democratic, humanistic project in all the places it had soured into mechanistic scientism, subordination of human values and rights to the demands and expectations of market forces, the idolatrous exaltation of money and consumer materialism on which the system of market economy had come to depend, and the glorification of war and violence that stood as a central prop under-girding the entire project. The thread of continuity running through Becker's earlier work is exactly his unflagging commitment to what he understood as the original, generative Enlightenment vision of democratic humanism, pinpointing and then liberating human beings from the chains of alienation that kept them bound to personal, social, ideological, and political forces that impeded or prevented true human freedom. His principled stand in favor of human freedom in the face of opposition cost him dearly in terms of his academic career, and quite probably in terms of his own physical health as well.

Also often misunderstood by those who read Becker's final works harshly is his general dialectic method of presentation. Becker's habit was to write on a subject in one way, only to turn around in a subsequent work and approach the same subject from a very different angle. In *The Denial of Death*, for example, Becker wrote of 'twin motivating factors' in human affairs, the denial of death and the denial of life. In his final books, he wrote primarily an explication of the denial of death. It is suggested, however, that the work would not finally be complete until the same topics had been approached from the angle of the denial of life as well. Unfortunately, cancer intervened before Becker could come around and produce the scholarly counterweight himself, although a few of his latest essays, published in scattered locations, strongly hint at the direction this more positive treatment of human possibilities might take.

Although many factors were considered in the selection and editing of Becker's writings for this anthology, a couple of factors weighed most heavily in the process. One of these was simply to make more easily available the most poignant portions of books and essays long out of print and difficult to locate. More importantly, however, it is hoped that these selections will allow the reader to see the threads of continuity between Ernest Becker's earlier and later ideas, sparking interest in the earlier works and offering the foundations for a more balanced interpretation of the later works. Finally, since Becker himself did not live to complete his scholarly project, the door is open wide to that growing group of subsequent researchers, scholars, and intelligent readers, who find in Becker's work that startling recognition of genius, themselves to move this line of interpretation forward. My greatest hope is that the selections offered in this anthology will point readers toward the background material necessary for this venture.

Becker wrote with humor, personality, and with generous citations of the work of others. Space limitations too often forced an editorial decision to retain basic content at the expense of allowing 'Ernie the man' to peek through the text and say hello. I can only ask forbearance from those readers who feel that a particularly delightful passage from this or that writing was not included in this anthology.

Daniel Liechty
Illinois State University

ERNEST BECKER HAS LONG BEEN SOMETHING OF AN ENIGMA in the world of scholarship. His academic career endured for less than 15 years. For all but the final few years of that career, Becker led a rather nomadic academic life, existing on short-term contracts, often not knowing when one year ended where he would be for the coming year. Even as article after article and book after book appeared, he was continually denied contract renewal and any pathway to the academic tenure track. When finally he was offered a position that included some security, it was in a rather contentious and experimental interdisciplinary program that eventually spun apart. In any case, cancer soon intervened to cut Becker's career short at the young age of 49 years. The absorbing question Ernest Becker pursued in all of his research and writing was simply, *What makes people act the way they do?* Although Becker certainly did receive some significant accolades, even these were not unambiguous. When in 1967, for example, students at the University of California at Berkeley heard that Becker's contract as a visiting lecturer would not be renewed by the administration, they voted to pay Becker's salary out of student funds in order to retain him, being the first and only time this gesture of student support has been given. Unfortunately, the administration understood this gesture as an attempt by students to intervene in the hiring and firing process and the offer was roundly rejected. This strong gesture of student support for Becker's teaching did nothing to endear him to the college administration. Similarly, as he was dying, Becker's book, *The Denial of Death* (1973), was awarded a Pulitzer Prize for Nonfiction. While this award would certainly be more than a feather in the cap of any writer, in the academic world in which Becker worked, a Pulitzer Prize was generally viewed as a 'literary' award for writing, rather than an academic or scientific award in recognition of a major contribution to an academic field.

We might have expected that once the excitement of the Pulitzer died down (and this happened quickly, since there was no book tour promotion or follow up work) whatever reputation Ernest Becker had would ebb, and his work would join the hundreds of thousands of others on the shelves of academic libraries, at best to make brief appearances in the obscure footnotes of dissertations, or worse, to be culled out and discarded from the library collection altogether. This, however, has not been Becker's fate. Sales of *The Denial of Death* have been steady and brisk enough to keep it continuously in print for the past three decades, even to be expanded in a recent printing with an able and informative introduction by public philosopher Sam Keen. At least two other of Becker's ten books have also remained continuously in print since his death. Generous tributes to Becker's influence have appeared in the writings and interviews of many very well-known serious authors, such as Annie Dillard, Anatole

Broyard, Woody Allen, Robert Jay Lifton, Irvin Yalom, Sam Keen, Molly Ivans, Don DeLillo, Percy Walker and many others. *The Denial of Death* appears as one of Bill Clinton's published list of most influential books.

In the academic world, as well, interest in Becker's work has been steady and growing. In many ways, Ernest Becker was too far ahead of his time in his academic work, a main source of his difficulties in finding a welcoming academic home base. At a time when sociologists and even theologians were extolling the arrival of the 'secular city' and the demise of an integrated religious worldview, Ernest Becker anticipated current 'post-secular' social theory in law and philosophy by insisting that all cultural worldviews are essentially 'sacred' in character, and that the choice was not between the sacred and the secular, but rather between religio-cultural visions that exacted differing tolls on human freedom and community, and demanded differing sacrifices of scapegoats required to keep us from focusing on the inevitable mystifications of the system. Likewise, while working in an era in social science infatuated with imitating mathematics and physics, in which ever-narrowing statistical studies bought access to grant money to conduct research, prestigious journals to publish findings, and the academic rewards that follow, Ernest Becker anticipated the postmodern turn by continuing to call his fellows back to a socially-engaged and values-centered vision of social science he associated with the vision of the disciplinary founders. In addition, Becker's insistence that first and foremost, human beings are animals, sharing completely in the evolutionary history of all animal species, while at the same time possessing a distinctly human psychology rooted not in a metaphysical realm but in the uniquely human awareness of death, he both anticipated and pointed beyond the subsequent interpretations of sociobiology and evolutionary psychology.

Although Becker's work has been read and appreciated by some within the academy, the pace for this reappropriation has increased in the past decade, aided by the founding of The Ernest Becker Foundation in Seattle. Many of those, like myself, who had been reading Becker, were convinced that there was something of central importance in this work, and who were making initial efforts to apply these ideas to our disciplines, often felt alone and isolated. Repeatedly, we faced skeptical dissertation, grant funding, hiring and promotion committees, publishers and journal editors, who were completely unaware of Becker's work, and too often were initially hostile to it when it was explained to them. It was not until the founding of the Ernest Becker Foundation, in 1993, that those with scholarly interest in Becker's work began to feel a break in their sense of isolation. For the past decade, through the work of this foundation, a growing community of scholars, professionals, activists, and serious readers working in many areas of the social sciences, the professions, the arts and humanities have been making contact with each other, learning from one another's perspectives, and in the process have laid the foundation for appropriating Becker's basic theory as the basis for fruitful interdisciplinary conversation and learning. In many ways, this anthology is an open invitation to join this venture of conversation and mutual learning.

ERNEST BECKER WAS BORN IN MASSACHUSETTS in September of 1924. Although the family practiced the Jewish faith, Becker himself reports that he was basically atheistic in his views for most of his early adult life. He served in the infantry during World War II and was part of a regiment that liberated a Nazi concentration camp. There Becker saw first hand the underside of Western civilization.

After discharge from the military, Becker attended Syracuse University. Fluent in French, he took a position as an attaché in the Parisian embassy of the United States upon graduation, where he spent the middle years of the 1950s. We know from an exchange of letters written at this time between Becker in Paris, and his close friend Phillip Singer in England, that Becker began to feel restless with his work in the diplomatic corps, and he and Singer began to explore various ideas, including various 'get rich quick' schemes as import/export entrepreneurs in the area of Far Eastern religious artifacts. When these schemes fell through (apparently, in Becker's view, because his own family did not see him as a settled and responsible person and refused to loan him the seed money he requested) Singer and Becker decided to return to the USA for graduate school. They chose anthropology, it appears, more or less on a whim, because it seemed to be a field that posed the broadest questions possible about human behavior.

They both enrolled as graduate students in anthropology at Syracuse University, studying under Japanese specialist Douglas Haring. Phillip Singer went on to an illustrious and productive career in medical anthropology. Today some of the most creative work in African shamanistic medical practice and ritual is associated with Singer's name.

Becker's dissertation focused on Japanese Zen Buddhism, drawing parallels and distinctions between the student/master relationship in Zen training, Chinese thought reform, and Western psychoanalysis. Becker also seemed destined for a career in medical anthropology, and upon receiving the Ph.D., he was hired to teach anthropology in the Department of Psychiatry at the Upstate Medical Center in Syracuse, at the time one of the most prestigious New York state medical teaching hospitals outside of New York City. Here Becker had the promise of tenure and a fine future in medical anthropology, and soon gained a reputation as a skilled mental health diagnostician. In the following two years Becker published two books (his dissertation and a book based on his initial lecture series at the Center) and a number of journal articles, more than enough for tenure, all else being equal.

It was during this time, however, that Becker developed an admiring relationship with Thomas Szasz, an unconventional senior professor of psychiatry in the department. Szasz was already known in the field for his antiauthoritarianism and protests against the medical model of mental illness. Becker joined a circle of junior faculty formed to study Szasz's ideas. Becker's association with Szasz was very productive in terms of providing him with a stimulating, extra-medical perspective on mental disorders. Becker's writings from this period reflect a broadly transactional view of mental illness, or what in current terms is called the 'psychosocial' view of mental illness and mental health. However, this association with Szasz also got Becker and others of the junior faculty into deeply troubled waters.

Thomas Szasz was and continues to be a genuine maverick in psychiatry. A radical civil libertarian, his two main books at the time, *The Myth of Mental Illness* (1961) and *Law, Liberty and Psychiatry* (1963) were direct attacks on some of the very basic assumptions of standard psychiatry, as well as the central pillar of psychiatry's social power, the power of involuntary commitment in psychiatric institutions. Needless to say, Szasz ruffled feathers and created real enemies in the world of academic psychiatry (Upstate Medical Center's program, for example, was largely dependent on involuntary commitment patients, both for state funding and subjects for teaching.)

In the second year of Becker's time at Upstate, the administration attempted to remove Szasz from his teaching duties. This move against Szasz ultimately failed, because Szasz was tenured and therefore protected. But Becker and the junior faculty associated with Szasz were not tenured, and were fired when they rallied to Szasz's support. Although Szasz undoubtedly influenced Becker strongly during this period of time, Becker was by no means simply an uncritical disciple of Szasz or exponent of Szasz's views. His support of Szasz at the time was as much a principled stand in favor of general academic freedom as it was for Szasz personally. (Direct reference to Szasz in Becker's writings were relatively few even during this period, and disappeared altogether soon thereafter.) The school administration, however, was not looking for nuanced distinctions. Becker was summarily dismissed from his teaching post.

His dismissal from the Upstate Center began for Becker a long period as an academic nomad, living on grants and short term teaching contracts in undergraduate departments of education, sociology, and psychology. All the while he persisted in producing nearly a book every year, along with various other writings. As a teacher, Becker was very engaging and theatrical. To make a point concerning the existential aspects of human choice, for example, Becker apparently took the amphitheater podium in full costume to perform a scene from Shakespeare's *King Lear*. Although such flamboyance endeared Becker to students (more than 2000 Berkeley students signed protests of Becker's dismissal in 1967, and they even voted to pay his salary out of student funds) it did not win him any particular favors with fellow faculty and college administration. More than once Becker ended a school year with no firm commitments at all for where he would be the following Fall.

It was not until the 1969-1970 school year that Becker found himself in a tenure track position, in the newly-formed interdisciplinary department combining sociology, anthropology and political science at Simon Fraser University in Vancouver, Canada. There Becker completed a second edition of *The Birth and Death of Meaning* (1972) and what would become his master work, *The Denial of Death* (1973). Also completed at this time were the notes and partial manuscript that would be published, posthumously, as *Escape From Evil* (1975). In late 1972, Becker was diagnosed with cancer, and he died in March 1974, at the age of 49 years.

THE GIST OF BECKER'S MATURE THEORY WAS BEST outlined by public philosopher Sam Keen, in his introductory preface to the 1997 printing of *The Denial of Death*. Keen summarized Becker's theory as containing four main strands of emphasis.

The world is a terrifying place. Here is it important to recognize that Becker purposely situated his views as a corrective to overly optimistic versions of evolutionary philosophies, in which increasing human perfection is our natural destiny. Becker pled humble ignorance on human destiny; we simply cannot know what aims the cosmic Life Force may have. But viewing our situation on this planet with jaundiced empiricism, we do know that we are inextricably bound up in a systemic food chain in which living organisms sustain themselves only by ingesting, digesting and creating fertilizer of other living organisms. For all but a very few of its organisms, this must be seen a nightmarish system of constant terror. Even for our own species, recent anthropological literature suggests that the transition from prey to predator took place only very recently in our evolutionary history. Accordingly, we may assume that the rumblings of a prey animal's terror, as well as the exaggerated human fascination with power and weaponry that facilitated this recent transition from prey to predator, remain very present in the collective unconscious of our species. The undeniable awe and wonder in nature's beauty aside, Becker insisted that there is real terror in the most basic structures of this world, terror that is echoed in the deepest recesses of our being. Even as we repeat our cultural narratives of conquest and comfort, we cannot mistake these narratives for empirical reality itself. We employ an array of culturally constructed 'necessary fictions' to aid us in the repression of our real anxiety of death and vulnerability, giving us as individuals and as societies a sense of purpose and forward movement. Yet because such narratives are bound to conflict across cultures and this will have real consequences, including overt violence between people, we must keep on our mental horizons the narrative nature of our transcending Truths.

The basic motivation for human behavior is the need to control our basic anxiety, to deny the terror of death. The most basic anxiety is not sexual urgency or aggressiveness. It is the anxious terror produced in an animal that has attained self-awareness and knows that it will die. Though in his own time, Becker's theories were not widely accepted by specialists, hypotheses derived from these theories (called 'Terror Management Theory' in the specialized literature) have been proving amazingly resilient under rigorous empirical testing.

Since the terror of death is so overwhelming we conspire to keep it unconscious. Death awareness and the anxiety it produces is not simply uncomfortable. It does not simply make us uneasy. It is so overwhelmingly threatening to the human psyche that it positively has to be repressed. The entire range of psychological defenses must be employed to keep this basic anxiety masked and disguised, and this need to repress death anxiety from consciousness may well have been, in fact, the stimulus at the origin of these psychological defense mechanisms. Individual and social character emerge from a dynamic unconscious, which must expend an enormous amount of energy in this positive repression of the terror of death from conscious awareness. The very definition of a successful culture is that it offers satisfactory, convincing and viable avenues for achieving triumphant sublimation of this basic anxiety in the form of cultural 'heroics.' The heroic drive is the varied and culturally-contoured drive to excellence, by which individuals 'make their mark,' prove their larger worth and value, and thereby earn self-esteem and symbolic immortality.

Our heroic projects, aimed at destroying evil, have the paradoxical effect of bringing more evil into the world. Because it remains unconscious and repressed, human beings will displace and scapegoat the terror of death almost willy-nilly. We are able to focus on almost any perceived threat, whether of people, political or economic ideology, race, religion, and blow it up psychologically into a life and death struggle against ultimate evil. In doing so, we lose the very faculties that allow us to place limits on the violence we are willing to employ against this perceived threat. This dynamic of spiraling violence, more than anything else, remains the underside of human social interaction at all levels, from personal interactions, to group interactions, to interactions between nation states.

Becker's theory of human behavioral motivation is not easily optimistic; if the ultimate human struggle is ultimately an unconscious fight against mortality itself, and therefore doomed to repeated defeat, it is hard to see how the spirals of violence can ever be eliminated from our behavior. On the other hand, if we are able to recognize the true nature of our struggles against evil, this may assist us in demythologizing the real threats posed by 'evil empires' and other perceived enemies, thus yielding at least some handle of rationality for setting controls and prior limits on our violence.

AS WILL BE SEEN IN THIS ANTHOLOGY, Becker returned again and again to similar problems of human behavior in his writings, each time exploring the problems from a different angle, and in conversation with a different set of authorial interlocutors. Becker was determined to approach his questions of human nature and human behavior from as broadly an 'empirical' perspective as possible. For Becker, this entailed a very conscious effort not to exclude from view any observational data on human reality, regardless of its source, including theological observations, observations rooted in literary sources, and other areas of the humanities. The resulting Theory of Generative Death Anxiety, as I call it, opens the doors of perception and interpretation of human reality in at least four interlocking levels.

The Personal Psychological Level. Freudian theory, as well as the more recent interpretations stemming from sociobiology and evolutionary psychology, presents the human unconscious as composed mainly of thwarted instinctual sexual and aggressive drives, which are in conflict with the norms and values of civil society. The socialization process is understood as the process by which the instinctually-driven individual finally capitulates to the behavioral demands of civil society, in recognition of the overwhelmingly inferior position of the individual in terms of raw physical power in relation to society. Defensively, the individual internalizes as his own the 'socially acceptable' values behaviors demanded by society and will eventually even accept such norms as freely chosen values. Yet a seething, defeated, defensive, self-ish, reactive, 'reptilian' anti-social character remains buried inside the individual, somewhere under the surface of civility. It occasionally reappears in various measure in response to particular circumstances and provocations.

Becker understood personal psychological development in broadly contrasting, *post-Freudian* terms. While he acknowledged the concept of a dynamic unconscious, he considerably downplayed the role of instinctual drives. The content of the dynamic unconscious largely consists of symbolic distortions of childhood perceptions of the actions of parents and other caregivers. Following Alfred Adler, Otto Rank, and others, Becker focused attentiveness to original ego-weakness and ego-inferiority in the context of the infant's relationship with caregivers, and the vicissitudes of the separation/individuation process. Becker pictured the individual child as naturally social with continuing needs for security, closeness, and affection. Spurred originally by the anxiety of physical separation from caregivers, the child is increasingly motivated by the need to maintain self-esteem. As the child grows and matures, it learns to expand its repertoire of maintaining its sense of security, closeness, and affection, which becomes increasingly less body-based and increasingly more based on symbolic-action, initially in the caregiver relationship, but finally extended to symbolic meanings connected with the larger society.

Thus Becker wrote not of a psychosexual *Oedipal Complex,* but rather of an relational/existential *Oedipal Transition*. The Oedipal Transition is a time in which the child must learn to seek and be satisfied with continued parental approval on a psychological and symbolic level, rather than on a direct physiological level. This process of socialization is culturally specific, but describes in very broad terms that which takes place in all cultures, the process of transforming the child from being primarily a biological actor into a person who is primarily a social actor. The process is mainly transactional rather than instinctual. The end result is that the individual learns to maintain a sense of personal self-esteem in the psychological, symbolic arena.

This process only occurs as the symbolic Self of the individual assumes evermore effective control of its own physical body. Thus one byproduct of this process is the emerging experience of a dualism of body and symbolic Self. The body becomes an object in the sphere of the ego or symbolic Self. The growing ability to delay reaction to bodily stimuli is the mechanism by which the symbolic Self comes to increasingly know itself and stretch toward further individuation. This experienced dualism of body and symbolic Self increases as the growing child begins to confront the fact of mortality and the related anxiety this produces. Quite early the child suspects that hope for continued existence on the physical level is finally doomed to failure, and in this realization the psyche is pushed toward constructions of psychological, symbolic (rather than physical) conquering of death.

Chronologically, therefore, the first anxiety is the anxiety of physical separation from the caregiver. As the child's ability to abstract and symbolize develops, this first anxiety is displaced by the existential anxiety of mortality awareness. From that point at which the child is able to understand that caregiver separation (object loss) = inability to thrive = death, it can be assumed that death anxiety has establishing itself as basic to the anxieties of abandonment. The experienced dualism of body and symbolic Self, along with the concomitant urge to conquer death symbolically, emerge during the Oedipal Transition, and largely define the problem of living itself, characterized psychologically by ego expansion on the one hand and safe anxiety avoidance on the other.

The Social Psychological Level. As implied above, in Becker's theory of Generative Death Anxiety, there is a smoothly integrated and logically compelling movement from the personal psychological to the social psychological levels. It is at the social psychological level that the need for continued individual self-esteem maintenance is carried into the social arena. There are several linking concepts between the sphere of the personal and social spheres, but the most important is Becker's category of the *immortality project*. Spurred by the need to repress awareness of mortality from consciousness, human beings spend enormous amounts of psychic energy creating symbols of immortality, the psychological mechanisms for taming of the terror of finitude, with which people identify themselves and through which people vicariously participate in a sense of immortality at the symbolic level. Viable cultures provide what Becker called an *immortality ideology,* a narrative of symbolic power that adequately satisfies the human need for security and protection. In a smoothly functioning society, the myriad individual immortality projects fit neatly into the overriding cultural immortality ideology, thus allowing each individual the sense that he or she is an important and valued actor in an historical drama of transcending significance. When this happens smoothly, the anxiety-allaying function of the social immortality ideology is mutually confirmed at the level of individual and collective experience.

Because the symbolic Self is largely linguistically (that is, socially) constructed, the grammar by which the symbolic Self maintains its sense of worth and value moves logically and compellingly into the social arena by way of the developed theory of role and status. There is a *public logic,* a dominant socially constructed ethos, which may differ from the private logic of individuals making up that particular public. Psychological and social 'character,' whether functional or dysfunctional, reflect rather directly the individual and group strategies for encompassing the gap between public and private logic, balancing both the social need to maintain the sanctity of public logic and the individual need to maintain maximum self-esteem. Here the importance of Becker's expanded category of *transference* can be seen. As individuals, we are finite, mortal, weak animals. Given the choice between accepting this reality or giving oneself over to illusions of greatness and importance which a leader imparts to followers, the mass of human beings will choose illusion over reality, lies over truth, fiction over fact. Transference describes the nature of the bond between leader and follower, between individual and group behavior. It is a bond rooted in the regressive, individual submission to 'power,' in the individual need to feel awe and protection by symbolic icons of power and thus deny and avoid recognition of finitude. People do not simply find themselves passively 'engulfed' by such feelings toward symbolic icons of power. People actively and all-but-consciously seek such symbolic icons of powers toward which they might submit themselves, even when, perhaps in our time especially when, this is done under the ideological cover of seeking independence, individuation, self-actualization, self-fulfillment, and autonomy.

The individual Oedipal Project is the life-long quest to establish independent sources for grounding ego expansion. It is finally a striving for a self-grounded ego. Yet very few are able to establish their own meanings (private logic as opposed to public logic) in an absolute sense and no one is able to sustain such personal meaning without interruption over time without socially available structures of plausibility. Therefore most people all of the time, and all people some of the time, must draw upon the established categories of culture (public logic) for a personal sense of worth and forward movement. Life is a constant movement between establishing personal meaning and seeking confirmation of that meaning from the group. The most prominent features of social life can best be understood as public striving for symbolic immortality. They are attempts to symbolically establish human worth, dignity, meaning and significance, thus to allay the anxious, gnawing, unconscious suspicion that, in the face of the reality of mortality, individual and species human life is but fleeting, perishable, transient, insignificant, and meaningless.

The Political Level. Though not an activist, Becker held generally progressive views for his time—he was an early voice against the Vietnam War and thought very highly of the Civil Rights movement. Yet Becker was, like Reinhold Niebuhr, no unambiguous friend to the conventional dichotomous politics of Left or Right, Liberal or Conservative, Democrat or Republican. He understood that all political movements gain power by fostering transference reactions among their target constituencies; all political movements engage to one extent or another in mesmerizing slight of hand, since none can actually produce the implied utopia of its immortality ideology. On the other hand, some political movements are less prone to deception and exact a lesser pound of flesh than others.

Becker drew directly from his philosophical anthropology to construct what we might call an *ideal/real* theory of democracy, which he defined briefly as a state in which each person strives to achieve *maximum individuality within maximum community*. In critical service of this ideal is the quest to provide a synthesis of knowledge leading to better solutions to the recurring problems of community, social morality, and an ordered but free society. Becker was cognizant of the fact that as buffers against anxiety, human beings will always be prone to following those leaders whose projected image is perceived as an adequate transference object. After all, a fully 'socialized' adult human in any society is exactly one who accepts authority in place of trial and error learning, and subsequently distrusts his or her own independent judgments if such judgments conflict with established authorities. Yet as Becker saw it, modern liberal democracy at its best has been an experiment to see if this aspect of socialization could be seriously ameliorated. Modern democracy is nothing less than a radical social experiment, especially when viewed against the backdrop of European monarchies and aristocracies, systems in which it was anything but self-evident that all people are created equal. It is an experiment to test whether a conceptual construct, self-governing human freedom, can itself function as a transference object adequate to hold a free and diverse people together in unity. Contrary to what many history books teach, however, this was not accomplished once and for all in 1776 or 1792, but is an ongoing experiment, subject to strong obstructing social forces. This experiment is of itself an heroic immortality ideology, in which the State itself encourages (especially in the form of protection of minority rights ensconced in the Bill of Rights) participation in multiple interlinking spheres of transcendent meaning that specifically undercut aggrandizement of the State. The common heroism is only the heroism of participation in the democratic experiment itself. Ideally, this sense of personal and social heroism allows a diverse and multicultural population a high degree of mutual respect, recognizing each other as free and equal citizens, seeking to curb the pursuit of naked self-interest at the expense of the commonweal. Much of the social malaise which many people feel in America today stems from the fact that, as a nation, we have largely lost the sense of personal and social heroism we once enjoyed as our right as participants in this noble political experiment. We now run in all directions seeking that sense of heroism, which is already ours by our heritage as citizens, even while our democracy itself falters.

In the ideal/real democracy, leaders emerge from the people, and leadership changes often enough that there is minimal opportunity for the establishment of oligarchy or demagoguery. People learn to trust their own independent judgments, and, through its system of public education, this is fostered and encouraged by the State itself. The State itself, both by strategic intervention, and by strategically keeping out of the way, becomes a mechanism for encouraging progressive social change.

This use of State power for what is actually the abolition of a powerful State is indeed a fragile experiment, easily driven off course. In America this experiment has been significantly derailed by an assumption that took hold in the late 19th century, by which for practical purposes the political system of liberal democracy and the economic system of free market capitalism were totally identified. This significantly narrowed the scope of hero-worthy pursuits supported by the public logic of the society, focusing social power on one main social project, material accumulation and consumption. The relative merit of all social institutions, as is confirmed by even a cursory look at the debates surrounding (as one example) current educational policy, is then judged by how well it contributes to this one social project.

Becker suggested that a unified educational curriculum might be the way to get our democratic experiment back on track. Recognizing the impossibility of defining the Good to the satisfaction of all, Becker counseled that at least we might find agreement in defining what is bad for human beings. The Bad would be anything that stands in the way of full human development, of achieving maximum individuality within maximum community. Becker here introduced the category of *alienation* as a short-hand for the Bad. He proposed that we examine the possibility of using the concept of an 'alienation curriculum' as a unifying force for education and learning. A general theory of alienation is an explanation for the evil in the world that is caused by human made arrangements. It points a finger at those evils, which could be ameliorated by human effort. Becker sometimes called this larger social scientific project anthropodicy and sometimes referred to it as a *Unified Science of Man(kind)*, a dynamic, inductive description of human values which evolves and is revised in response to the concerns of each generation as new aspects of human alienation are recognized.

In service of a revival of what he took to be the true spirit of liberal democracy, Becker suggested that a unified theory of alienation could become the single unifying principle for our whole curriculum and the foundation for a genuine synthesis of knowledge. Education would seek to show students the history of alienation in one's personal life development, how alienation arises as a result of the law of individual development. It would seek to show the history of alienation in society, how alienation arises as a result of the workings of society and the evolution of society in history. And finally, it would seek to show the total problem of alienation under the conditions of existence, how evil arises as a result of the condition of life itself, which is finitude and mortality.

Becker characterized the educational system in the ideal/real democracy as a *Great Conversation* carried on by a community of scientist-scholar-investigators. This was also his basic description of an ideal social existence in the ideal/real democratic state, in which the expansion of maximum individuality within maximum community would itself serve as the socio-cultural immortality project—the only kind of immortality project that by its nature will not displace freedom with servitude in the process of achieving its actualization.

The Religious and Spiritual Level. Becker is one of only a few social scientists who took great care to foster a perspective in which the theological knowledge and religious or spiritual aspect of human experience is given a place of full integrity beside other fields of knowledge and experience. Becker neither bracketed out such knowledge and experience, nor treated it reductively. On the other hand, he did not privilege it either. He listened to what was being said in this area for what it could contribute to a more well-rounded view of human nature and behavioral motivation.

One of the central points Becker made in this regard is that because all personal and cultural immortality projects, strategies and ideologies (collectively the stuff of *culture*) function to allay the terror of mortality, finitude, insignificance and nothingness, in a very real sense even secular societies are *religious* to the core. Culture helps us confront the mysteries of life and death, of mortality and immortality, and makes it deeply religious or sacred. Any legitimate distinction between the secular and sacred at the social level quickly collapses at the psychological level. Religious faith in the broadest sense is the inevitable human response to mortality awareness.

Becker followed especially Soren Kierkegaard and Paul Tillich in his formulations. The concept of a Creator God is our ultimate transference object. The concept of a Creator God offers real hope of transcendence over the terror of mortality. A Creator God gives human life significance, meaning and value in a world of suffering and pain, a world in which death finally rules. In this world, any sense of significance, meaning and value, of transcendence over the terror of mortality, comes as a free gift of the Creator God and can only be accepted as an act of faith.

Wittingly or unwittingly, Becker stepped directly into the thick of postmodern theological debate. For the very Creator God who is able to act as the ultimate transference object as Becker outlined it—who bestows human freedom but does not aggress against human freedom in reciprocal expectation—is an ideal/real aesthetic construction. This construction of the Creator God always stands *ahead of human history,* calling humanity toward new achievements of maximum individuality within maximum community. This God cannot be calcified in descriptions of divine nature and attributes, nor ever be fully known. No 'graven image' can be made of this God. As soon as an individual or community claims to know this God, to speak for this God, they have created an idol, a human-made God, which will sooner or later displace human freedom with alienating subservience.

Because cultural immortality ideologies function to protect us from mortality, from that which we perceive in ourselves as ultimate powerlessness, human beings have always been drawn to images of power, the possibility of victory over our ultimate powerlessness. Becker's theory accounts for the *dark side of human spiritual experience*—the ongoing fascination we have with violence; the attraction to blood rituals of sacrifice; worship of symbols of wealth; the religious need for reverence and servitude; and attraction to the awesomeness (the horror!) of raw, amoral power. This dark side of human religious experience persists and flourishes in conditions of modernity, long after its 'irrational' nature has been well exposed.

Human spirituality is presented in Becker's theory in a very real sense as the age-old struggle with idolatry. God, as ultimate transference object, cannot be materialized, cannot be possessed, cannot even be with us (against them) in history; rather God stands *ahead of us* as an aesthetic ideal/real conceptual construction. God requires above all else endurance of anxiety, on faith. Those gods which can be materialized, possessed, known exhaustively, located in time and space, offering power for anxiety-free living are exposed as idols. Only too late we learn that servitude to such gods entails sacrifice and displacement of human freedom and creative expansion. The drama of human spirituality, the sense of true heroism it offers, is contained in the possibility that in each day and in each moment, we may choose the security of idols or the adventure of faith.

ALTHOUGH THIS INTRODUCTORY PRESENTATION of Ernest Becker's ideas is necessarily sketchy, the positive value of his central Theory of Generative Death Anxiety as an organizing principle in the social sciences and humanities is clear. It accounts for much of human motivation and behavior in at least four large fields of experience, and does so in a way that treats each field autonomously and with integrity, neither ignoring any field of experience, nor reducing or collapsing all fields into one. Furthermore, in the form of *Terror Management Theory,* important aspects of this theory have been tested using established, sophisticated, empirical methods and the results have been demonstrated to be reliable, predictable and repeatable across a spectrum of research teams, age groups and nationalities. While such research cannot prove absolutely the truth of Becker's ideas, it has shown that among a field of alternative theories, Becker's theory best accounts for the demonstrated research results.

Becker's own work warns of the potential dangers inherent to any ideological *grand narrative* statement of human knowledge. This is certainly not being advocated here. Yet even as a pendulum reaches its apex in one direction, forces are being gathered for a return swing in the opposite direction. We have already seen the apex of a trend in knowledge construction emphasizing the distinctive, difference, the deconstruction and tribalization of knowledge, and we already see the forces gathering for a swing back toward an integration of knowledge. Too much of this returning trend appears to be more than willing to embrace various forms of exactly those ideological grand narratives, along with the inherent dangers contained within them. My hope in presenting this anthology is for wider recognition that in Becker's Theory of Generative Death Anxiety, we may find a way forward, toward a respectful, unified, interdisciplinary integration of knowledge, which does not simply steamroll over distinction and difference.

PART ONE
A PSYCHOSOCIAL VIEW OF MENTAL HEALTH
(1960–1963)

The chapters in this section present selections written while Ernest Becker was a lecturer in anthropology in the Department of Psychiatry at the Upstate Medical Center in Syracuse, New York. This was a plum position for a newly minted Ph.D. Becker's Ph.D. dissertation compared the master/student and analyst/analysand relationship in Japanese Zen Buddhism and Western psychoanalysis. This research was the basis for his first book and a few articles, also published during this period. Although this work contains some interesting ideas, including in seed form the beginnings of Becker's later formulations on social transference, Becker left this work undeveloped, and in subsequent years took a very different view of Buddhism (though not necessarily of Zen) than is expressed in this work.

The work that consumed Becker during these years was that of formulating a consistently transactional, or psychosocial, theory of mental health and mental illness. Always writing with Freud and psychoanalysis within his peripheral vision, Becker set out to demonstrate that mental health and mental illness are relatively fluid categories. Particularly keen to reject Freud's instinct theory, Becker set forth a view of the unconscious consisting of the individual residue of early social learning and experience. This early material creates habits of behavior, habits of reactions to stimuli, and these habitual behaviors collectively do form general character types. But just as these behaviors are formed as habitual patterns based on early social learning and experience, they are amenable to change based on new social learning. The difference between conceiving behavior as rooted in thwarted natural instincts, and conceiving behavior as rooted in habitual responses to early social learning, may seem insignificant and semantic at first glance. But in Becker's view the differences in conception were crucial, particularly in that the instinctual view sees the individual as antisocial at the deepest level, held in line only by the naked social power of society. The latter view accounts for the worst of human behavior, yet holds onto the idea that humans are at the deepest level social animals. Social bonds are those of mammalian connection, not the implied violence of social power.

These writings reflect Becker's ongoing attempt to find in Freud that which is really valuable and enduring, while rejecting what he considered to be Freud's uncritical acceptance of the biologism and instinctivism in the nineteenth-century intellectual milieu.

Chapter 1

ANTHROPOLOGY, PSYCHOANALYSIS, AND MENTAL ILLNESS

Socialization, Command of Performance, and Mental Illness (1962)*

THE ESSENTIALS FOR A SOCIOLOGICAL UNDERSTANDING of behavioral malfunction presented here underline a crucial but simple consideration, which has not been sufficiently stressed in discussions of mental illness. It is clear that whatever the origin of malfunction—in biological substrata or in conventional social definition of desirable norm—there are individuals who will not meet the behavioral requirements of their fellows. But in addition to this consideration, there is a less obvious one, namely, that to a self-reflexive, symbol-using animal, *the purely symbolic social definition of normative behavior* is as crucial to action as is instinctive patterning to any lower organism. . . .

[I]t is becoming increasingly obvious—or should be—that a comprehensive theory of human behavior will draw upon those discoveries of Freud which figure less prominently in clinical matters and which are of more general import. I am referring specifically to the genesis of the self and the ego, and to the fact of the Oedipal transition—a transition from biological proximal relationship to a succoring figure, to a distanced, symbolic relationship to the internalized values of that figure. These two general, universal developmental trends are crucial in the humanization of *Homo sapiens*. It is important to underscore that they are based upon one continuous thread: the change from a stimulus-response reaction to primitive anxiety, to an ego-controlled reaction. The latter interposes a series of complex mechanisms between anxiety and the organism, which we have come to know as the self-system. The bootstraps, so to speak, by which man lifts himself above the other animals are those which enable him to handle primitive animal annihilation-anxiety with a durative defense. The self-system is an anxiety-buffering motor that is always idling.

Now it is well known that this unique development in the animal kingdom is possible for only one reason: the development of language, which permits a self-referential existence. As the infant learns 'mine–me–I' in that order, he fixes himself in a

---

*Original, full text: E. Becker, "Socialization, command of performance, and mental illness." *American Journal of Sociology,* 67: 494-501 (1962). Reprinted with permission from The University of Chicago Press.

space-time world populated by named, identifiable objects. [Harry Stack] Sullivan referred to the self-system as largely a series of linguistic tricks by which the human conciliates his environment—allays his anxiety, that is. Thus, self-reflexivity and anxiety avoidance are two sides of the same coin. They create symbolic action possibilities by making the world safe for a symbolic, self-reflexive animal. . . .

If the behavioral world of the self-reflexive animal is based on a pronominal 'I,' then the 'I' must be separated from the 'not-I.' In other words, the motivational goals, and the proper actions for reaching those goals, must be jointly defined as more desirable than other alternatives. The animal must have, in brief, a feeling of primary value in a world of meaningful objects. Culture, in this sense, is a symbolic fiction without which the psychological animal could not act. The basis of this fiction is a pattern of values, which gives vital meaning and permits action. . . . When we say that an individual is properly socialized, we mean simply that the process of formation of the self-system has been secure enough to enable him to sustain interaction with someone other than the agents of his immediate socialization. If he can do this, society provides him with a conventional code of rules for interaction, by which to sustain his own face and to protect the face of others. . . .

The problem, from a social point of view, is to respect the privacy and integrity of the individual and, at the very same time, to include him in social interaction. Society does this by a series of conventions which [Erving] Goffman includes under two main headings: deferential rituals of avoidance and deferential rituals of presentation. The body privacy, separateness, and the integral self of the individual must be accorded a degree of avoidance behavior. Avoidance implies that everyone has the right to keep others at a certain distance and recognizes that the self is personal. Presentation, on the other hand, implies that everyone has the right to engage others, *if it is done properly;* the self is recognized as social. Thus, all the conventions of salutation, farewell, quick formal smiles of acknowledgment, facile compliments, brief adjustments of another's tie or brushing his clothing, and so on, are presentation rituals which engage his self in social intercourse. . . .

The further problem is that the gestures of presentation which engage the individuals in social intercourse must not encroach too much on their private selves; a peculiar tension must be maintained between avoidance and presentation rituals. The individual, in sum, must be assured that if he entrusts his fallible face to society, it will take good care of it for him. . . . If this all seems axiomatic, its simplicity is deceptive. It is only when we consider the complement to deference, the phenomenon of demeanor, that the fictional fabric of social life becomes transparently clear. Demeanor refers to the problem of social action from the point of view of the individual. Demeanor means proper deportment, dress, bearing—in a word, self-regard. The individual is tasked to respect and maintain a sense of self. For an individual to have a sense of self—and this is of fundamental importance—means sustaining a named, identifiable locus of symbolic causality, which can be counted on to communicate within the social conventions. Demeanor is the *obligation to have a self,* so that there is something *socially transactable*. But the self-contained locus of communication must behave in an expected manner, so that his inclusion within the larger plot is a matter of facility. Otherwise, people would endanger themselves in undertaking interaction with someone who does not present a socially viable self. They would expose their fragile self-esteem to entirely capricious monstrosity.

Crucial to our understanding of the delicately staged plot of social actors within a social fiction of learned meanings, goals, and values is this: An individual who engages us by manifesting the proper deference must have an equally appropriate sense of demeanor to make the deference socially meaningful—he must present a credible stage personality. If our interlocutor does not have proper self-regard, he threatens us at the very core of our artificial action. It is fundamental to the implicit rules of social life that there must be no hint or revelation of the *unbelievably flimsy* basis for our impassioned life-and-death actions: the revelation that the self is merely an attitude of self-regard and a learned set of arbitrary conventions designed to facilitate symbolic action. The hopeful enjoinder that upholds the social fiction is: 'Let us all protect each other by sincere demeanor and convincing presentations, so that we can carry on the business of living.' The self-esteem of plural numbers of anxiety-prone animals must be protected so that symbolic action can continue. Not only must it be protected, it must in fact be enhanced by an intricate web of rituals for delicate handling of the self. Man must make provision for the utmost sensitivity in social intercourse. This fine social sensitivity is, as Goffman observes, largely what we mean when we speak of 'universal human nature' . . . .

The culture protects social action in two ways. By providing a strict code of social ritual, it makes available an adaptational device designed to prevent the contamination of social intercourse with private data. The more or less 'proper' thing to say in each situation is provided. At the same time, it protects the ongoing action situation by ablating the irrelevancies of private data. The socially awkward person is one who is not 'successfully' socialized from roughly two points of view: (1) His reaction-sensitivity prevents effective communication, and the forward motion of social action in a situation. (2) He has not learned to use with facility the social ritual rules for interaction. We can ask of an individual in this context: How much 'reaction-sensitivity' is present in his social presentation of face (of his positive self valuation)? To what extent do his needs and susceptibilities risk contaminating the smooth flow of face-saving ritual that the culture needs in order to function? . . . .

It is not widely enough recognized that easy handling of the verbal context of action gives the possibility of *direct exercise of power over others*. The individual who uses with facility "I'm terribly sorry," "Good show!" "Good to see you," and so on, creates the context of action for his interlocutor, by his confident manipulation of the conventional ritual verbiage. The parent's enjoinder "Say 'thank you' to the man" is not an inculcation of obsequiousness so much as it is a training in control . . . since action within shared meaning provides the only framework for the continual social validation of the actors, we can understand that deference is the means we have of enhancing one another. The ability to use its formulas with facility actually means the power to manipulate others by providing the symbolic context of their action. . . .

[U]sing the deference-demeanor model, we can see how identity and self-experience are *social created:* only by exercising demeanor and experiencing deference does the person fashion and renew himself by purposeful action in meaningful contexts. Thus, loneliness is not only a suspension in self-acquaintance, it is a suspension in the very fashioning of identity, because, cut off from one's fellows, one cannot exercise demeanor or experience deference. Therefore, he cannot experience his own powers and come to know himself as agent of them. In this sense, identity is simply the measure of power and participation of the individual in the joint cultural staging of self-enhancing ceremony. . . . It is important to realize that the delicate balance of avoidance and presentation rituals is not an easy one to manipulate. And, in order to have any skill at it at all, one needs a clear definition of the situation. It is precisely this that is obscured by poor socialization. A clear definition of the situation demands an apprehension of one's private self, a sensitivity to needs and expectancies in the interaction, and last but not least, a sure cognizance of self-other discreteness. Thus, in simplest terms, we might say that the basis for social ineptitude is the failure to form an adequate phenomenological self. A feeling of primary value, separation, and de-identification of self from the succoring figure, sure possession of one's body—these have all to be under the individual's control if he is at all to get started in the complicated game of role-playing. Otherwise, we have the familiar gaucheries of an overdoing of avoidance ritual, as, for example, by not allowing oneself to be touched when it is quite in order; or overdoing of presentation ritual by overpersonal manipulations and attentions. . . .

In the last analysis, *power over others* consists in presenting an infallible self and in commanding dexterous performance of deference. The power of the 'natural leader' resides perhaps in such fortunate socialization that a convincing self is invariably put forth, with sharp separation of personal and reality needs. By putting forth a convincing self, the actor obliges others to a more careful deference. The strong self forces others to make an effort at performance that may often be beyond their means. . . .

Socialization, then, is a preparation for *social performance* of the individual actor. Using this scheme (deference-demeanor) we might ask two key sociological questions of this individual preparation, questions familiar to the clinician: 'With what behavioral style has the individual *learned* to get his self-rights respected?' How, in other words, has the child obtained appreciation from significant adults of his discrete social self? The manner of obtaining respect for self would be his basic method of comportment, or demeanor. The other important question has to do with determining his basic pattern of orientation to deference: 'How has he learned to react to the hierarchialized status of others?' In other words, what kind of cognizance does he have of the plot, the fiction of social action in which he will be expected to perform? These two sets of questions are separated for conceptual purposes; actually they are part of the same judgment: *How has the actor been trained as a performer?* The social judgment of the individual can be phrased in stark terms of his rule-following ability. . . .

One cannot overemphasize the fact that the basic pattern of deference-demeanor in a society is the necessary social nutrient for the continuing creation of the personal significance of the social actors—a sort of public *mana* in which everyone is rejuvenated and supplied. There is a continuing affirmation of meaning in deference-demeanor social transactions which, although purely on a fictional-symbolic level of discourse, seems vital to the very organization of the self. This symbolic sustenance, in other words, seems a *sine qua non* for creating and maintaining an integral symbolic animal. This idea in itself is certainly not new, but its consequences have still not been followed through broadly enough in psychiatry, nor with the requisite theoretical relentlessness: that we cogitate this whole problem on the organism's purely symbolic functioning. . . .

The view that social life is a symbolic, fictional nutrient for a self-reflexive, symbolic animal represents one direct, theoretical approach to the problems of behavioral malfunction. Seen from the individual point of view, this problem presents itself in terms of the individual's ability to sustain a self of positive value in a world of meaning and to act according to the social conventions for sustaining and reinforcing that meaning by mutual support. When we realize that the action world of a symbolic animal is fictional and continually fabricated, nourished, and validated, this does not diminish the importance of that world to the behavior of *Homo sapiens*. There remains the problem of individuals who *cannot follow* the social ritual rules. Questions to which behavioral specialists should be sensitized are: In what ways is the manner in which this individual has learned to handle anxiety a hindrance in his performance of the ceremonial that permits sustenance of the social fiction of shared meaning? What are the rules for performance which society itself projects? Alertness to questions such as these would lead to a more sensitive understanding of the variations in performance ability of the individual actors, and (as in existing research) the reasons for that variation. Finally, and not least important, it would contribute to a greater flexibility of appraisal of the conditions for social becoming in an open democratic society.

Anthropological Notes on the Concept of Aggression (1962)*

ESPECIALLY RELEVANT TO THE DISCUSSION here is [Sigmund Freud's] sharply delineated subject-object polarity—a man-against-nature ontology—and his infusion of man's opposition with a powerful, aggressive instinct. . . . Of all animals, man alone filters his action-responses with the conceptual screen provided by culturally learned conventions. This idea is the keynote of my subsequent discussion, which is designed to contribute to the thoroughgoing cultural view of human action that has been in the mak-

*Original, full text: E. Becker, "Anthropological notes on the concept of aggression." *Psychiatry*, 25: 327-338 (1962). Copyright © 1962 Reprinted with permission from The Guilford Press.

ing for over fifty years but has long been restrained from full fruition. . . .

Judging from anthropological materials, there is every reason to consider aggression in large measure to be a learned reaction in the service of the ego. But this is not a new or surprising discovery. It is merely field evidence which anthropology contributes to the broad convergence of twentieth-century thinking on a view of man as a plastic, symbolic animal shaped by culture. . . .

The intimate connection of aggression with depression seems another good reason to suppose that it is largely a cognitively mediated response to fluctuations in total personality self-esteem. In [Edward] Bibring's reformulation of the mechanism of depression, which accords a central role to self-esteem, he cites a case that showed the marked sequence of depression, self-accusation, hypomania, and then aggression directed to the outside. He points out that fluctuation in self-esteem is the thread of continuity here, and not aggression as attempted mastery. Bibring says that the patient's aggressive fantasies were secondary to her exaggerated self-esteem, just as her turning of aggression within was secondary to lowered self-esteem. . . .

In sum, in many situations, aggression might be understood as an inept, sporadic way of creating a positive, acting self, of exaggerating or affirming self-esteem. Hate, after all, creates a valued self vis-à-vis an object. Paranoia functions similarly, but it is a relatively sophisticated mechanism, requiring a degree of imagination and control. In individuals whose organization is so faulty that they cannot fashion a positively valued self, rage and helplessness may replace the action possibilities of a focused hate. In situations where it is not culturally possible to sustain such a self—for example, the discovery of fraud at the Balinese cockfight—the outburst of rage may create and support self-affirmation. Hate-aggression is a moment of paranoia, which by creating a fiction—a hostile environment—permits a positively valued self, along with ongoing action in an encapsulated world. In this sense, it is a creative act. . . .

As I mentioned earlier, Bibring, in describing the clinical sequence of depression, self-accusation, hypomania, and aggression directed to the outside, says that the patient's aggressive fantasies were secondary to her exaggerated self-esteem, just as her turning of aggression within was secondary to lowered self-esteem. Thus, it is possible to understand the two aspects of aggression, turned within and without, as concomitants of the same drive-for-mastery function of the ego. But one can wonder how it is permissible to postulate—as is often done—aggression turned within, simply because there is no manifestation toward external objects. The theoretical encapsulation based on a constant drive is very neat. But the problem is only skirted, it seems to me, when the psychiatrist assumes that the aggression is turned within toward an introjected object. The self-accusations and delusional guilt of the depressed patient, which are taken to be a self-directed rather than object-directed aggression may really be, as [Alfred] Adler observed long ago, desperate attempts at sustained affirmation—even if negatively expressed.

When Sullivan stressed that anger is a cover for anxiety, he meant that anger is an affirmation that blocks helplessness. It is possible to imagine that the sense of positive self-value can be so low in the individual that self-affirmation vis-à-vis objects is no longer possible, not even by a creative act of aggression. 'Self-directed aggression' and 'latent hostility' may in some cases describe an individual who so lacks self-esteem that he is unable to affirm himself by aggressive behavior toward objects. Instead, some motivational coherence of the ego is sustained by self-denigration—a negative identity is created which in itself is an act of affirmation. In psychoanalytic terms, one can say that the creation of an overbearing superego permits the affirmation of an identity. But this is not the same as saying that the external aggression against objects is continued in an intrapsychic battle.

There seems to be every reason for a final, complete departure from the traditional Freudian idea of aggression as a primary destructive drive. Among other benefits, this would allow for a more sensitive treatment of the behavioral phenomena in the individual clinical case. Thus, as suggested above, aggression need not be a constant quality, or even due to simple reactions to frustration, but may in some instances be an attempt toward self-affirmation by a fragmented ego. Aggression can also be considered as due to cultural learning; as such, in some contexts, it may be the only way— or the most direct way—for an individual to get a feeling of self-value and socially recognized power; one might understand aggression to exist where alternative creative means of deriving a feeling of self-value have not been made available in a particular cultural context. Accepting these alternative impetuses to the creation and expression of aggression necessitates departing from a dualistic, mechanistic formulation, and progressing to a more holistic approach to social phenomena, a more mature, problem-oriented view of the subject matter of social science.

Psychotherapeutic Observation on the Zen Discipline (1960)*

PSYCHOTHERAPEUTIC OBSERVATIONS ON ZEN, which attempt to equate its result with that effected by psychoanalysis, have generally been uncritical. Obviously, no word can be final in the present state of knowledge, and the entire question is open to and in need of much more thorough study. But there is one need which is not being met, it seems, and that is for a critical antidote, at the very outset, to a too complete equation of Zen with psychoanalysis. . . .

Aspects of Zen which have "striking counterparts in current psychotherapeutic practice" are enumerated. The first such element is the necessity for the presence of a master. . . . The manner in which the master acts upon the student is compared to the psychoanalytic method: the need to maintain a "delicate balance" between the "encouragement necessary to maintain the subject's participation, and the frustration required for his continued self-examination." . . . The need for a resolution of ambivalence in the interpersonal relationship is particularly clear to the psychiatrist—

*Original, full text: E. Becker. "Psychotherapeutic observations on the Zen discipline: One point of view." *Psychologia*, 3: 100-112 (1960). Copright © 1960. Reprinted by permission of the Psychologia Society.

interpersonal adaptation under stress, and not reality-testing, is the main issue at stake for the disciple. . . .

The new task before the disciple is to win over the forbidding authority figure of the master, and it is this that becomes all-important. . . . In psychoanalysis, on the other hand, a premium is put on symbol recall in free association, "if for no other reason than for the purpose of communication between the analysand and analyst." . . . [Albert] Stunkard's observation on satori is that it seems to involve "no special insight." Rather, what occurs, is a change in the functioning of the individual. . . . [This change] in functioning is not immediate—satori is best understood as final introjection of the new value system, or superego of the master. One of the tasks Stunkard sets himself to is the psychiatric explanation of the arbitrary and irresponsible conduct described in the mondos (description in the literature, of persons who got satori). The novice may hit or otherwise mock the master, etc. The author uses [Karl] Abraham's view that "the goal of therapy is the resolution of the patient's ambivalence and narcissism."

The origins of ambivalence are found "in the state of infantile helplessness and consequent dependence upon an outside source of security and satisfaction." Ingratiating techniques alternate with hostility toward authority; the hostility gives way to attempts at conciliation, and the cycle "tends to perpetuate itself." Resolution of this ambivalence must be achieved by a resolution of the "infantile dependence upon symbols of authority.". . .

Stunkard sees in the Zen accounts of irreverence for authority reported in the mondos a therapeutic result precisely in Abraham's terms—a resolution of the ambivalence in the master-disciple relationship: the student slaps the master, and both laugh, etc. [Gregory] Bateson, et al., in their discussion of the "double bind" seem to agree with this point of view. Referring to the situation in which a stick is held over the pupil's head by the master, they compare it to the double-bind situation. The master says, "If you say this stick is real, I will strike you with it. If you say this stick is not real, I will strike you with it. If you don't say anything I will strike you it." In the double-bind situation, the schizophrenic is disoriented. But, in the Zen situation, they claim that the disciple can achieve enlightenment by an assertive action. . . .

Again, Zen is understood as having definite therapeutic results in its resolution of ambivalence toward authority. Stunkard finds this all the more remarkable, in that it comes against a background of "strongly patriarchal cultures of China and particularly Japan," where there is "painful acceptance of the traditional" on the part of the submissive individual.

Several qualifications are needed to this interpretation of a worthwhile therapeutic resolution of ambivalence in Zen—a result that closely parallels the aims of psychoanalysis. This point is crucial, since most of the acceptance of Zen as a therapy, in the view of Westerners, is based on such all interpretation: spontaneous individuation and freedom derived from a resolution of ambivalence. From a psychoanalytic point of view, such all interpretation is quite natural. Gordon W. Allport has called attention to the general need for shock in personality change. . . .

Clearly, the utterance of shocking and blasphemous ideas is a part of Zen training. From the Zen anecdotes there is little doubt that a psychological shock treatment is taking place. Obviously, what new materials the ego can incorporate which were previously "shocking" are culturally defined. In Freud's culture, Oedipus and latent homosexuality are powerful confrontations which, when admitted by the individual, give a sense of self-mastery. For the oriental, a burning of a statue of the Buddha, or a reply that the Buddha is only "three pounds of flax" are conceivably quite contrary to childhood learning. The incorporation of this blasphemy into the ego signals a kind of adult maturity and freedom—a relief of previous superego restraints. . . .

When the disciple seizes the stick with which he is threatened, or when he slaps the master in answer to a question—it is evidently up to the master to determine whether this represents a true grasp of the new value system—direct, uninhibited action in the place of cerebration. Or whether, on the other hand, it represents an aggressive acting out, in exercise of one's impulses quite independent of any understanding as to what they mean or should mean. In any case, the acceptance of the slap, or of the aggressive act of the disciple cannot mean the end of the Master's authority. . . . At best, resolution of the ambivalence to authority is bought at the price of introjecting the superego of that authority. One is free from the domination of the particular mortal person of a master, but one has become a convert to his value system. In terms of a religious conversion, one replaces a more personally constraining superego by a more permissive, more symbolic one. . . .

Let us grant to the specialist the veracity of his observations on the noncognitive nature of the psychoanalytic "insight" that causes a changed functioning; although it seems that this is the change that takes place after the emotional catharsis in analysis, which, after all, is agreed upon by all as having primacy over any "intellectual" understanding by the patient.

But, to equate the discipline of the koan, and its destroying of a logical causal view of reality, to the psychoanalytic taking away of the rationalizations and distortions of reality of the neurotic personality, seems to overlook an important distinction: The koan discipline does away with an habitual way of viewing external reality, via a dominance-submission relationship. In psychoanalysis, the primacy of the emotional catharsis is indisputable, but the mind is used, in accustomed logical, causal thinking, to reinforce this catharsis via understanding: one is dispelling rationalizations about oneself—not abolishing a way of seeing the entire world of external reality. Now it may well be argued—in line with Stunkard's observation—that the psychoanalyst sees "paratactic distortion" whereas the Zennist sees "illusion," and can take his choice. In other words, "what reality is one obscuring with what distortion?" Nor is a "logical, causal view of reality" an absolute: The Zennist scoffs at a logic that seeks to equate subjects in order to establish identities, whereas the psychoanalyst scoffs at a logic that seeks to equate predicates in order to arrive at the same result. But, the impression of absolute relativity that is conveyed is false. Paleologic, the equation of predicates, is a logic of emotionally determined premises. . . . And emotionally determined premises are not the best means for coping with external reality—however effective they may be in providing comforting beliefs in stressful areas of living.

[Erich] Fromm holds that the psychoanalytic "insight" does not appear "in our brain but . . . in our belly." Of course, the psychoanalytic experience, as an emotional catharsis, creates a new individual, or rather one who functions differently. But can this be equated with Zen? After all, the psychoanalytic reorientation is a clarification, a new orientation to one's own superego, effected, optimally, by understanding one's repressions and self-constraints; it is not an entirely new superego, effected by supportive, suggested methods. Repression is lifted and self-understanding created by examining unconscious materials, not by reorienting the individual to a new view of external reality. . . .

The crux of the matter is here, and evidently Fromm's option for the Zen value system prevents him from seeing it: if you abolish the theoretical structural system— unconscious versus conscious—then you are no longer talking about therapeutic un-repression as the bringing up of unconscious materials. You are talking, rather, about a total "eu-function" within a new value framework that utilizes the "total man," regardless of what the individual learns about himself. . . . This may be achieved by insightful, critical transference analysis. But one doesn't get this awareness by using [D.T.] Suzuki's methods: one simply gets a new package view of reality that replaces the old view. One does not exercise insight, but simply employs newly adopted symbols. . . .

Insisting on the priority of "total experience" over "intellectual insight," Fromm points out that Freud, in his earlier years, believed that giving the patient the proper information was enough to cure him, and Fromm bemoans the fact that some analysts still have not abandoned this concept of intellection. He adds that Freud never expressed himself "with full clarity" on the difference between intellectual insight and the total experience which occurs in "working through." "But this new and not intellectual insight is the aim of psychoanalysis." But surely, even in transference analysis where un-repression is only incidental, the working-through is characterized, in [Franz] Alexander's terms, by a "more and more precise verbalization of all the details of the emotional patterns." Working-through without any intellectual insight at all would not be psychoanalysis—even if that insight takes a minor second place to the purely emotional aspects of the working-through. In psychoanalysis, the working-through is rendered profitable to the individual by punctuation with insights that are purely cognitive—that make all appeal to the patient's logic as his defenses crumble: "You are acting this way because you think I am your father," etc. In Zen, too, there is an alternative reality offered in explanation of one's emotional frustrations—"you cannot get off a good shot because you have too much will," etc. But the difference is obvious and vital. The latter is an imposed view of reality which, in order to be accepted by the individual, requires a total change in his logical, causal apprehension of the world. Psychoanalysis, in its revelation of insights, appeals to a logic already possessed by the healthy part of the patient—the individual is being communicated with, in part at least, in terms which he can understand. He has only to unlearn the distorted part of his reality apprehension. . . .

In spite of the widening of the sector of the unconscious to be uncovered, by [Carl] Jung, Adler, [Otto] Rank, and the other neo-Freudians, the extent of it to be therapeutically handled was determined by the desire to cure this or that symptom or this or that neurotic character trait. Unconscious contents representing unsuccessful repressions which affected one's ability to cope consciously were considered the cause of one's illness—treatment was confined to that sector of the unconscious. . . . Id is replaced by Ego by means of working-through and insight. Or, in transference analysis, attention is confined to interpersonal processes largely. How, then, does one make the entire unconscious conscious? One is obliged to stick to the sector of the unconscious that has therapeutic significance because that is the part of the unconscious that is troublesome. If, however, one takes for granted that the unconscious possesses creative powers, then a value is attached to revealing those powers. But, how is this to be effected? Not, obviously, by the same methods of therapeutic uprooting of the repressed sector. There is no way of effecting, logically, a release of something that is not repressed. Therefore, the original aim of Freud cannot be followed to its last consequences by using the psychoanalytic method. In order to effect a release of something that is not repressed—in order to give full creative power to the total individual, he must acquire a new value system as a total individual. If this is the case, then one has no business either using the psychoanalytic terminology, or equating the psychoanalytic method with this goal—psychoanalysis and Zen are not comparable. . . .

The extreme authoritarian figure of the support analyst is duplicated in Zen, to a degree that surely no psychoanalyst would sanction. From accounts in the literature, there is no restraining the intensity of the transference into which the novice is plunged—a restraint that present-day analysts advise. The transference neurosis seems much more intense then any real-life situation, probably due to the fact that the disciple never knows what exactly is demanded of him until his regression becomes so complete that he simply surrenders to the new superego after a long conditioning process. The pupil's old authoritarian frustrations are re-enacted with heightened intensity in the master-disciple dyad—and the pupil has only one choice: to yield by incorporating the new superego. He is not led to any clarification of his old conflicts or of his unconscious contents.

Nor do sharp differences between Zen and psychoanalytic technique end here. One of the most recurrent problems in psychoanalytic literature is the problem of counter-transference—the emotional entering into the analysis on the part of the therapist himself. His aloofness and objectivity are not compromised by sympathetic friendliness, but his usefulness as an impartial helper is seriously impaired by any personal, emotional involvement in the therapy. Despite all claims of impartiality and disinterested objectivity made for the master, he seems to enter emotionally into the situation to a degree that would not be sanctioned in psychoanalysis: Accounts in the literature in which the master administers affectionate strokings on the back of the dis-

ciple, or the breaking off of the therapy because of an "affront" by the disciple. . . .
That the Zen therapy 'works' in a very real sense, that it creates an individual who is
convinced of a new-found strength and contentment, is not unexplainable in psychotherapeutic terms. Incorporation of a new superego does not have to be accompanied by insight and self-knowledge—this is the well-known technique of support therapy. Support therapy aims at a strengthening of the ego in reference to the other structures. . . . One way of strengthening the ego is to bring it into line with "the claims of
the superego." . . . [I]t would seem that Zen effects precisely this alignment: the new
functioning ego, emerging in a mastery of the skill being learned, meets approval of
the superego in a ready explanation of every success—and disapproval for every failure. As long as the ego continues to expand by proper learning within this new value
system, the superego continues to be approving and permissive. . . .

One of the difficulties in Zen is the distinguishing of "true" from "false" satori—
real apprehension of the value system versus the simple exercise of imagined new
powers. In other words, the ego that is built up must derive and use its powers within the superego that is inculcated. The old superego is replaced concomitantly with
the build-up of ego strength operating within the new value framework. Conscious
understanding, or insight by the patient into his unconscious, is sacrificed to the need
to obliterate the old superego. Ego replacing Id is not an absolute dictum of therapy
where the enhancing of ego strength via re-repression is the goal. An individual
whose psychic "economy" has been re-arranged by re-repression, ego strength, and a
new superego, can function perfectly well without the need for any insight into himself. But this is not psychoanalysis.

Ego strength in Zen seems to be built up by increased progress and proficiency in
the Zen skill. But the environment of the Zen master-disciple interaction is a true
subculture, isolated from the widespread values of the world at large. There is a magical quality surrounding the esoterics prototaxically and verbally imported by the master to the disciple. And the creative activity of the Zen skill seems to provide experiential confirmation of the otherworldly values of the Zen sub-culture. Effective adjustment
to environment and role responsibilities can be maintained by periodic, rejuvenating
withdrawal; it is perhaps here that Zen can be said to be therapeutic in a true sense, and
is at the same time at a polar remove from the result effected by psychoanalysis.

Private Versus Public Logic (1961)*

THE MAIN TASK OF THE EMERGING INDIVIDUAL is the discovery of himself
and world. Reality-oriented from the first, the infant tries to surmise boundaries and
depths, especially of self and objects. By taking the attitudes of others toward himself, by 'identifying' with the object, the child gives his own body an outside and at

*Original, full text: E. Becker, "Private versus public logic: Some anthropological notes on the problem of
mental health." American Journal of Psychiatry, 118: 205-211 (1961). Reprinted with permission from the
American Journal of Psychiatry, Copyright (1961) American Psychiatric Association.

the same time apprises the inside of the flat, external object ministering to his needs. The world comes to be seen in the round.

But reality testing does not continue smoothly. The environment causes frustrations, which give rise to conflicting impulses and inhibitions, and a new task is posed. The infant must find out what the novel features are in the new frustrating situation, in order to organize a response. This response, once organized, follows the conservatism of all organisms: it tends to be pertinent not only for the particular individual but also for others. Thus, two new ideational components come into being: analysis of the unfamiliar, and representation of it in a generalizable direction. This play of ideas for coping with reality—analysis and representation—is internalized as a trial-and-error method within the individual, and thought and reflection become new tools for facilitating conduct.

These are George Herbert Mead's ideas, and he extended them in his understanding of the scientific method itself, and so put the method back into proper, exoteric perspective. Frustration arises when we meet a problem in thought, action or feeling, or an inhibition or exception to accustomed conduct. Our reaction to the new situation is characterized by a certain opposition of feelings—the same inhibition that the infant feels in the face of his frustration at something new and constricting. A problem, whatever its nature, can only come into existence when forward momentum in a particular situation has been stopped. Now, the statement of appraisal of just what it is in the situation that calls out the inhibiting reactions is what we call gathering the data or facts by analyzing the situation. The hypothesis is merely a mental reconstruction of the situation, taking into account its presumed unusual aspects, and designed to eliminate what was previously inhibiting. The hypothesis serves to unplug the situation, with the facts duly taken note of, so that forward action can continue. The problem is solved when the momentum resumes. In other words—and this is important—the unplugging of the situation depends initially on the problem being resolved *in the mind* of the hypothesizer. External reality gives its assent to our appraisal of the facts only later on, when we experiment by acting on the hypothesis. . . .

Thus, the primary character of thought . . . is its function as a proof of reality. The scientific method is a method of natural inference which grows out of a more primitive 'attitude taking.' To get a proper appraisal of a social situation in order to act, the individual tries to get as many perspectives as he can on the situation, so that his behavior will be based on sound inference. It is to the great merit of the sociologists to have insisted that the simple operation of role-taking is integral to social living: role-taking simply means taking the attitude of others toward oneself and toward the objective situation, so that behavior will be based on a many-sided pattern of inferred facts. Role taking is an anticipation of the situation for valid action. It is because everyone has roles and can imagine the roles of others that social behavior is at all possible with a minimum of confusion. Role taking, in sum, is a fundamental source of data obtained by the trial-and-error method practiced within the individual by thought. It is a natural means of providing information by inference. Ultimately, then, we can see that the individual is *forced to become social in order to function:* his behavior cannot take place independently of thoughtful identification with the behavior of others, i.e., role taking. . . .

[S]ome forms of behavioral dysfunction, especially paranoia, arise through the individual's inability to take roles. Thus, instead of constantly validating his action and thought by sound social inference, he comes to create a purely private delusion; at no points in this delusion do the real attitudes and roles of others break through. The individual has effectively isolated himself, and has determined his own eventual destruction, by his inability to see himself and the social situation from a many-faceted view.

Role-taking skill can, in fact, be considered a pivotal criterion for mental health. In his ability to take roles, the individual allows himself a flexibility, an adaptability and re-adaptability, that make for a constantly buoyant orientation to a changing social field. An individual who cannot take roles, risks submerging himself in unverifiable private thoughts and delusions, as his suspicions and susceptibilities are reinforced into a false dogma, which is unquestioningly adhered to. In his inability to throw fresh social light upon his private preoccupations, by taking the role of others, the paranoid becomes a dogmatist. His theory (delusion) was initially a mental release from an intolerably uncertain situation, but he becomes hedged in by the dogma itself. Now paranoia is a very graphic illustration of how social isolation is effected by the inability to use thought properly in reality testing. The main function of natural scientific inference is thereby defeated. We are tempted, therefore, to support the view that here, indeed, is an objective criterion for pathological behavior. The question is prompted: Can the idea of mental health be considered a phenomenon purely relative to cultural norms, when role-taking skill defines the individual's flexibility and adaptability, and therefore his sound social functioning? . . .

[M]ind is an evolution in nature, and [sociality] gives form to emergent mind. Mind, in other words, is first formed in the infant's taking the role of others to orient his own action by natural inference. So that, evolved on its highest level, consciousness is wholly socially reflexive: the individual apprehends as wide a variety of generalized standpoints as possible. By taking the role of the other in thought, the mind can be projected to any part of the universe. . . . Meaning in life is fashioned from the perspectives which thought can encompass. Beginning as painful inference to overcome physiological helplessness, the infant's mind becomes, ultimately, an impersonal, socially reflexive entity, projecting disembodied scientific concepts. Through impersonal rational mind, man becomes wholly social.

But he does not become *personally* social. Here is the rub. Implicit in our discussion of role taking is the idea that it may serve two kinds of thought processes: 1. That process whereby the individual assumes the attitudes of others, inferentially, in a social situation; 2. That process whereby the individual makes various inferences in systematized abstract thinking. In order for science and logic to luxuriate, literacy and symbolic manipulations had to succeed a constricting illiteracy, so that the dexterity of mind in inferring complementary propositions could be given free rein. The consequences of this for the individual may now be considered ominous. Role taking in science and logic, the rapid leafing through mentally of complementary and opposing attitudes, releases the mind from inhibition. But in his juggling of abstract symbols, the individual formulates problems and hypotheses that have no relationship to present, external reality. The impasse one reaches in a private, logical problem is an introverted one. It does not need social proving out. When literacy enabled the rise of science, man could proceed to unbridled use of role taking in inferential logical analysis, independent of his own organismic experience. Mind, in other words, loses its primary social function, as it becomes peopled with systems of visual abstract symbols. Logic becomes internally uninhibiting, and the social proving out of the most esoteric products of mind is totally unnecessary. Einsteinian generations of thinkers could live a part of each day taking the role of light beams around the sun, and thus be truly lost to the social community a good part of the time.

Emergent mind seems to operate with a vengeance against the animal's boundness to the here and now. When the 'superego' is implanted in the child, his mind is claimed for society. Paradoxically, the further development of rational thought serves to separate the individual more and more from his early symbolic identifications, whether as the growth of the scientific thinker or the religious convert. The self-custodial function of the superego runs its full course: as rational scientific mind becomes thoroughly social, the *individual* is given the possibility of becoming asocial. The written word and the development of logic serve to free man from a personal dependence upon the immediate social world. . . .

Despite the abstract level of our discussion thus far, its import to a practical psychiatry is quite clear. As private logic enables the luxuriation of a symbolic world that is idiosyncratic, the individual is allowed to create a psychological behavioral world as fantastic as that of the legendary 'primitive.' In other words, though we should like to imagine that the growth of literacy has permitted an unprecedented realism, we may be as far from it, individually, as ever—and perhaps even a good deal further. If the separation of public and private logic represents a growing historical dichotomy, the subjective and objective worlds are no nearer to determination by realistic standards.

Margaret Mead once observed that in our culture, cause-and-effect thinking is *culturally learned*. Quite naturally, we link present happenings to past causes, even if thereby we really learn or explain nothing. The psychiatrist is best witness to the patient who painstakingly links present malfunction to minute sexual trauma of the past, when in reality these have nothing to do with his basic problem. Furthermore, although we culturally value the idea of realism, the testing and proving-out of propositions, it might be found that we are quite off the mark in most of our thinking. At the present point in history, it would probably take a visitor from an uncorrupted planet to discover the illogic in our minute checking out of the mechanical details in a new car, which we may have never needed yearly-renewed in the first place. . . .

[C]ulture provides the self-reflexive human with a psychological behavioral world designed to furnish him with the one premise without which he cannot live: the conviction that he is an object of primary value in a world of objects. Culture, in brief, provides the symbolic myth of meaning to an otherwise impossible world. Since man is the only animal who can reflect, who can objectify himself, he is thus also the only one who must infuse his self-objectification with a sense of primary value. This basic function of culture is well known and unassailable. It follows, of course, that if each individual must assign himself a sphere of primary value in a psychological behavioral world, each society tends to arrogate unto itself the pretension to a symbolic meaning system that is unimpeachable—if it is at all approachable by others. . . .

[T]here are at least two very trenchant reasons for doubting that widespread realism is characteristic of our culture. In the first place, as indicated above, the private world of the literate thinker may never be socially proven-out. The logical manipulations of the scientific theorist may provide both himself and a good percentage of his fellows with a full-time activity that may only be proven *totally unreal* several generations later. Not only does the individual's private logic permit him a socially accepted positive self-valuation on the basis of his 'scientific genius,' but his real alienation from the world of reality can, like paranoia, proceed without check. In the second place—and this is really the crux of the matter—this alienation *has nothing to do with survival in an immediate sense.*

[Paul] Radin's Winnebago could afford to be tolerant of the individual's deviation by private thoughts. Besides, where community survival hinges on some sound everyday logic in hunting and fishing, and everyone usually pitches in on the task, social testing of individual preoccupations is never long delayed. Shared activities upon which life and death depend are more immediate; they demand a more strict adherence to logical rules that can be perceived by all. The individual who demonstrates subjective deviation or nonsense in the dangerously exacting job of offshore communal fishing will often be quickly dispatched into unconsciousness by an alert group.

In civilized living . . . social survival [is] assured in a society of plenty, and with the products of private logic susceptible of remaining untested during an entire lifetime, the individual can no longer destroy himself, like Radin's Winnebago.

Thus, our society is unique in that, not only is the individual immune to self-destruction by following his private logic, but even were he to follow it to the point of extreme catatonia, *we do not let him die.* Our society places a positive value on neonates, aged and maladjusted that in itself might be considered culturally and historically somewhat peculiar. . . . The primitive, in other words, tolerates the aberrant private logic because he also tolerates the self-destruction it entails. By the very same cause and effect, we do not tolerate the self-destruction, and *therefore do not tolerate the private worldview.* . . . [T]o the extent that private logic is considered dangerous to a society, it will be controlled. In those instances in which magical thoughts are a menace to the whole community, the individual's own death may be unimportant, but the damage he can do with his mind is. . . .

The ineluctable historical innovation of literacy, private logic and an economy of plenty seem to exacerbate the problem of mental health. To what extent can we clarify, by attempting to view objectively, the peculiar rationalizations of our culture as it copes with these innovations? This is a research problem of no small import. For example, a lobotomy not only prevents individual 'death,' it also prevents cultural death. The primitive, by allowing his deviant to die, forestalled thereby any living reproof to the sacrosanct symbolico-cultural system of sustained meaning upon which society depended. The cultural myth of action and meaning had to be unshakable, since deviation from it demonstrably meant death. But the living mental deviant in our society permits no such ready reinforcement. Allowed to live, his private distorted meanings assume an unnatural discordance; they threaten to illuminate the transparency of the culturally fabricated meaning from which humans draw sustenance. We can rejoice when the disease-ridden patient triumphs over natural biological limitations. But it is quite otherwise with culture: man cannot allow triumph over or indifference to his own fabrications of meaning.

Toward a Comprehensive Theory of Depression (1962)*

UNTIL EDWARD BIBRING'S THEORY, SELF-DIRECTED aggression was considered a primary mechanism in depression. Bibring signaled a radical departure from previous theory when he postulated that self-directed aggression was secondary to an undermining of self-esteem. Thereby, he delivered an apparently telling blow to formulations around the concepts of orality and aggression—in fact, to any predominantly instinctual formulation of the syndrome. Bibring conceived depression primarily as an ego phenomenon. . . . If self-esteem is the primary focus of depression, then it is evident that symbols play a larger role in its dynamics than does physiology. The Oedipal transition is defined precisely as a changeover from physiological to symbolic derivation of self-esteem. No matter what biological residues remain as predicates for self-esteem, it is difficult now to conceive how these can be of overriding importance.

It would, I think, be impossible to overestimate the significance of this shift in emphasis. Indeed, one may wonder that it was so long in coming. Part of the reason is, of course, the historical neglect of [Alfred] Adler's early views. An ego-based theory of depression broadens the area of its dynamics from a purely intrapsychic battlefield to the entire range of social phenomena. Since the ego is rooted in social reality, depression becomes a direct function of a cognitively apprehended symbolic world. Nothing less than a full sweep of cultural activity is brought

*Original, full text: E. Becker, "Toward a comprehensive theory of depression: A cross-disciplinary appraisal of objects, games and meaning." *Journal of Nervous and Mental Disease,* 135: 26-35 (1962). Reprinted with permission of Lippincott, Williams & Wilkins.

into consideration in any single case of depression.

The full fruits of this broader view of depression have still to be gathered. It is amazing that human action could have been so consistently and thoroughly conceived in instinctual and compartmentalized terms. . . . Even in sociology, which views the self-image as inseparable from the symbolic social roles and structure, there are those who remain overawed by the simplicity of a 'man *versus* society' dialectic. . . .

In the classical psychoanalytic formulation of depression, mourning and melancholic states, loss of a loved object was considered to be a crucial dynamic. The ego which (theoretically) grows by ideationally gathering objects into itself, was thought to be subject to sometimes massive trauma when loved objects had to be relinquished. The loss of an object in the real world meant a corresponding depletion of the ego. Freud theorized beautifully on the rather elaborate procedures set up to ease this relinquishing of objects—the funeral rites, mourning states and so on. There is nothing fundamentally wrong with the view of depression—it explains a good deal. Its principal drawback is that it is used to explain too much. . . .

With this broadening out of traditional object-loss theory, [Thomas] Szasz links this area of psychoanalysis fully with social science. In fact, he equates depression as game-loss with sociological 'anomie' as norm-loss. Objects and games, as he insists, are not mutually exclusive: they are inseparably joined. They provide man with a staged drama of significance, which is the theater for his action. When an object is lost, often an entire game is undermined; especially if *appeal to that object* was a principal predicate for one's action.

Thus, depression, understood as loss of self-esteem and as game-loss, is all of a piece with the traditional sociological view of human action: namely, a view of man as social performer [whose] ... identity is created and validated in the social arena. Man discovers himself by making appeal for his identity to the society in which he performs. To lose an object, then, is to lose someone to whom one has made appeal for self-validation. To lose a game is to lose a performance part in which identity has been fabricated and sustained. . . .

The fact is that self-esteem *is the basic predicate* for human action. The fascination of psychoanalytic characterology and its cogency in explaining much human conduct stems from its relatively straightforward formulation: the various characters are all idiosyncratic means of maintaining and maximizing self-esteem. Nothing could be simpler, once the Oedipal transition is understood as a learning period in which self-esteem comes to be derived from symbolic rule-prescriptions for behavior, in place of physiological transitions with the mother.

Anthropology has confirmed the fundamental place of self-esteem in human action. It seems that nowhere on this once-vast globe has man been able to act unless he had a basic sentiment of self-value. The primary task of culture is precisely to construct the individual as a locus of primary value. Unless the actor feels worthwhile, and unless his action is considered worthwhile, the zest for living will surely disappear. . . .

By focusing on the symbolic and linguistic aspects of meaning-loss, we can explain the relentless self-accusations and guilt of the depressed that seem evasive to formulations around self-esteem-loss and game-loss. Thereby we counter the possible objection to simplicity raised above. Cross-cultural data are especially relevant here.

It was formerly thought that depression was rare among the 'simpler' peoples, for several reasons. For one thing, traditional societies enjoyed firmly institutionalized rituals and practices that provided dependable and ready catharsis for object-loss. For another, it was thought that the absence of a Christian tradition of sinfulness lessened the accumulation of guilt so prominent in the depressive syndrome. . . . But contrary to this accumulated mythology, [Margaret J.] Field's recent study of rural Ghana shows that depression can be quite common there. Depressed women in considerable numbers travel to Ashanti religious shrines, and there hurl accusations of vile witchcraft against themselves. They present a guilt-laden syndrome which appears to be quite like that of our culture. Field postulates that depression has probably had a long historical connection with witchcraft. The self-accusation of witchcraft seems to provide the perfect justification for failure and worthlessness. In the case of the Ashanti woman, the explanation seems quite clear. She raises large families with extreme care, is an excellent housekeeper and business woman as well. There is enough significant action on her life to provide ample self-justification. But often when the wife grows old the fruit of her labor is lavished by the husband on a younger bride.

How is the individual then to justify this utter subversion of life-meaning? A life-plot that had consistency, integrity and full social support is suddenly undermined. Fortunately, the culture provides a ready rationalization. The continuity of the staged drama of one's life-experience need not be broken—the woman can simply acknowledge that *all along* she has been a witch. The culture provides a reasonable explanation for an otherwise cruel turnabout: "I have become useless because I have always been evil. I deserve to be hated." Thus it would seem that, in any culture, depressive self-accusation serves to supply a meaning to one's life-plot in the event that all other props for meaning are pulled away. Let it be stressed emphatically that the most difficult realization for man is the possibility that life *has no meaning*. This apprehension comes to very few. Even then it is perhaps easier to speculate that *all* life may be in vain, than to admit that *one's own* life has been. It seems paradoxical that even in opting out of life, a meaning must be supplied: "Let me die *because* I am worthless." The problem of fashioning a coherent identity remains to the end.

The ego, after all, strives to create a continuity of integrated experience. As [Erik] Erikson's work shows so eloquently, the identity is a painstakingly fashioned work of art. It is symbolically constructed, continually refashioned, never complete. The individual can be compared to a movie director who is saddled with a lifetime job of staging a plot, the outcome of which he never knows. Indeed, he never knows what will happen *in the very next scene,* but he must strive to give the whole thing credibility

and self-consistency. This he can only accomplish by reworking the previous material as new events joggle his creation. When one gets down to the last twenty years of
a life drama, it becomes more and more difficult to justify abrupt changes in continuity: there is too much preceding plot for it to be re-manipulated with ease. Whole portions cannot be re-interpreted with credibility, much less re-staged. Hence, if the continuity is radically undermined, the individual grasps at whatever straws his ingenuity can muster. No movie director would accept such an assignment, yet each individual is burdened with this ultimately and perilously creative task. The remark that an
individual cannot know if his life has been satisfactory until the moment before he
expires then becomes understandable. Life is symbolically re-appraisable until its
very last second. The proverbial drowning man who passes his life in review is merely exercising the last impulsion of the reclaiming artist.

It is important to realize that man possesses only one tool for his highly critical
appraisal of experience, namely, words. Life's meaning is contained, fabricated and
elaborated primarily in words. Words give man the motivation to act, and words justify the act. Life-meaning for man is predominantly an edifice of words and word
sounds.

The power of words lies in the fact that they dress our action with meaning—
frosting the cake, so to speak. Action and forward momentum are primary for
energy-converting organisms. Meaning does not need language. Possibilities for the
forward momentum of action exist *in nature*. Action gives experience which provides meaning because it commands attention and leads to *further* action. Language
merely makes action more meaningful for a symbolic animal. But something curious happens in the case of man. Since we have grown up learning verbal motivation
for most of our acts, an unprecedented thing occurs: for man alone among all animals there is no cake if the frosting is missing. We are paralyzed to act unless there
is a verbal prescription for the situation. Non-verbal situations do not commit our
attention and hence do not call up action. (Obviously I am omitting consideration of
the non-discursive arts, which do not apply in this context.) In other words, man
loses very early the capacity to 'act in nature' as it were. For the infant, each of his
acts becomes dressed in words. Words serve to convey to him the consequences of
his action and thus to make anxiety-free conduct possible. As a child, lacking a
word, he lacks a safe action. Action and word-prescriptions become inseparable. As
an adult, lacking a word, he lacks a meaningful action. The simplest act has to take
on meaning, has to point to something beyond itself, exist in a wider referential
context.

The upshot of all this is crucial for our discussion of depression and self-accusation, where the depressed person employs witchcraft or other rationalizations. It is
simply this: when action bogs down, meaning dies. For man, it suffices that verbal
action bog down in order for meaning to die. In other words, *if the individual can keep
verbal referents going in a consistent scheme,* action remains possible and life retains
its meaning.

In the face of sharp changes in object relationships, the individual has two control tasks: 1) to maintain the continuity of identity, and 2) to continue action in the situation. Both of these tasks are accomplished by finding a proper framework of words which will sustain the identity and the action. Self-esteem, symbolic integrity of the identity and the plot, and possibilities for continued action must all be provided for. This is no mean job, and the burden of it all is on the *proper word formula*. Small wonder that private justifications so often become 'paranoid': words have manifold meanings. Take, for example, the woman in our culture who helps her husband through college, gives up her own education to do it, and then finds that she is growing old and useless while he is becoming more successful and independent. She is in roughly the same position as the Ashanti woman, except that she has no witchcraft tradition to fall back on for ready rationalization of her sense of utter uselessness and worthlessness. One justification the culture provides her with to maintain her self-esteem and identity is the possibility that her husband is 'cheating on her.' For him to be adulterous means he is failing to uphold his part of the marriage bargain. This is obviously the *closest she can come* to adumbrating that he is 'cheating her,' *since the culture does not give voice* to the idea that the frustrated career wife of a successful businessman should feel cheated when she has been well provided for. She may go to any lengths to imagine adulterous affairs of her husband, even in her own home while she sleeps upstairs—the picture is familiar. It is noteworthy that in these cases the person rarely attempts to surprise 'the lovers,' even though ample opportunity presents itself. It is as though one fears undermining a rationalization that so perfectly sustains meaning.

The narrower the performance scene, the more precarious is the situation. That is, the more people to whom one can make appeal for his identity, the easier it is to sustain life-meaning. Object-loss hits hardest when self-justification is limited to a few objects. But object-loss is not crucial (or even necessarily important) *per se*, when there is the possibility of sustaining one's performance as before. Further support for Szasz's view of the theoretical primacy of game-loss over object-loss is the situation in the extended family of traditional society. The life-chances and life-meaning of the individual do not depend on only a few parental objects. Rather, they are generalized to a whole range of kin. The extended family provides a continuing source of esteem and affirmation for the individual actor, *even though significant figures drop out*. In our culture, we are familiar with the case of the person who lives his life for the wishes of his parents and becomes depressed when they die and he has reached the age of forty or fifty. Obviously, he has lost the audience for whom the plot in which he is performing is valid. He is left in the hopeless despair of not having anyone to appreciate his lifelong surrender to the dictates of others. He is truly left in the lurch. The extended family conceivably skirts this problem: even though behavioral prescriptions for the individual are rigid, still he can count on a continuing audience for his performance even after his parents die.

When we hear of those who cannot for several days leave the grave of a loved one who has just died, it is often because the grave contains the only one to whom they can appeal for their identity. They no longer have anyone for whom to perform meaningfully—and it may be too late to start one's own show, develop a new part. Normally, the work of mourning takes place without great difficulty, because the death of a loved one always contains one *positive* element. It removes an actor who is part of the old plot. Therefore, the urge to ego mastery and the continual fashioning of identity is satisfied by the new possibility of changing one's performance. One need no longer refer in his identity performance to certain past events. This is another way of describing the work of mourning, which in psychoanalytic terms takes place as 'introjecting the lost object' and the gradually 'working it through.' One continues to perform in the old plot with the lost object's image and cues familiarly in mind. Gradually, this old performance inhibits the challenge of newness and change, and the old plot is transformed as the object is 'worked through.' An altered life style and identity ends the work of mourning. However, despair, and the inability to 'extroject' the object, may mean simply that the departed object so controlled one's performance that continuing the play in any altered manner is unthinkable or impossible. The meaning in one's life so belonged with the object that it has died with the object, and the development of an altered life style is impossible. . . .

In sum, the preservation and creation of meaning is basic to human action. And conversely, the bogging down of action and meaning signals human failure. It is convenient to pin syndrome labels in these action failures, because they define a point of clinical approach to the problem. . . . But these labels should not obscure the full reach of these failures into high-level cognitive integrations, as well as into a total social performance world. . . . Man makes a cognitive synthesis of experiences and joins to it his own feeling of worth. When action bogs down and experience becomes unsatisfying and frustrating, self-esteem is directly threatened. *Homo sapiens* maintains his self-esteem predominantly by symbolic words and word sounds. Where there is a poverty of word justification for one's known failures and inchoate dissatisfactions, any convincing rationalization will do.

Toward a Theory of Schizophrenia (1962)*

ONE OF THE MOST SUGGESTIVE AND ECONOMICAL schematizations of the precise problems to which humans everywhere must find an answer is that of Florence Kluckhohn. Her *5 common human problems* seem directly to clarify the question of 'stupidity' in primary enculturation data. These are problems to which every culture must provide an answer, and although I have never seen them detailed in reference to possible schizophrenic shortcomings, they seem particularly applicable to him. The function of answers to these problems is basic to the organism,

*Original, full text: E. Becker, "Toward a theory of schizophrenia: External objects and the creation of meaning." *Archives of General Psychiatry,* 7: 170-181 (1962). Reprinted with permission of the American Medical Association.

because they clear the world for action. Though they appear simple, answers to them are vital to peculiarly human, symbolic action:

1. What are the innate dispositions of men?
2. What is the relation of man to nature?
3. What is the direction in time of the action process?
4. What type of personality is most valued?
5. What is the dominant modality of relationships of man to other men?

Variations in primary enculturation may be approached on this 5-problem basis. Thus, when [Harry Stack] Sullivan observed that the schizophrenic never knows what the next person will be like, and never suspects that he can be pleasant, it is permissible to conclude that the schizophrenic has not resolved the first human problem. On this view, the well-known double-bind theory of [Gregory] Bateson *et al.* could be a focus on the area responsible for the basic stimulus to uncertainty: continuing, severe double-bind creates a disposition to confusion.

As regards Problem 2, it is characteristic of many schizophrenics that their hold on the meaning and purpose of life is weak. The loss of a loved object will often suffice to cause extreme bewilderment over why man is here and what life is all about. This could be conceived as resulting from a deficiency of internal objects. The individual poses one out of a meager 'store' of objects and has little left of close identifications to fall back on. But as we shall see in our subsequent discussion, it can be conceived in much broader perspective.

Problem 3 concerns the well-known and crucial basic function of the ego as a time-binder by means of which a pronominal identity fixes itself in a meaningful past-present-future and can confidently find its place in a time stream. Accordingly, it happens that a schizophrenic, in his inability to securely fix time, often cannot control memories: he cannot hold the past at bay or envision a future. . . . [O]ne definition of regression is merely the relinquishing of temporal perspective by the ego. [O]ne could say that a difference in the inner relation to the time experience alone is the regression. Unrepression of unconscious contents and ego-strength may be two poles of the same self-referential fixing in time and space. Variations in ego strength, that is, seem to place time perspective in different values. The future may seem far to a weaker ego, and the past may seem immediate in the present. Regression might be defined from one point of view as a composite of those events in relation to which the ego does not possess any experiential fullness and which it cannot keep out of the present. This would apply to past trauma, or to a future that does not seem controllable. Allowance may have to be made in [Donald L.] Burnham's postulate that the schizophrenic peoples his present environment with known faces from his past in order to orient himself. Actually, this may not be wholly a process of comfortable orientation at all, but rather also an inability to keep the past out of the present world. Faces keep popping up, toward which the schizophrenic could not create an experiential distance in time. Finally, it is this lack of control of self within the time process that is in large meas-

ure responsible for the oft-noted inability to plan, and consequent 'aimlessness.' . . .
As regards Problem 4, the schizophrenic often has the vaguest and most idealized
images, untempered by rational critical assessment of detail. [And finally,] Problem
5 is actually a part of Problem 1.

Answers to these 5 common problems permit human action. By means of these
answers, the individual constructs himself (a) as an object of primary value (Problems
2, 4, and 5); (b) who acts without anxiety (Problems 1 to 5); (c) in a world of meaning (Problems 1 to 5). And acting without anxiety in a world of meaningful objects
contributes to and reinforces the sentiment of primary value and the urge to masterful action.

We are disposing rather quickly of these problems at this time, hoping that they
will become more meaningful in the light of the subsequent discussion. Suffice it to
stress here that the most important fact about these common problems, for our subsequent discussion, is simply this: they can never be adequately *imparted* to anyone.
They must be lived and achieved by the individual himself. . . . If one refrains from
using the word 'schizoid' in a pejorative sense—as it obviously cannot be used—it
refers to a multitude of individuals who have had difficulties specifically in one or
even several of the above experiential ranges; individuals who, nevertheless, have
gone unnoticed in (or achieved distinction from) the social melee. . . .

The social-psychological contributions of George Herbert Mead to our knowledge of human behavior are becoming increasingly well known. His elaboration of
the concept of 'role' has already a wide currency and has stimulated considerable and
continuing research and theory. His view of the social genesis of mind—common currency in philosophy—has also entered social science, where it promises ultimately
(and belatedly) to displace Freud's rigid mechanism, essentialism, and physicalism.
Less well known perhaps, but of especial interest here, is Mead's behavioristic view
of meaning. Without doing violence to Mead's carefully elaborated and subtly
detailed ideas, I think we can sum up briefly the essence of his view on meaning.

For Mead, meaning has its locus in the adjustment of an organism to other
organisms and objects. In other words, meaning arises when something occurs in the
environment to which the organism can react. In social intercourse among the lower
organisms, reactivity meaning is triggered by the gesture of another: a dog responds
to the bark of another, a bird to a cry, and so on. . . . But since man is a self-reflexive animal, he reacts to his own internal environment. He is not dependent upon concrete objects to sustain meaning. By means of symbols, the human being is self-
stimulating and self-responsive, as Mead says. We create a world of symbolic movement, using objects as a referential base. But in private soliloquy, the symbols themselves become objects to which we can respond. While all animals are dependent
upon action to create and sustain meaning, the human animal can substitute symbolic elaboration as a form of action. Thus, the individual has two sources of meaning:
environmental and interpersonal action-meaning; and self-stimulating, intrapersonal,
word action-meaning.

However, this distinction . . . is less important for our discussion at this point than the fact that meaning exists entirely within the field of action and experience—within the field of behavioral response. In fact, Mead stressed that meaning exists prior to the symbol. The symbol merely serves to make meaning conscious to the acting organism. Meanings are already in nature, in the form of objects, which can be responded to. . . . Meaning is not primarily a content of mind; it is only derivatively a conscious phenomenon. *Meaning exists within behavior and only within behavior. Any object which does not organize behavior has no meaning.* . . .

The relevance to schizophrenia of the behaviorist view of meaning is perhaps already obvious. Let us consider the more important external action world of meaning. For the individual, action goes forward and individuation takes place by reducing problematic situations to habitual ones. (Mead's and [John] Dewey's view.) The individual, in other worlds, overcomes a problematic situation *by finding a dependable response* which he can make to it. Until a response is found for a problematic sector of experience, it may be said that this sector does not fully exist. By attempting to predict what will happen in a problematic situation, the individual searches himself for a potential response to that situation, by means of which it can be overcome. The process of individuation, therefore, is one in which problematic situations *are converted into objects.* If a response cannot be summoned for a particular problematic situation, the situation does not attain the status of an experiential object. . . . We must conclude from this that constituting oneself an object of primary value in a world of meaningful objects cannot be only a function of 'transmission' of cultural values. It is directly a function of experientially *converting* that world into meaningful objects, by being able to overcome problematic situations through the reduction of them to habit. By his inability to organize dependable behavioral responses to an anxiety-laden environment in flux, the schizophrenic lives in a relatively objectless world. His answers to the five common problems *never become meaningful* because no pattern of dependable behavioral response can be organized around them.

Now when the schizophrenic tells us that things are relatively without meaning for him, we *infer* that he is deficient in internal objects. Because, we imagine that meaningful action is patterned wholly on the values embodied in ideal representations. Actually, we need not (and perhaps should not) limit ourselves to so narrow an inference, if we consider values (meaning) to be composed of organized behavioral responses to objects in the external (and also the self-reflexive) world. Short of metaphysical idealism, there is no other way to consider them. This view of meaning brings it back to a phenomenological level, from which it was shifted by the internal object theory. It should be possible to devise ways to *determine* the relative extent of a schizophrenic's external object world, whereas it is possible only to *infer* the extent of the internal object world.

It is permissible to say that a conviction of meaning in life has to be built up, day by day, and built into the organism, by overcoming problematic situations and thus *creating* meaning. Early peer contacts, in baseball, playing hooky, and in the myriad 'inconsequential' events of childhood, are a process of converting the world in expe-riential objects; an environment is created for the individual by fashioning a range of responses to it. And as this creation and fashioning take place, life becomes meaning-ful. Other individuals and interpersonal situations become meaningful objects as one learns to fashion dependable and organized behavioral responses to them. We might say that an individual is indoctrinated into meaning by being obliged to take part in a continuing hierarchy of problematic, cultural situations, by means of which *he builds himself* into the experiential world of that culture.

Furthermore, as the youth learns the rules of the cultural staging, the proper roles, ceremonials, and performance parts, he develops a critical sense by which to analyze problematic situations in the conduct of others, especially. Then, the creation of meaning is furthered by sharpening visual acuity to details. In the very process of judging the conduct of others, of calibrating their deficiencies (and one's own) in the attempt to overcome interpersonal problems, measuring scales are created which fur-ther refine meaning by committing perception to greater symbolic acuity. Critical scrutiny of ideals in problematic performance, in other words, inculcates a realistic sense of values. . . .

The external world provides neither adequate meaning nor motivation, which is why events in it are so overpowering and incomprehensible. The tenuous grip on interpersonal meanings lies in the fact that the external object world is poor, which explains directly why object loss can be so overwhelming and threatening. Thus, in glancing back to the five common problems, we can see that they are . . . data which relate the individual *primarily* to an interpersonal, external object world. Knowledge of these common problems is built up in action in an interpersonal, behavioral world. It is easy to see that when an individual has not done so, he may compensate for his 'stupidity' by developing a secondary fluency in the abstract aspects of these five problems. He may attempt to systematize an internal object world, encompassing problems like the second—'What is the relation of man to nature?'—in an abstract metaphysics that has little relation to external experiential reality. . . .

The sociological approach to motivation has grown out of the idea of the social behavioral genesis of mind. The view of motives as a vocabulary appropriate to a given social action situation is not new, but it is fair to say this is one of the most sore-ly neglected areas of research in our thinking about identity problems. [C. Wright] Mills made a serious and provocative attempt to systematize this view as early as 1940, and he reiterated it in 1953. In the sociological view, motives are words. . . . This is again a behavioral view of human meaning, this time as motivation. Dewey indicated that people confronted with alternative acts choose between them on the basis of the consequences they anticipate. Mills elaborates on this view of Dewey's and stresses the important fact that these anticipated consequences *appear in linguis-tic form* . . . . In other words, the social dimension of motives is the implicit names for the consequences of action that takes place in society. Therefore, for the individ-ual, motive may be defined as Max Weber understood it: as a complex of meaning which appears to be adequate ground for action. And the only way a symbolic animal can know whether a situation is adequate ground for action is by being able to frame words appropriate to it. Motives are the words by which we dress our acts in meaning. . . . Adequate motivation is contained in the word, in the vocabulary which refers to an action situation, because thereby action in the situation is facilitated both without anxiety and with a symbolic for self-enhancement.

As the individual grows, he learns a vocabulary of motives appropriate to each experiential situation. As the child learns a number of various performances in different roles—starting, say, with 'cops and robbers' or 'cowboys and Indians'—he learns the proper vocabulary accompanying the roles, and thus the correct motivation. The symbolic self is a role actor, and it is by means of exercising powers in the motivational vocabulary of the role that the individual comes to discover himself. That is, he discovers himself in the meaningful action of the social performance part. The sense of identity does not proceed from 'built-in' motives, but rather is elaborated from 'role-accompanying' motives.

Now if the schizophrenic is one who does not take full part in an extrafamilial interpersonal performance world, the upshot of this discussion is apparent: Motivational aspects of his *identity have little reference to interpersonal cultural situations.* Questions that he may pose in reference to his own identity can then only be answered in terms of internal fantasy reveries and private symbolic elaborations. His motivation, in other words, is in terms of a purely private vocabulary. He has acquired no meaningful social motivation. . . . His nuances and motivational justifications are personal. It is this self-justification of meaningful action, rather than social justification, which gives the schizophrenic such a tenuous hold on the interpersonal world. . . .

This view of motivational vocabulary and identity is part of a conceptualization of the socially symbolic self as an entity in a continual state of formation. It explains how an individual can feel totally different from one moment to the next in the *same unchanged role.* For example, he can feel hate toward a mistress, at one moment, when examining his performance part from a symbolic point of view of motivational justification in which, say, phallic-narcissistic strivings (symbolic justifications) are not involved. He can feel extreme tenderness for her the next moment, when certain other of his symbolic self-justifications monopolize the field of attention and exclude those alternates formerly in awareness. Thus, the seeming duplicity and 'inconsistency' of the identity is not a question of 'change,' but a question of partitive attentional field, and the particular symbolic of motives which is referred to the self-image at any given moment. One can conceive of the harassing 'inconstancy of love' as a question of the richness of symbolic justifications available as motives for a particular performance part in which a loved object is concerned. Admittedly, there is nothing in these explanations that will be new to a student of the human personality; but the contention here is that they can be phrased solely in terms of a vocabulary of motives, without making appeal to unknown 'drives' or 'needs.'

When one talks about the 'automaticity of the unconscious' or, in other words, about the constriction of built-in rule-following behavior in a style precipitated during the confusions of the Oedipal transition, he is referring to: A symbolic of motivation which prevents behavior from being guided by alternative vocabularies of motivation. Thus, automaticity of the unconscious means simply *the poverty of motivational vocabulary in a world of performance complexity.* On this view, the confusions of identity, or rather, the insecurity of identity of the schizophrenic, comes not from the possibilities of plural choice and 'other-directedness,' but rather from the continuing restriction of possibilities of symbolic justification beyond those formed in early childhood. . . .

The schizophrenic, especially, can find himself tortured by the problem of which is the 'real' me. He stands to be doubly confused by the multiplicity of roles in modern society, but he needs to clutch firmly to whatever identity his fantasy can muster. And because of the poverty of his external object world, and his consequent real self-ignorance, he falls even further behind in the capability of modern man to be glibly facile and to juggle with ease a random array of situational motives. Only in this limited sense can one agree that schizophrenia is sociological, that it represents a bafflement in orientation in a complex world. But it is more accurate to say that schizophrenia represents a desperate attempt privately to fabricate meaning in a world that is poor rather than rich in complex objects. It is an attempt to build up an identity by motivational vocabularies that are divorced from the real interpersonal activities by which such an identity can be most convincingly fashioned. The court of last appeal for man's identity is composed of the systematized reactions by means of which he creates an object world. True spectatorship, to which he appeals for verification, depends on painstaking authorship of lived situations. Schizophrenia best shows up the old fallacious philosophical split of idealism versus realism. Without an external world with which to come into contact, the self cannot be brought into being. But the self also fashions out of that world a sector to which it makes appeal. Schizophrenia is a poverty in external objects and, consequently, in selfhood and meaning.

Chapter 2

THE ENDURING VALUE IN FREUD

A Note on Freud's Primal Horde Theory (1961)*

FREUD'S IDEA WAS THAT BOTH TOTEMISM and primitive taboo have their origin in Darwin's 'primal horde.' In this hominid group, the strongest tyrannical male dominated the females, and as his young approached maturity they were driven off by him. His offspring, dispossessed, one day united, killed and ate the father, and liberated the women, whom they took for themselves. At this point, as guilt and remorse led the brothers to renounce the ill-gained females as well as any future partaking of a father-displacing totem animal, both taboo and totem were said to have arisen. Thus, the almost homogeneously universal incest taboos and the widespread primitive idea of totemism were given ready explanation. . . .

Freud had already so qualified his account, and cleared away the implication that the totem and the taboo had been instituted *sur le coup* in evolutionary development. This leaves the psychological potential of his account very much alive, although, curiously, nothing has been done with it. . . . It is precisely a salient feature of Freud's conclusions in *Totem and Taboo* that they can integrate with contemporary science. Admittedly, there is need for more research, but some thirty years of careful observations of the subhuman primates have brought out some very suggestive facts.

It is these facts, derived from observations of the subhuman primates and from new discoveries of fossil hominids, that anthropologists are hopefully marshaling in an attempt to determine the Rubicon between man and his prehuman ancestors. The tremendous gap in knowledge is filled with careful speculation, and one may justifiably wonder whether the picture can ever be complete enough to dispense with speculation altogether. At any rate, in the present state of knowledge, fossil findings are little more than inanimate jigsaw pieces, and even the layman knows that we did not descend from our contemporary anthropoid cousins.

But these anthropoids give extremely valuable and suggestive clues to prehis-

*Original, full text: E. Becker, "A note on Freud's primal horde theory." *Psychoanalytic Quarterly,* 30: 413-419 (1961). Reprinted with permission from The Psychoanalytic Quarterly.

toric prehuman behavior, possibly to those times when *Zinjanthropus boisei* roamed East Africa, with a brain little bigger than the gorilla but with the ability to use tools and make fire. Subhuman primates, for one thing, live in sharply mutually antagonistic groups. These groups, while organized, are prevented from combining for greater environmental exploitation, and they are even prevented from migrating by territorial fixity and marked hostility to proximate groups. Within the group, dominance-subordination is rife. Only the chimpanzee seems close to the human in its relative mildness of character; [Meredith] Crawford reported, on the basis of an experiment, that only four-tenths per cent of chimpanzee social behavior could be described as aggressive. Perhaps a basic impetus to the softening of aggressive ingroup relations, and to the cooperative socialization of the human primates, is the phenomenon of reciprocal social grooming. There seems to be evidence that this social grooming increases on a continuum from the New World monkeys to the Old World monkeys, and thence to the higher anthropoids.

While these facts disclose nothing of fossil man, they are suggestive of a gradual mellowing of social behavior in the primate line. However, this behavior never attains the true cooperativeness characteristic of human social life. Freud's theory and contemporary primate studies seem to have isolated for research a most significant area of behavior that may demarcate the Rubicon line.

The fundamental feature of human society—cooperation and teamwork—is absent even among the higher anthropoids. Neither mutual aid nor spontaneous cooperation has been observed. While some chimpanzees have been trained to cooperate in problem-solving, monkeys apparently cannot even be taught. It seems justifiable to consider this the outstanding disparity between subhuman and human society. The crux of the matter is that spontaneous teamwork assumes the use of symbols. . . . In other words, we can make the striking equation of teamwork with man's superego and symbolic faculty the outstanding difference between him and his prehuman forebears.

I submit that the crucial merit of Freud's account is his insistence on precisely this point, and that this insistence has been overlooked to the detriment of the true cogency of his interpretation of the origins of human society. . . . Freud apparently knew little about lack of teamwork in the subhuman primates. The cultural advance may well have been the gradual growth of the faculty to symbolize, developing *pari passu* with another, apparently decidedly new factor—cooperativeness. Indeed, in the chimpanzee, where dominance-submission behavior is observed least, there is a hint of reliance of one chimpanzee upon another of its choosing. Friends so developed can be counted on for aid and protection.

It is conceivable that beyond a certain point in primate social life increasing brain size and psychological complexity succeeded simple brute dominance, and that the strength of single individuals no longer served to define behavior. Throughout the mammalian class, age-peer association is the rule during maturation. Growing psychological identifications and the possibility of concerted action could wreak havoc with single male dominance, and with group organization as well. Furthermore, it is in this kind of complex atmosphere—young relating to mothers, to each other, to adult males, and so on—that roles and status arise. The function of status is to define the psychological environment to which the individual must adjust. According to the principle of energy conservatism, it is possible that an animal with a large brain could not function if it had to define each psychological situation anew. Thus, roles and statuses provide an economical behavioral definition of the situation for a larger brained animal. Intraspecies combats and ecological rivalries would serve to select naturally those societies who made the transition from simple dominance, through increasing psychological complexity, to smoothly working statuses and large, complex brains.

Nor can Freud be accused of the naive assumption that this happened as an event. He makes plain the developmental evolutionary nature of cooperativeness—its adaptive significance over a long stretch of time . . . [This] new faculty, teamwork, presented as great a danger as it presented an advance—new organization of the band into a truly cooperative, exploitative society was endangered by patricidal bands in fratricidal strife. If one adopts the necessary time perspective, he can see this problem in its full import: the organization versus the destruction permitted by the growing symbolic faculty and ability to cooperate. . . .

Of course, in developing cooperativeness, the new, symbolizing animal developed concomitant affective sensitivity to close objects. The two are inseparable, and Freud fully comprehended this very inseparability. . . . The new, symbolizing animal . . . had to give as much priority to his new affective sensitivity to the objects with whom he was cooperating as to his omnipotent aggressive desires. In instituting the social taboos—the law against incest—a new, group-maximizing cooperativeness was ineluctably established as an evolutionary coping device. . . .

There is no need to belabor the point. Superego affectivity and primary process omnipotence cannot have arrived at their tenuous *modus vivendi* easily. Little wonder that Freud stuck to the underlying soundness of his conceptualization, later again qualifying the father-killing as 'not a unique event'. However, the psychoanalytic reader would be amiss to keep to the whole totemic package while insisting on the cogency of the main point. Freud, in fact, failed to understand what the anthropologists have really learned from the incest taboo. He observed that the sexual needs were divisive, self-defeating, that they were "not capable of uniting men in the same way as are the demands of self-preservation." "Sexual satisfaction," he maintained, "is essentially the private affair of each individual." But it is precisely the sexual need that was put to work by the incest taboo. By elaborating a rigorous kinship organization of mutual rights, duties, obligations, and taboos, primitive man created an unparalleled exploitative structure over the natural environment. The original functional cooperativeness based on the taboo was achieved by making sexual satisfaction a social affair.

The Significance of Freudian Psychology (1963)*

The Oedipus Complex

Freud, it will be remembered, used this concept to explain the phobia of a five-year-old boy, and went on to postulate that everyone had an Oedipus complex. In his view the Oedipus complex arose in the close nuclear family, and it summed up a variety of factors. Freud's view was that the precociously maturing child had sexual strivings which could not be tolerated. These strivings would arouse jealousy and ill feelings, and generally disrupt family authority. Thus, Freud postulated that the child is forced to repress his 'natural urges' to possess the mother and do away with the father. This repression is induced by repeated castration threats and enjoinders to abandon sexual assertiveness. It is only when the child willingly proceeds to a new kind of obedient relationship, in which he models his conduct on the more social roles of one or the other of his parents, that the anxieties, sexual urges and confusions which characterize the Oedipus complex are resolved. Freud's theory, in sum, held that each individual must resolve his Oedipus complex if he is to be a fully social actor.

This brief sketch should suffice to introduce a theory that is well-known; however, we will come back to it from a broader point of view below. Freud also claimed other things for his idea. In addition to being a crucial phase of childhood development, it was also considered an allegorical historical event, by which to explain phylogenetic development out of subhuman species. Freud postulated that over a period of time, it was necessary for proto-hominids to suppress their natural, anti-paternal aggressiveness, in order for cooperative human society to take shape. But this speculation is less important than the accent which Freud put on the events of the Oedipal phase in contemporary society. In clinical practice itself, the Oedipus complex took fatal reified shape as a disease entity. It was now less an abstract concept that imaginatively bared certain unobservable relationships between child and parents; rather, it came to be a 'thing'—a complex aggregate that the patient had to resolve and 'work through,' with the aid of a psychoanalyst.

These shifting definitions of a single concept cover considerable ground. However, when the psychoanalyst is pressed by the philosopher of science to justify the purported universality of this concept, the psychoanalyst inevitably falls back on the broader definition—namely, the Oedipus complex as a 'phase,' rather than as an actual 'complex.' As such, it is considered to be a universal developmental sequence in the higher primates, a natural history description of part of human development. Seen in this light, it can be rephrased in somewhat more abstract form. The outstanding feature of this phase is this: By means of language, the biologically dependent, physiologically performing child develops a behavioral style unique in the animal kingdom. During his early training period, he learns to pattern his conduct upon a

*Original, full text: E. Becker, "The significance of Freudian psychology." *Main Currents*, 19: 45-50, 61-66 (1963). Reprinted by permission.

symbolic code of rules transmitted by the parents; he becomes a value-responsive actor, for the most part, rather than a physiologically responsive actor. Biological systematization of his conduct is discouraged, symbolic codification is encouraged, by threats, cajoling, and enticements to new forms of mastery. The end result of this process is the formation of a socially obedient actor who has repressed certain of his 'basic drives' and who is now fit to assume his place in 'civilized' society.

Now this shift in emphasis, from a 'complex' to a 'phase' seems minor, but it has important—indeed crucial—consequences. In effect, the idea is taken right out of the clinical situation, and Oedipus, instead of being a disease entity, becomes a natural history description of all human actors, a description of part of the process that *Homo sapiens* must undergo in order to become a fully human, symbolic animal. It is little wonder, then, that Freud was convinced of the fundamental value of his discovery. No matter what evidence anthropologists might marshal against the universality of the Oedipus complex, human development was surely not to be restricted to turn-of-the-century Vienna.

Social scientists, too, were quick to recognize the basic importance of this idea, and Talcott Parsons has included it in his theory of action. A human social system can only exist if each of the actors has internalized a code of symbolic rules and values for behavior, which makes social life possible. Parsons paid full tribute to Freud for revealing his process of internalization; he understood Freud's 'superego' to be the outstanding contribution to the interdisciplinary current of modern social science. Freud thereby joins [Emile] Durkheim, [Charles H.] Cooley, [John] Dewey, [William] James, George Mead, and others like [Jean] Piaget, in a solid front convergence on the social nature of human action.

Thus Parsons . . . sees no discrepancy between Freud's real contribution and that of James and Dewey. In a sense, they [Parsons and Norman Cameron] are both correct—Cameron to assume that Freudianism is incompatible with a broad view of human behavior; and Parsons to assume that Freud's theory of the superego is a fundamental contribution to understanding the nature of man. However, no one has yet carried through an examination of the full consequences of viewing the Oedipus as a phase rather than a complex. Only when this is done can we see Freud's true contribution to the nascent human sciences, as well as the crippling limitations of his system. Neither Cameron nor Parsons—indeed no one to my knowledge—has proceeded to a proper appraisal of Freudian psychology. At least this is the view proposed here, and which I will now attempt to elaborate.

The Ego as a Linguistic, Value Locus

Parsons, stressing the linkage between the superego and the social system as Freud's great contribution, assigned less importance to the id—the instinctive reservoir of action—than did Freud. In order to show man in his full plasticity as a social actor, biological drive components of action must be given very little weight. Thus, Parsons is repeating, in a sense, Harry Stack Sullivan's modification of the Freudian tripartite psyche: Ego-Id-Superego became for Sullivan the 'self-system' simply. The Sullivanian model is clearly superior to the Freudian not only because it supersedes a biological, entelechistic view of human action, but for an even more crucial reason: With the Sullivanian view, we are brought to understand the important fact that the self-system is largely a system of linguistic conventions. The personality is constructed of words and the ability to use them. The self-system is a locus of linguistic causality, by means of which man animates himself and his environment, and lays the ground for action by others. Sullivan considered the personality as largely a series of 'linguistic tricks' by which man conciliates his environment, stressing the fact that language was developed in good measure to avoid anxiety, as a means of manipulating others to cater to one's wants and to secure their good will.

If the self-system is largely a series of linguistic tricks, initially a 'good-bad' 'do-don't' vocabulary by means of which the child learns to navigate in a social environment, one fact becomes strikingly apparent: The linguistic self-system is largely an aggregate of social rules for behavior. The self-system is a response-delaying 'psychological' organ, which holds alternative courses of action steady in awareness, so as to permit choice in response to stimuli. But these alternative courses of action are linguistic, they are words among which the individual must choose. Thus, it is proper to say that what we term 'person' is largely an aggregate of vocabularies, of behavioral prescriptions that permit social action. By 'individual human nature' we mean a distillate of social conventions as they are manifest in the behavioral style of a particular person.

This important modification of orthodox Freudian doctrine is familiar but it has not enjoyed wide enough currency in social science thinking. We have placed it first in our reinterpretation of Freud because it is familiar, and because it ties directly into a more crucial proposition, which is the core of this discussion.

Anxiety and Self-Esteem

The ego takes shape as an aggregate of words for action that will be agreeable to the parents; the self-system is largely an action-potentiating entity composed of symbolic rule-prescriptions for anxiety-free behavior. The fundamental underlying factor in this early developmental process is the phenomenon of anxiety. Freud, [Alfred] Adler, and Sullivan made it central to their systems. Initially, anxiety seems to be a part of the child's extended mammalian helpless dependence on a succoring source of nutrition. It manifests itself as a fear of object loss. The child can only successfully ward off what appears to be a primitive annihilation anxiety by means of secure ministrations from the mother. Later, any threat of separation revives this anxiety; any conduct which threatens to alienate the parents is referred to as the anxiety of object-loss. As Adler observed, the child's natural inferiority and consequent helplessness and anxiety over separation are the basic materials for his humanization.

It seems necessary, for secure development of symbolic powers and mastery over the environment, to develop a buffering system with which to handle anxiety. It is worth stressing that the whole process of early development seems to center on this, and the ego or self-system is largely evolved as a psychological organ which permits anxiety-free operation. (I am stressing this because it makes understandable the crucial role of the next concept.)

Now there is one fundamental factor in all this, which seems necessary *in order for the whole development to take place.* This is the sentiment of 'self-value' or 'self-esteem,' as the psychoanalysts term it, but which, unfortunately, is not sufficiently stressed in their exegeses. It is neglected in favor of 'aggression' and 'sexuality.' Self-esteem is a quality (for want of a better word) that is basic to human development. It is a warm feeling of being right with the world, which performs the crucial function of allaying anxiety, and at the same time permitting a secure, curious probing for mastery of the environment. It begins, theoretically, with early maternal milk and care, and continues through the close, physiological transactions with both parents. The confusions and the crises of the Oedipal transition center precisely on this self-esteem. The child finds that he can no longer keep this anxiety-buffering feeling by his old mode of relating to the parents. Instead, he is now enjoined to proceed to a new type of symbolic, rule-following action. At the end of the Oedipal transition, the self-esteem comes to be derived in an entirely new way: by implicitly following the verbal commands of the parents, which have been 'internalized' into the self-system—indeed which form it. The child retains possession of the love and protection of the parents simply by shaping himself into a pattern of conduct and self-justification which does not alienate them. Thus, even though he remains inferior and helpless, he is still permitted to feel self-righteous and comfortable in his action. This is the basic function of qualitative self-esteem. *An ego-governed organism cannot act without it.* And in all of nature, man is the only ego-controlled animal.

Real and Spurious Invariants of the Oedipal History

This is a brief view of the genesis of the self-system. It conveys the basics in the natural history of the fashioning symbol-responsive actors. However, when we try to extricate the important invariants in this historical process, something curious occurs: *We find that there are any number of abstract constructs which one can choose as the invariants.* The basic process lends itself readily to adornment, as it were, with one's own concepts. Of course, this concept formation is a fundamental procedure of all science, but it has been a real difficulty for psychoanalytic theory up to now. The invariants which have been stressed as crucial by the psychoanalysts have been disputed by others—as well as among themselves to a certain extent; and, as we noted earlier, there has been no successful linking of these abstract concepts, via operational definitions, to situations where they might be falsified by testing.

Freud was permitted by his own rare talents, and by history, to be one of the first systematic interpreters of this process. (James Mark Baldwin was another.) He eagerly extracted a number of invariants from this natural history—or better, read them into it. As an innovator, he had undisputed claim to this privilege. There is no point in detailing his familiar system; suffice it to mention the highlights of it here, in order to proceed to our next conclusion. Freud saw human nature as part of a man—society dichotomy, ruled by antithetical forces like 'eros' and 'thanatos.' Man's sociality was bought at the price of frustration of deep-seated instinctual drives, in his view. Thus, infantile sexuality and innate aggression were thought by him to be crucial invariants in the humanization process. (Furthermore, as we saw, he reified the whole Oedipal development into an invariant, which became a disease entity for the clinician to test.)

The history of the last half-century has been witness to the vicissitudes of these concepts: Freud's physiological drive invariants have been all but wholly discredited by researchers in a variety of disciplines. . . . And the Oedipus complex, as we have seen in some detail, is rather to be interpreted as an historical description of part of human development than as a disease entity. The conclusion, then, is long overdue: *most of the major invariants which Freud derived from his theory of human development are spurious.* The only thing we are sure of is the linguistic self-system or ego which results from the historical development.

The implications of this are far-reaching. Freud's inability to conceive invariants acceptable to science has been a major reason for skepticism in scientific circles about the value of the whole of his theory. But even more important, these dogmatic and heavily invested false starts in explaining human psychology have made it seem beyond the possibility of simple, scientific explanation. . . . [Yet] Freud did discover something extremely simple, and fundamentally important to human behavior—a universal that provides grounds for concluding that Freud is the Newton for psychology. His work did disclose just that basic concept which is a fundamental insight into all human behavior, everywhere.

But we can only get at this universal when we peel away the disguise which Freud himself erected, when we return from the laborious detours made necessary by his own spurious constructs. *Freud's discoveries all center around the idea of self-esteem maintenance by the growing organism. In other words, his discoveries all pointed to one crucial fact: namely, that the basic predicate for human action is a qualitative feeling of self-value.*

Not surprisingly, therefore, everyone has been quite correct in their response to the fascination of the Oedipus complex construct, however much the emphasis on its true significance has been wrongly stressed. Freud properly felt it to be one of his outstanding discoveries. It is by means of the Oedipal transition that we are enabled to see that the most crucial problem in early human development centers around the maintenance of self-esteem. The Oedipal problem is one of switching modes of maintaining self-esteem in the face of environmental changes. Each actor must learn to switch from a physiological behavioral mode to a symbolic-linguistic, rule-following mode. From the massive amount of clinical and observational material accumulated on this process we have been able to postulate that *the human organism cannot act unless it constitutes itself an object of primary value in a meaningful world.* And it is precisely the training in fashioning and maintaining this sentiment of self-value that takes place during the Oedipal period. It cannot be overstressed that the self-system is a locus from which the individual derives self-value symbolically, a derivation achieved by following internalized social rules for behavior.

Admittedly, the centrality of self-value as the universal predicate for human action is not altogether a new idea. It has been variously stressed before, as 'self-seeking,' 'self-interest;' 'egotism,' 'the search for prestige and self-aggrandizement,' and so on. As such, the idea is part of most religious systems and traditional philosophical systems. But the further contention of our discussion is this: that the notion of the fundamental nature of self-value to human action was worthless as long as it remained a metaphysical postulate. Nothing could be done with it scientifically until Freud's work took it out of the realm of the 'naturally given,' and plotted the exact *correlates by which it comes into being and is maintained.* The careful study of the Oedipal transition, as we have seen, does exactly this: it traces the rise of self-esteem from early dependence on the mother, as a buffer against the annihilation anxiety of object loss; it follows self-esteem in the crucial change in behavior by which it comes to be maintained in largely symbolic fashion, as a distillate of rules for perception and action. Never before had the human need for a basic sentiment of self-value been mapped out in behavioral terms of its genesis and sustenance. It is this truly revolutionary achievement to which Freud's work pointed.

It is not accurate to say that Freud himself made any break from the traditional way of viewing man's basic nature, even while he went about making his observations and postulates. Freud's own attempt was to establish this very egotism of man, by stressing self-seeking, physiological drives. Thus, he suffered a fate common to many scientists: namely, *unawareness of his own fundamental discovery.* Freud thought that he was mapping out the correlates of basic drives and an entelechistic universal human nature. Actually, he was plotting the invariable of man's need for a sentiment of self-value by which to infuse all his acts—a sentiment achieved in a uniquely rule-predicted behavioral formula. *Freud laid bare the point of contact between culture and biology in the human animal by linking anxiety-proneness with prescriptions for right conduct.* It remained for the later ego-psychology to stress the cultural side of this point of contact, which is an emphasis that represented a complete reversal of what Freud actually proposed, and a challenge to his whole earlier system. . . . We are, then, reinterpreting Freud in order to emphasize that he discovered man's need for a sense of primary value—rather than the physicalist entities upon which he so firmly insisted. Thus, to equate Freud with Newton is to overlook the fact that the universals they discovered are totally dissimilar. Man's sense of primary self-esteem is non-quantifiable and value-predicated; it is based on the linguistic conventions which sustain it; it is a symbolic aggregate, in sum.

George Herbert Mead showed brilliantly how the self comes into being: it can develop only through the inculcation of symbols from another human being; further, the very feelings that one has of oneself are initially the feelings of another toward one. The implications of this process of building a self are far-reaching and profound: *the self is rooted in an interpersonal context,* it is a social creation. Hence even the adult's need to fashion an identity is at all times dependent on the reflection he receives from significant people around him.

The human animal, having become symbolic, muses upon the body casing in which the identity of the self resides. The body assumes the guise of a chafing delimitation on the psychological action world of the self—it is a drag on a being who finds his fullness in this psychological world. The self is a symbolic construction that throbs with experiences that mere flesh and blood could never relay. (I do not mean to imply a phenomenological dichotomy here, but merely a logical one.) The self trails its body into old age, after a lifetime of daily scrutiny in a mirror, of a biological aging process it does not understand. Approaching death, the magnificent, intricate symbolic creation of history—the self—can only show resignation. *To the self-reflexive animal death is an absurd injustice, which thousands of years and unnumbered systems of thought have labored to explain.*

How are we to apply physical science criteria to a symbolic aggregate that is infused with self-value? If self-esteem is to be an invariant point of reference in social science theory, can it at the same time be wholly normative? There seems to be no defense that can be offered if we are to continue using criteria of the physical sciences in our study of man. The question now is whether we need any defense at all. The cumulative current of recent critical thinking in the social sciences has built up to a creative rebelliousness. There seems no reason for further accepting the dictates of the physical sciences. It is becoming widely agreed that their research problems are not ours, their cartons of rigorous quantifiability and total abstraction from values are not possible in the social sciences. Facilitation of research (instrumentalism), ordering of data for explanation and prediction, are the goals of modern science, rather than the starry-eyed search for 'truth.' These can be achieved by the human sciences *with the use of a qualitative human factor universal as an invariant point of reference in all theory.* The fundamental uniqueness of any explanation of human behavior must be on its own terms; and these terms, as we are perhaps tediously aware by now, are that self-esteem (a non-quantifiable and value-predicated construct) is the basic predicate for human action. There is no *a priori* reason to deny quality its proper place in the social sciences.

The difficulty in fashioning abstract constructs in the social sciences has stemmed precisely from the fact that man, unlike atoms, is a qualitative organism in nature. As Dewey observed, the physical sciences have as an ideal aim the elimination of precisely that which is dependent upon the distinctively human response. Abstract constructs that establish relationships in social science must include these qualitative human factors so recalcitrant to physical science method. It seems plainly necessary to introduce the idea of a qualitative self-esteem in order to establish relations of dependence between what we observe in human action and what we do not observe. Freud probably overlooked the real significance of his discovery because he stood firmly in the nineteenth-century physicalist tradition. *In sum, it seems fair to say that social science has lagged so far behind physical science because it has been reluctant to fix upon its own proper subject matter: the qualitative facilitation of action.*

Further Problems: Operational Predicates
. . . It should, therefore, be apparent that one can prescribe clinical changes in [. . .] behavioral style only from a normative, and not from a scientific posture. *An historical theory cannot prescribe a desirable development on the basis of the descriptive history.* The analyst, of course, aims to be concerned with 'pathological' processes, like the 'automaticity of the unconscious,' from which the patient must be 'cured.' Undeniably, the unconscious or non-verbalized aspects of the behavioral style each person develops lends it a certain automaticity. What takes place in the Oedipal training is actually an adaptation by the individual to a conditioning process of which he is largely unaware. When this automatic behavioral style becomes binding, and prevents intelligent adaptation to new ranges of experience in later life, the psychoanalyst terms it 'neurosis.' For this reason alone, the source of neurosis is sought in the 'Oedipus complex.' But what actually is being sought is the particular adaptation that the individual has made in order to keep his self-esteem constant. A prescribed change in this adaptation can only be normative.

It is for these reasons that we consider the Sullivan model to be superior to the Freudian, as was mentioned earlier. The only thing the psychoanalyst really has to work with, if he refrains from reifying human behavior, is the self-system as a value-aggregate. The self-system provides an explanatory model for human behavior that has the virtue of eliminating explanatory concepts about things often not found in reality. These imaginary things—namely, the idea of an inborn infantile sexuality, and an innate aggression—directly undermine the model. The self-system model seems faithful to the empirical world. It groups the results of the entire early learning process, and omits mysterious 'inner forces.' At this time in the development of the human sciences, it is plain that the famous 'mechanisms of defense' are not defenses against instincts, but rather against any learned source of conflict and hence anxiety.

Now if this is correct, it leads to a further important conclusion. The mechanisms of defense—projection, repression, denial, introjection, and so on—are the behavioral aspects of the self-system. As such, we might erroneously suppose that they are the intervening variables which link up with the self-value locus. But, and here is the important qualification, if these defense mechanisms are not protective against spurious 'instincts,' but rather against learned conflicts and anxieties, then they are integral components of the self-system. To change them is to effect a change in the self-system itself, *without reference to any other constructs but the total behavioral style which is a unique creation of the individual.*

The purport of this is clear. Once we have rid Freudian theory of spurious reifications and drive constructs, it becomes abundantly clear that any prescribed change in human behavior must derive from a purely normative definition for the life style that one desires. The mechanisms of defense are not 'intervening variables' in any value-free, systematized scientific sense. Rather, they are 'intervening' in a conceptual sense: from one normative definition of behavior to another—from the behavioral style the patient manifests, to that which the clinician desires to promote. This raises further havoc with the possibility of a traditional scientific approach to human subject matter. With unique, value-laden operations, the situation is hopelessly compounded: How can one look for 'operational predicates' from a value locus (the patient) to a value prescription (the new behavior promoted by the therapist)?

There is obviously only one way out of this dilemma, and that is to accept the radical reorientation suggested by Freud's basic discovery, and focus on the self-system within a value-explicit science. Such a science has long been championed in some quarters. It would correlate values within values, weigh means for given ends.

Self-Esteem and the Social System

What are some of the implications of this for broad social theory? [Anatol] Rapoport has observed that the theory of evolution was a windfall which enabled natural scientists to distinguish homologies in the structure of organisms. It might be permissible to conclude that so too was Freud's theory of human development a windfall which enables social scientists to distinguish invariants in human action. But, as we have seen, quite the contrary is the case. To recapitulate, when we clear away Freud's spurious physiological invariants and reifications, we are left with only one invariant in human development: the behavioral style that each individual develops as a mode of maintaining his self-esteem—a style predicated upon a symbolic, value definition for action. In the Oedipal transition as an historical process, *this behavioral style is a unique creation in each case;* it is not a repetitive phenomenon. If we seek to standardize certain elements in it, so that we can focus on changing them, we must do so from some normative prescription for the kind of behavior we want. Thus, we have been able to conclude that the human sciences are inescapably value sciences: they must include values as an integral invariant point of reference in their theories.

This fundamental difference from physical science, once accepted by social science theorists, should result in wide benefits in theory building. Consider, as an illustration, the impasse in which functional theory—once so promising—is now caught. The idea of the functional interdependence of the institutions of a society has not provided much in the way of causal explanations. It has remained at the stage of mapping the formal and comparative levels of social structure. In effect, the very idea that a functional analysis of society is possible seems little more than a belief, an inference about the interrelationships of the institutions of a society. Many sociologists have put their trust in the hope that another Max Weber will soon be born, to make new, salient conceptualizations of total societies. This is an attitude that [Ernest] Gellner summed up as 'The Interregnum Theory' or waiting for the great man.

There seems to be only one way to give functional theory the historical dimension which it so glaringly lacks, and without which it cannot attain to full cause and effect explanatory power. And that is by including social actors who possess some invariant universal point of reference. Self-esteem needs within a particular value system would, of course, be such a point of reference. This would also make possible the up-to-now fruitless quest for some sound basis for comparative, cross-cultural studies. Furthermore, if we include self-esteem as an invariant point of reference predicated on a symbolic code of action, it solves a major problem that has plagued functional analysis: namely, the inclusion of history. It is evident that the historic moment itself is a component of self-esteem: the individual is tied directly to symbolic history, through his institutional action and allegiance. A major shortcoming of functional theory stands thereby to be remedied. Self-esteem is relational in the broadest sense, since it is a precipitate of symbols.

Max Weber still looms so large on the horizon of social theory because he saw that motivation was inseparable from symbolically meaningful action. Whereas [Karl] Marx had stressed the determinism of economics, Weber insisted that the purely ideational urges to action can be cause as well as effect in determining the institutional structure of a society. Motives were not to be considered simply as a reflex of economics, but could in turn shape it. Marx overlooked the importance of early symbolic motivations, and their direct relation to self-esteem. In fact, the dispute between Russian and American personality theorists centers still around this fact: that early conditioning in maintenance of self-esteem is considered crucial by the Americans; whereas the adult's relationship to the realistic ties of his economic situation are considered vital by the Russians. Russian theorists violently dispute the value of [Abram] Kardiner's contributions to social science theory. They understand his insistence on the various modes of maintaining self-esteem in different societies to be a reactionary dwelling on the deterministic nature of childhood experience, to the detriment of a view of the adult as rational and changeable.

Let us grant that the case of the Russian theorists is not blind ideological dogma. Under the influence of Freud, we have given too much weight to childhood experiences. William James, as usual, went beautifully and directly to the heart of the matter: "By their fruits ye shall know them, not by their roots." In effect, it is only by considering self-esteem as continually potentially modifiable, *pari passu* with the changes in symbolic history and structural arrangements of a given society, that a full picture of human action is possible. Thus, self-esteem provides a behavioral link that can be looked at simultaneously from both the psychological and the social view—it retains the theoretical postulates of both psychology and sociology.

However, explanatory models of the Weberian *Verstehen* type have been unsatisfactory, in the opinion of many. Social science, to build good theory, will have to progress from the merely hypothetically explanatory to the grossly predictive. In that event, it will be necessary to subject certain crucial constructs of social system theory to controlled inquiry, and to possible falsification, so that hypotheses can be progressively refined or superseded. Some form of social engineering, as Dewey stressed long ago, will be necessary to build social science theory. A science can be fashioned only by examining the experimental results of the theories it puts forth.

It is in this context that we can disagree with the final observation by [Michael] Scriven, namely, that he considered Freud's turning to abnormal psychology, for the major application of his insights, a drawback of his theory. Quite to the contrary, it becomes evident that the psychiatric situation can be *par excellence* the nexus of controlled inquiry, within a value theory of human behavior. Abnormal psychology is to Freud's theory what the inclined plane was to Galileo: the test situation wherein the universal point of reference is revealed. There is even now indication that psychiatric theory can be conceived as unifying around the notion of self-esteem.

At the present time, psychiatry is the institution most apt to provide the focus for study within controlled manipulation of human subject matter. Psychiatry has been given the mandate to manipulate in the interest of reducing suffering. What has hindered, up to now, the use of psychiatry as an indispensable applied focus in a unified social science, is that psychiatric operations were *covertly* value laden. Its aim has been to fit people back into a social system whose basic values were not questioned. It remains to make the values upon which psychiatry operates explicit, so that manipulation is related to a conscious appraisal of the symbolic correlates of self-esteem. These correlates can then be traced to their ramifications throughout the social structure. In this way, psychiatry becomes a focal point for controlled inquiry at the junction of psychology and sociology; that is, at the point where the dependence of self-esteem upon social motives can be examined. Thus, a unified social science, appraising values within values, would theoretically have the following four components:

1. Invariant points of reference in the individual actors: man's need for a symbolically predicated sense of primary self-value.

2. A structural-functional model of the institutions of society.

3. A problem for analysis at the present moment in historical time.

4. A focus for controlled inquiry, perhaps best provided by a value-explicit psychiatry, working within legal, democratic safeguards.

This kind of social science structure would not, admittedly, permit the same kind of fine predictability enjoyed in the physical sciences. But social science need not attempt this task. Its contribution could be enormous even if it contented itself merely with making accurate assessments of the limits and possibilities of effective human behavior (within a given value system).

In sum, a radical review of the significance of Freudian psychology has led to some equally novel prescriptions for the fashioning of social theory. There seems to be no other way for adequate theory to take shape than to be problem-oriented within an historical frame of reference. A comprehensive view of the interrelations of the social structure must include the motivations of value-responsive individual actors.

Thereby, individual conduct can be linked to large-scale abstractions, in a cause-and-effect manner. Finally, mature, hypothetico-deductive theory can only be shaped by providing a focus of controlled inquiry, in which hypothetical propositions can be subjected to possible falsification. A self-conscious, value-explicit psychiatry seems to provide one such focus.

Admittedly, this framework is at present little more than a utopian vision. Directive rationality and free democratic process are reluctant partners. . . . The frame of reference outlined here is essentially that which philosophers of mature vision— like Dewey, and social scientists like R. S. Lynd—might have championed. It is possible for man to study himself, and apply his thought to the problems of life, at one and the same time. Whether it will be done is quite another matter.

The Validity of 'Oedipus Complex' as an Abstract Scientific Construct (1964)*

PROPONENTS OF THE CONSTRUCT CALLED 'OEDIPUS COMPLEX' have claimed that this has the status of precisely the kind of bold abstraction that science fashions and with which it explains so much. And psychoanalytic clinicians have amassed a half-century of case histories to support the validity of their claim. Critics of the 'Oedipus complex' have countered by citing indisputable evidence from the history of science showing that the explanatory power of a construct has no relationship to its truth or falsity: the metaphysics of man's sinfulness, for example, has a high and durable explanatory potential and little relationship to the findings of science. The only way out of the dilemma of validity, they claim, is to fashion abstract constructs that can be connected to some form of controlled inquiry, so that these constructs may be proven assertable or false. . . .

When we look back at Freud's early formulation of the concept, two things stand out. In the first place, his procedure was scientific, in the way some understand the term. In the second place, Freud, flushed with the explanatory power of an imaginative abstract construct, succumbed to the fallibility of many theorists: he went on to claim too much. . . . What took shape as an ethereal abstraction in clinical practice became truly protean: 'Oedipus complex' was generalized to describe the crucial developmental phase of childhood. Every human child must pass through it on the way to adulthood. He must give way to castration threats and become a nonsexual performer. Thereby, he exchanges continuing biological dependence on his parents and (all this according to Freud) early sexual precocity for symbolic performance according to the commands of a social world. He becomes a social actor who must repress or otherwise defend himself against his biological tendencies. Thus, the 'Oedipus complex' is postulated as a natural history description of human development in all cultures and in all times.

*Original, full text: E. Becker, "The validity of 'Oedipus Complex' as an abstract scientific construct," in Earl W. Count and Gordon T. Bowles (eds.), *Fact and Theory in Social Science* (pp. 165-179). Syracuse University Press. Reprinted with permission from University College, Syracuse University.

Secondly, Freud, in *Totem and Taboo*, made the 'Oedipus complex' an *allegorical historical event* to explain phylogenetic development out of subhuman species. Freud postulated that over a period of time it was necessary for proto-hominids to suppress their natural, anti-paternal aggressiveness in order for cooperative human society to take shape.

Finally, in clinical practice itself, the 'Oedipus complex' took fatal reified shape as a disease entity. It was now less an abstract concept that imaginatively laid bare certain unobservable relationships between child and parents; rather, it came to be 'thing,' a complex aggregate that the patient had to resolve and 'work through' with the aid of the psychoanalyst—indeed with him alone. Everyone 'had' an 'Oedipus complex' if only he could be trained to see it or persuaded to avow it.

There is little wonder that contemporary philosophers, trained, for the most part, in rigorousness and parsimoniousness of thought, have found easy targets among the psychoanalysts, although one might suspect that the acidity of their attacks may have been motivated in part by the similarity of Freudian conceptual imperialism to that of certain speculative philosophers in their own historical ranks. However that may be, the philosopher would be wrong to imagine that vulnerability to attack is, in this case, indication of utter bankruptcy of concept. . . .

The psychoanalyst has urged us to consider the 'Oedipus' as a developmental phase rather than as a complex in order to stress its universality. So considered, he is unquestionably correct—the 'Oedipal phase' is part of the natural history of all human actors. But in winning the skirmish he has done himself out of the battle. If we define the 'Oedipal phase' as that behavior by which a potential *Homo sapiens* becomes human, where are we to observe it? In the style of behavior which we term human, of course: in other words, 'Oedipus' becomes a behavioral style which everyone possesses. It is the human mold for action, an adaptation in the higher primates that permits symbolic action. 'Oedipal phase' as a description of human behavior actually tells us much less than it seems to promise: that is, it is tantamount to saying, "All animals which undergo a stage of development in which proximal, biological relationships give way to relationships based on symbolic derivation of action-rules will manifest value-responsive, symbolic functioning." In other words, "All humans show human behavior."

If we accept this analysis, it becomes plain that the 'Oedipus complex' can no longer be considered a scientific 'problem.' The 'Oedipal phase' is like archaeology and evolutionary theory: it is an historical theory. As such, it has, of course, full claim to scientific status. But in asserting this claim, the scientific status of the clinical problem must vanish. It is difficult to conjecture what the psychoanalyst might counter here. Perhaps he would say, as he has done, that the clinical problem represents the individual who is not actualizing his full human potential—that is, one who experienced such great difficulties during the 'Oedipal phase' of development that his consequent 'neurotic' behavioral style represents an undesirable pattern of conduct. It is precisely at this point that psychoanalysts cause irritation and undermine further their own case. An historical theory cannot prescribe a desirable development on the basis of the descriptive history alone. . . .

The 'Oedipal phase,' then, is a unique adaptation in the higher primates in which human symbolic action is fashioned. Therefore, a clinical appraisal of the other, more limited problem, the 'Oedipus complex,' is of necessity always an evaluative prescription. It calls for a type of desired action which would or should replace it in any given case. It is no longer tenable to hold that a term descriptive of a developmental phase can also serve to refer to a reified entity that would or should somehow disintegrate under analysis.

The broader construct 'Oedipal phase' is potentially valuable because of the possibility it offers of disclosing invariant points of reference. . . . Dissatisfaction with Freud centers on his attempts to define certain crucial invariants in man arising out of his clinical work with the 'Oedipus complex.' Considerable cumulative evidence is being brought to bear against his most favorite invariants. Thus, his sexual instinct and aggressive drive theories are no longer widely supported, even among psychoanalysts. Freud's main difficulty in the formulation of invariants appears now to have been his carrying over of the nineteenth-century mechanism and essentialism. He clung tenaciously to a libidinal energy theory of human functioning that derived from nineteenth-century physics and viewed man in terms of irreducible energies, instincts and strivings.

It was this, in fact, that prevented him from carrying forward his sounder abstract formulations to the point where they would do full work in disclosing a broader pattern of relationships. His belated treatment of the crucial problem of anxiety and his later ego psychology remained bound to his earlier thing-in-itself framework. All of this is well known and needs no expansion here. Rather, I want to stress the full and as yet insufficiently fructified consequences of the recognition of the 'Oedipus' as a phase rather than a complex. This shift in emphasis, combined with an abandonment of the instinct theory, makes possible the formulation of abstract concepts that are more broadly relational than perhaps Freud himself might have liked. Indeed, he seems to have revealed, in his early dispute with [Alfred] Adler, that psychoanalysis had the choice of merging with a broad social science or remaining a vested-interest clinical grouping. By excluding Adler and his ideas, Freud chose the latter course. A truly staggering output of work has since gone into modifying or refuting dogmatic Freudian notions that were untenable from the start but that retained vitality partly because of this organizational move. Thus, it is fair to say that thereby social science has been considerably retarded.

When 'Oedipus' is considered as a developmental phase, certain other abstract constructs can be understood in their full relational scope. In the first place, the whole developmental sequence pivots on one key abstract entity, the self-system (or ego). This is the major psychological organ in the higher primates, by means of which the organism mediates responses to stimuli. It is a response-delaying mechanism which acts on the basis of information fed into the cerebral cortex. The self-system, or ego, thus permits man to hold constant in awareness several alternative responses and action possibilities and to choose among them. It makes possible a complete break from slavish stimulus-response reactivity characteristic of the lower animals.

Harry Stack Sullivan conceptualized the 'self-system,' and he preferred it to the Freudian legacy of id-ego-superego. . . . With the Sullivanian view, we are brought to understand the crucial fact that the self-system is largely a series of linguistic conventions. The personality, in other words, is constructed of words and the ability to use them. . . . The self-system is also a locus of linguistic causality, by means of which man animates his environment and lays the ground for action by others. It cannot be overstressed that that which we call 'personality' is largely a linguistic style or behavioral style of initiating communication and a style of reacting to it verbally.

Phrased in these terms, it is already possible to see the conceptual fruits of the abstract concept 'self-system.' Let us develop this somewhat. For both Freud and Sullivan, the idea of anxiety was basic. Sullivan understood that the development of language was in large measure directed toward the avoidance of anxiety. Thus, the self-system was conceived as a series of linguistic 'tricks.' In the child's helpless dependence for survival upon his parents, an undercurrent of anxiety over possible separation has to be overcome by loving care. Adler understood that it is this anxiety of helpless dependence that is used by the parents as a lever in training the child. Early anxiety in humans seems to be akin to primitive annihilation anxiety that one divines in animals. As long as it is allayed, the child can proceed securely to a development of his potential for symbolic mastery. Early ministrations from the mother provide for a warm sense of goodness in the child, which the psychoanalysts call the early supplies of self-esteem. Later supplies of self-esteem must be won by the child himself in the form of proper linguistic performance and symbolically mediated conduct that meets the approval of the adults. Self-esteem is a constant factor in human development, because it reflects at all times a secure mastery of the environment—a triumph over anxiety.

The 'Oedipal phase' can be understood then, from one point of view, as that developmental process in which the self-system achieves a radical reorientation with respect to keeping self-esteem. The 'Oedipal phase,' in other words, is a developmental training period in which the child learns to *switch modes of maintaining self-esteem* from an early mode of proximal, biological relationship to a later mode of symbolic, linguistic performance, according to an internalized code of rules. Thus, we can parsimoniously conceptualize two abstract invariants in human development: the self-system as a response-delaying psychological organ and the self-esteem as a basic quality within which the self-system develops.

Now, we can consider the self-system from still another point of view. If all the above is warranted, it becomes clear that the symbolic composition of the self-system is a series of codified rule-prescriptions for action capable of being held in awareness and of being put into linguistic form. The self-system is largely an action-potentiating entity composed of symbolic rule-prescriptions for anxiety-free behavior. This is what Freud meant by the superego, although he did not use the term to include the whole personality. We undoubtedly slight certain accents by viewing the self-system as a codification of symbolic rules for action; but the gain in conceptualization is enormous. We are enabled to see man in his fully relational nature; that is, the very predicates for action that compose the self-system are rules for viewing and treating the world. In other words, the ego is a precipitate of value prescriptions, which marks the appearance of *Homo sapiens* on the evolutionary scene. . . .

The significance of this view is that it permits us to understand that the cultural constitution of the self-system is itself a symbolic value constitution. . . . [The] self-system fashioned in this transition is fundamentally a value locus; that human action is value, or it is not human action. Thus, the self-system, like any good abstract concept, cannot be analyzed as a thing-in-itself. It has utility because of the relations which it establishes. A full break with Freudian essences was necessary in order to shift to what [Ludwig] von Bertalanffy would call a deanthropomorphization of the social world picture. With this deanthropomorphization, we have left far behind serious consideration of the 'Oedipus complex' as a scientific problem. It is now abundantly clear that any problem dealing with the mode of functioning of the self-system is a value problem, and as such it is inseparably embedded in a broad socio-cultural prescription for normative behavior. The mainsprings for human action are rooted in an extra-individual context, even though they may be manifest only in individual behavior. In passing beyond Freud, we have taken another step in deanthropomorphizing the individual as a central locus of natural causality. . . .

It may seem inept for us to accuse a theory of being too close to common sense, whose concepts did, in fact, so outrage common sense. But the common sense of Freud's time is not that of ours, and sexuality and aggressiveness have become banal components in today's world view.

But the problem of the introduction of quality—the idea of self-esteem—needs further justification. . . . [It] is necessary to introduce the idea of a qualitative self-esteem to establish relations of dependence between what we observe in human action and what we do not observe. The difficulty in fashioning abstract constructs in the social sciences has stemmed precisely from the fact that man, unlike atoms, is a qualitative organism in nature. As Dewey observed on the physical sciences, their ideal of knowledge is to eliminate precisely that which is dependent upon the distinctively human response. Thus, abstract constructs that establish relationships in social science must include human factors so recalcitrant to physical science method. One of the most important of these qualitative human factors is, as we repeatedly noted, the concept of self-esteem, the basic predicate for purposive human action. In addition, to complicate the problem even more for a physical science approach, self-esteem is invariably a function of symbolic value prescription for action.

Furthermore, self-esteem performs a task in establishing certain relationships that we would otherwise be at a loss to explain. Since it is symbolically animated, as it should be if the 'Oedipal phase' was negotiated, it remains bound to symbols. It is a direct link to historical and social events. Self-esteem is a quality that can be demolished by a single symbolic event or immeasurably multiplied by another symbolic event. Stock-market fluctuations can break lives, if point variations are great enough. Thus, self-esteem as an invariant point of reference is meaningful within a larger theory because it can be integrated into a logically coherent system. Perhaps social science has so lagged behind physical science in establishing invariant points of reference because it has shied away from fixing upon qualities. And perhaps we can only deal with qualities in social science when we include values as an integral invariant in our theories. . . .

The use of self-esteem as a qualitative concept may lead to the formulation of deductions testable in controlled inquiry. It might be operationally predictable in the individual, deviant case which the psychiatrist treats. Admittedly, this would have to take place within a value definition for normative behavior. The symbolic self-system cannot be otherwise than continually grounded in the fabrication of meaning appropriate to a particular cultural system.

But by all physical science criteria, an operationally predicated construct cannot at the same time be a purely normative derivative. It would seem, however, that in some areas of social science, this must be the case. The formulations of abstract constructs and invariants, linked operationally to behavioral styles and interpersonal events, are inevitably value-laden when we deal with individual human behavior. This realization, if it is not fanciful, bids fair to cause discomfort among both some psychoanalysts and some philosophers, although there have been those, like Dewey, who would acknowledge it with a wink.

Chapter 3

PERSONALITY, COMMUNICATION, AND
EDUCATION FOR DEMOCRACY

Personality Development in the Modern World (1963)*

W E LIVE, AS C. WRIGHT MILLS SO TIRELESSLY pointed out, in a society whose institutions are frighteningly mechanical. How can we find a foe where everyone not only protests his good intentions, but actually demonstrates them? Everyone is honestly building for the good life, and yet we know that something is radically wrong with our combined, well-intentioned efforts. . . . I want to help extricate educators somewhat from the growing, stifling disciplinary confusion, so that we can fashion some clear educational directives on the problem of personality development. The question, then, will be this: What do we know basically in the second half of the twentieth century about personality formation — straightforward knowledge that educators can use to do something about the human condition? . . .

Instinct Theory: An Historical Curio

The major whittling down of Freud has struck at the very heart of his system — the spurious instinct theory of human motivation. Most social scientists abandoned this long ago . . . but it managed to linger on. With Freud, the French Enlightenment view of man had given way to the influence of [Arthur] Schopenhauer and [Charles] Darwin: it was no longer society, but man's animal nature that had to bear the blame for human evil. Many people were helped to explain human misery in a simple way, by believing that man was somehow frustrated in his real basic urges by society. Human aggression and sexuality were plain facts, taking place every day on any city block; thus they could hardly be denied. We all know what Freud made of them. He said that every child has basic sexual and aggressive drives that sought outlet in the family circle. The parents could have none of this, and they actively

*Original, full text: E. Becker, "Personality development in the modern world: Beyond Freud and Marx," in H. W. Burns (ed.), *Education and the Development of Nations* (pp. 83-105). Syracuse University Press. Reprinted with permission from University College, Syracuse University.

frustrated these would-be primal drives. The result was that each parental couple shaped a self-conscious and sensitive human actor, who did what society expected of him, but who suffered quietly from his frustrations in the form of a deep-seated Oedipus complex.

Without going into technical details it can safely be said that the instinct theory of human behavior is now quite dead—if indeed it ever had to be born. We have any number of ways of explaining such behaviors as aggression, without having recourse to an instinctive drive formulation; and we have, furthermore, quite good authority for discounting any innate sexual drive on the part of the infant. There is no sexual instinct that is driving the child; rather, there is an environment which is not shaping him intelligently or wisely. This is what Erich Fromm observed, in effect, in his early criticism of Freud's view that the Oedipus complex was the result of sexual repression. Fromm thought that the Oedipus complex represented, rather, the child's fight with authority.

The 'Dynamic Unconscious' as Formed by a Learning Process

Many psychoanalysts themselves will accept this belated return to an Enlightenment view of man, as a very malleable creature free of instincts. But they will insist that Freud's basic discovery was really the 'dynamic unconscious.' In which case we have to ask: What is the dynamic unconscious if man is free of instincts? It can no longer be the 'seat of the instinctual life' as Freud understood it. In the modern psychoanalytic understanding the focus is accordingly shifted, and the dynamic unconscious can be thought to be made up of early 'repressions.' That is, the parents frustrate many of the child's activities—interrupted breast-feeding, scheduled waste elimination, and so on; in hundreds of ways he is trained to be self-reliant, careful, and compliant. All this takes place long before he is able to understand what is happening to him. So, we can say that the child gains control of his world without being fully aware of the why's and how's of the process. This kind of training leads him to perceive the world in certain automatic ways, so we could say that he has an 'unconscious'; which can then be understood, in one shorthand way, as the distortions in perception formed during the early conditioning process. In this view, then, Freud's basic discovery, even without the instinct theory, would be that man is largely an irrational creature, rather than a rational one, because he has no clear idea of his real motivations. The early learning process would call the quiet tune to which each individual jumps, whether he knows it or not.

Now this is a quite reasonable modification in breadth and emphasis, and most of us can agree on it. Once we throw out the instincts, the dynamic unconscious loses its mystery. Instead of being a fatal subterranean core which we inherited from Paleozoic times, it is something we earn through our early experience. Instead of being saddled by a phylogenetic fate, we are merely burdened by our early indiscretions and the results of our parents' tyranny, impatience, or simply their own limited world view.

Oedipus and Neurosis

In discovering the constrictions of early experience, symbolized in the Oedipus complex, Freud also discovered what we have come to call neurosis. Continuing our simplification, we find there is nothing mysterious either about this characteristic human ill: Man is burdened by his early learning. What does 'burdened' mean exactly here? It means that the child learns to conduct himself, and to execute choices, in a manner that will be pleasing to his parents. He learns to gain his feeling of self-value by performing according to codes that are thrust upon him by his parents. By neurosis, then, we mean to indicate the fact that early learning remains inadequate to meet the varied demands of adult experience, that it constricts the choices and the action of the adult in some ways. The child had made, in other words, a sacrifice in learning in order to please the parents at the expense of his own broad action. Neurosis signifies simply that there is a basic dichotomy in human experience, an incompatibility between early training and adult needs. . . . We might say that neurosis, in effect, is a kind of behavioral stupidity in the face of the new.

To carry the modern reinterpretation to its conclusion, we can hold, then, with Talcott Parsons, that the notorious Oedipus complex is not a complex at all; it is a transition, a *developmental phase* in the higher primates. As a phase, we have seen that it refers to a long period of training in which the child learns to perform as a member of society, and in which he develops certain habits and perceptions which partially cripple him for certain ranges of later experience. Instead of discovering human nature . . . Freud actually accomplished something more realistic and more scientific: he made some connections and saw some relationships between things that had previously been largely ignored, specifically, as we said, between early training and later experience. This is the basic dichotomy that has gone under the obfuscating name Oedipus complex. I have been somewhat didactic because these plain facts are something that educators can use, as we will see further on.

Now, at this point, a perplexing question may occur to us. If Freudian theory can be so handily rephrased and reoriented, and if we thus dispel its mysteries and get rather wide agreement on this reappraisal, then why have so many sparks flown in the process over the last fifty years? The question is crucial, and the answer I think is partly this: Freud not only offered a theory of neurosis, but he also claimed to have perfected the best instrument for a cure: the psychoanalytic treatment. In effect, the psychoanalyst tells us that if the individual wants to be more rational, and take command of his own destiny, then he must find out what happened to him in his early conditioning process. The psychoanalytic treatment boils down to this: during long hours of free reminiscence and talk, one is led to bring up and review the history and the results of his early training, somewhat like a pet dog would—if he could—be made to reflect on why he had always been enticed to jump through a hoop, and why as a puppy he got such a kick from it.

Psychoanalysis, in other words, offers us a theoretical interpretation of our fate and at the same time, paradoxically, tells us that, practically, this fate is implacable unless we put ourselves in the analyst's hands. Instincts or not, we are said to be the helpless creatures of the first five years of manipulations of our lives. . . .

Once we see human experience in terms of the basic dichotomy that Freud discovered, it becomes possible to aim to be rational without the technique he offers. In other words, and more directly: *it becomes possible for the educator to take the place of the psychoanalyst.*

Let us briefly review the twofold aspect of Freud's legacy, before expanding this contention. In the first place we must grant that Freud highlighted the basic dichotomy in human experience, the hiatus that causes neurosis. We sketched briefly what this means: neurosis is another way of talking about the constricting effects of early learning on potential adult choices. Neurosis, quite bluntly, as we implied above, is a kind of stupidity; it reflects the inability to match appropriate means to freely chosen ends. We could go on and elaborate on this at some length, but there is surprisingly little that need be added to this basic formulation of neurosis. The early training cripples us in certain areas of awareness, and we meet problems that consequently we cannot cope with. The commonest example is perhaps the sexual one: having been taught, say, that sex is bad, and that we are evil if we practice it, many people find considerable difficulty in fulfilling the marriage role freely and without guilt. The person may simply not be aware that he can function in other ways than those he has been taught. In terms of a simple formula we could say: Lack of awareness of alternate modes of behavior = neurosis = stupidity.

In the second place, let us grant that Freud discovered a technique that permits the person to gain considerable awareness about himself. By talking to an analyst about his present problems and his earlier experiences, the individual actually permits two pairs of eyes to focus on his blind spots. The result, as we well know, is a learning process in which old ways of looking at the world are abandoned, or modified and broadened. Stupidity, in other words, is lifted in certain crucial areas of personality functioning. The process, as we also well know, is long and costly—an analysis may take five years or more. Furthermore, as is becoming increasingly apparent, its success is hardly to be taken for granted: the analyst can promise nothing and very often gives little or nothing.

So, we have the discovery of human stupidity and a technique for doing away with it. At this point, then, I want to pose a very basic question, which is part of my radical suggestion: What other ways are there to overcome human stupidity? The direct problem is: What other ways are there for the individual to gain awareness of himself and the world?

We are much better armed than was Freud at the turn of the century to realize one thing, namely, that there is nothing fated about the shape of human society. If instincts do not provide the impetus to making man then society must provide it; and if society shapes man, then each society must shape him differently. Stupidity, in other words, is relative to the cultural and social structural context in which individuals are trained and raised. Freud certainly realized this, but it needed over fifty years of anthropological study of diverse societies to fill out exactly what we might call the shapes and forms of human stupidity.

The Social Aggravation of Neurosis

The next important question that we must ask, then, is this: How do societies differentially foster stupidity, or lack of awareness, in certain crucial areas of personality functioning? What is there in human training that aggravates the individual's alienation from his own executive powers?

We know, in the first place, that every society brainwashes its young, or, to put it more euphemistically, seduces them into the world view of the parents. I don't of course mean this exactly as a condemnation: realistically, we take it for granted that some curb must be put on human spontaneity and free development, in order to have social obedience at all.

Once we realize this, we can go on to examine the ways in which this early warping for the purposes of minimum humanization becomes intensified in some societies, and actually cripples a good many people. Ruth Benedict focused on this problem some time ago, and wrote an important paper which somehow failed to goad us into any major efforts along the lines she illuminated. Citing contrasting data from several societies, Benedict saw that our own society puts some severe burdens on the child, and it does this in four major ways. To refresh our memory let us list them:

1) *Training in non-responsibility:* During the long period of childhood, 'latency,' and pre-adolescence (and including adolescence for the most part), the child is actively encouraged to forego responsibility for his own initiatory powers. He is not expected to be a person in his own right, but continues to function as a protected appendage of the family.

2) *Training in submission:* The child is actively encouraged to suffer penalties, remain docile, relinquish most personal rights; for example, he dare not strike back or overly assert himself in defense of his own interests.

3) *Training in sexual repression:* We are familiar enough with the contrast here between our society and others.

All these curbs on the child serve to interrupt the free development of his responsible powers; this leads Benedict to condemn what she called 'discontinuities' in cultural conditioning—discontinuities would exist wherever the child is prevented from experiencing a continuing sequence in the training and promoting of his abilities.

4) Now, these discontinuities and prohibitions exist in many cultures; but Benedict makes the final point that *their ill effects can be diminished:* at least among primitives, especially, this is done by clearly marking off, by means of social rituals, the stages of individual growth. So that if there is some confusion or some new behavior is suddenly thrust upon the unprepared child or youth, he is pointedly shown by means of some ritual of age passage that he has reached a clear new stage of growth in which he is a different individual, and can now function differently. Very little is left to his imagination about who he is, and to the possibilities of confusion between

what is permitted and what is not—even if, for a long time, his responsibilities had been in limbo. We have only to contrast, as Benedict does, this situation with that in our own society. We might describe our methods as those of cultivated confusion, or growing up by the technique of heroic blundering. . . .

The Twilight of the Psychoanalytic Cure

As educators, you will see the splendid point to which our discussion has brought us, and why I said earlier that the educator can take the place of the psychoanalyst. We can now define the Oedipus complex, the dynamic unconscious, or neurosis, in terms of two basic and related deficits:

1) The paralysis of the ability to learn by natural trial and error.

2) The distrust of one's powers of independent judgment throughout life.

What was the educational answer to these two 'Oedipal' deficits? Progressive, experimental education, of course. The early vision of progressive education was one of the continual engagement of the child in real problematic experiences in a continuing hierarchy of such experience. *This is how he effaces the sham dichotomy between constricting parental training and broad social challenge.* In Dewey's view, the child must be encouraged to make his own adjustment. He overcomes his Oedipus, if we still want to use this term, by direct refashioning of himself and his perceptions in ongoing problematic situations.

Dewey's whole protest, in fact, was against the educational atmosphere of societies like that of Freud's Victorian Vienna: the old educational technique simply reinforced the early authoritarian family training; the child was trained to acquiesce in his passivity by browbeating, emotional appeals, sermons, and so on. Hence, as Dewey saw, true democracy is the only atmosphere in which man can grow because it is against nonreflective action at all times. It is geared to meeting with the full force of reason continually new, problematic situations. The old authoritarian, faculty education, in other words, enforced the early perceptions of the child in their accustomed rut, by not allowing him to exercise and develop his own spontaneous organizing perceptions. Thus the moratorium on original perceptions and on the exercise of self-powers came to *last from the age of the Oedipal transition to late adolescence.* Freud's famous cases on hysteria, as a modern theorist has shown, reflected exactly what we would expect: not people who were 'sick' in any medical sense, but confused and purblind children who had been raised as uncritical slaves of their domineering parents and constricting society.

We would have understood all this much earlier if we had been less worshipful of medicine and more critical of culture. The great literary critic I. A. Richards certainly spelled out very clearly the artificial fixation of attitudes that takes place as the child is removed from the free play of experience. And he pointed out that this exile often makes of the adult a less aware individual than the child. Surely this is as clear a statement of 'Oedipus' or 'neurosis' as any educators would need—the whole theory of literature and art as preparations for life is validly based on it. . . .

Progressive Education as Naturalistic Psychoanalysis

Nevertheless, when psychoanalysis is at its (rare) best, its aims are those of radical education, even though its scope and method are not. Otto Rank summed up the deeper implications of psychoanalysis as education when he frankly said that it "must be opposed to every prevailing community ideology." More recently, we see this same spirit in the radical proposals of a maverick psychotherapist like Robert Lindner. Lindner, we will remember, was strongly opposed to the ideology of adjustment that we preach in our society, and he outlined a program of training in which children would be encouraged to rebel by developing capacities suited to rebellion. He listed six qualities which enable the child to meet the world in terms of maximum efficiency and satisfaction; the child should be trained to be *aware, identified, skeptical, responsible, employed,* and, finally (curiously perhaps to the ears of those in the adjustment camp), the child should be *tense.*

These qualities hardly need elaboration, but as I understand them they mean progressive education: To be *aware* means to bring reason continually to bear on problems in real-life situations; to be identified means to know who one is in relation to his own powers and to others around him; to be skeptical means just that—to be critical of any automatic authority; to be responsible means to be able to act as an autonomous agent, and to be prepared to bear the consequences for that action; to be employed means simply to be engaged in something meaningful rather than trivial; to be tense means that one believes there is something serious and dramatic about life, that it is a cause for real concern and for the best efforts one can produce.

The most immediate and crucial of these qualities, for Lindner, was the need to provide for the continuing growth and development of awareness, from early childhood, without interruption, right up to the end of one's days. We can thus see what these qualities are designed to effect: not rebellion in the destructive sense, but the kind of continual psychoanalysis that progressive education should be: in a word, a naturalistic resolution of neurosis, the wiping out of the sharp dichotomy between early training and adult experience, the lifting of the long moratorium on the exercise of self-powers to which the old, faculty, rote learning condemned the child. With training such as this, not only would a naturalistic psychoanalysis be freely accomplished, but the very idea of psychoanalysis would not be necessary. At best, it would be a poor substitute for what real education could and should provide. Psychoanalysis would only linger, as an educative technique, for the same reason it is now with us: by social default.

The Failure of Naturalistic Psychoanalysis

It is one thing to say that progressive education takes over naturally from the historically accidental technique of psychoanalysis; it is quite another thing to explain why its results have been even less satisfactory than psychoanalysis in fashioning alert, self-critical individuals. If by neurosis we mean the paralysis of the ability to learn by natural trial and error, and the distrust of one's own powers of independent judgment, then why hasn't progressive education been able really to attack neurosis?

The question ultimately hinges around the kind of definition we give to the six qualities listed above, and we will return to this subsequently. Here it is enough to remind ourselves once again that socially we have not dared to put real meat on the skeleton of progressive education. It is not that Dewey was a visionary or a Vermont rustic whose program was bound to run afoul of the hard facts of sophisticated modern life. Rather, as we know, it has been the case that socially we have been cowards.

Certainly the original vision of progressive education was the correct prescription for shaping modern man. Democracy needed citizens who were capable of independent judgment, free uninhibited cooperation; what better way to fashion them than by letting them use their own judgment in the situations and problems of everyday living? The best way to resolve the constricting effects of authoritarian training was to teach the child to master his own situations. We can see now that the stumbling block to this program was perhaps inevitable in any educational or re-educational program: In order to fashion a social animal some early constriction of perceptions is necessary. In order to fashion an independent, self-critical, and fully aware individual, many of these early perceptions must be almost wholly unconstricted. Progressive education was faced with Penelope's task, of having to undo what had to be done. The psychoanalyst, too, is faced with the same dilemma. He has to undo the parental constrictions, and still not create an irresponsible libertine. Small wonder that progressive education, trying to meet a broad and total cultural challenge, was likely to bungle the job. It was led to opt for creating automatically compliant social animals *primarily, and individuals only secondarily, which is equivalent to saying that it did not create independent and fully aware individuals.* Here certainly we recognize the gravamen of Arthur Bestor's criticisms of progressive education: it has become a mass technique for brainwashing the child into automatic obedience to social conventions—even hard intellectual effort has had to go down the drain, where the child doesn't need it in order to become acceptably social.

Progressive Education and Social Neurosis

Neurosis . . . takes two forms. This is very important to be clear about. In its first form it results from the abrogation of individual awareness and choice, due to the long surrender of one's active powers—a surrender that in our society we call latency and adolescence. In its other guise, neurosis results from a similar abrogation, which takes the form of the continued exercise of one's powers in automatically socially approved ways. The individual suffers no discontinuity in conditioning, and becomes a normal member of society only to lose his potential uniqueness in the process. . . . [W]e create more cheerful robots, simply, to borrow a phrase from C. Wright Mills. We will have to do better than merely creating smiling salesmen of our uncritical way of life; let us see both why this is necessary and how it might be done.

Beyond Marx

The problems of educating for living in the modern world are staggering. But surprisingly, the basic choices seem to be few and very clear-cut. The reason that the choices are clear-cut is that industrial society seems to grind relentlessly in one direction—in one frightening direction. For the last one hundred years, sociologists of the stature of [Karl] Marx, [Ferdinand] Toennies, Max Weber, [Thorstein] Veblen, and recently C. Wright Mills, have analyzed aspects of this unmistakable and relentless current. Industrial society as it has taken shape under both free and controlled enterprise is tending to become more and more bureaucratized, which means simply that its functioning becomes more automatic and uncritical. The job of any bureaucracy is to get things done easily and efficiently, and what tends to be overlooked are the more basic questions of whether the job is worth doing in the first place, or what its relationship is to desired human values and freely chosen goals. The smooth functioning of bureaucracy, in other words, tends to obscure the very purposes which it is designed to serve, and man gets lost in the process.

In our society, corporate economy feeds upon the energies of each new generation and quietly sucks up their skills and personalities to further its own forms. We are familiar with the words which describe this process: organization man, executive suite, Madison Avenue, mass society, and so on. We no longer ask whether it is good for General Motors to gamble a billion dollars on retooling for a new model car—whether this money might not be better spent for education and housing, or whether we need a new model in the first place. We take it for granted, automatically, that this is a good end, and the problem becomes one of gearing a whole bureaucratic organization to making the gamble pay off. People in the organization seem to be doing rational and logical things, life has meaning, and one can feel good about a job expeditiously and efficiently accomplished. In all this the individual gets lost—he doesn't have a chance, because he doesn't have a choice. He is automatically formed, recruited, and boxed, in order to keep the wheels of corporation economy running.

When Jacques Barzun said he saw a sign of health in juvenile delinquency, he was not trying for the startling effect. The matter of blind conformity has become so serious that we cannot even hope that our youth will violently rebel, that they will show some spontaneous, creative energy, even negatively expressed. This is the real underlying tragedy of our time, the quiet sapping of human vigor, on which everyone turns his back in fatalistic acceptance. There is a growing agreement on the part of the best analysts of modern industrial society that we are now ruthlessly completing what was begun at the beginning of the industrial revolution—namely, the abject surrender of man to the machine. . . .

This is what inspires the growing cry against alienation, the fact that the individual is no longer an end in himself, but is uncritically used for ends he does not even examine. When Kant said that man must be an end in himself and not a means, he meant that the individual should be allowed to regulate himself. Instead, we now see man dancing to the tune of mass consumer production. We pride ourselves on equality, and as we understand this term, it means something pitifully abasing: it means, to all intents and purposes, equal right to consumer goods. But true equality for man should mean that each individual has the free choice to determine his own purposes, not those that are handed down to him—he must be free to choose his own genuine ends. How can he achieve this freedom? Unfailingly, the burden falls on education: *man must be provided with a fund of critical knowledge, and be encouraged and allowed to bring it to bear.*

Educating for Real Awareness

All this, then, is by way of briefly introducing and affirming the fact that we have but one fundamental choice in our educative programs—choice, that is, if we value man. . . . The six qualities that we would strive to cultivate in our youth would have to be defined in entirely new ways, really meaty ways, as we suggested earlier. We have only to sketch them to see the real problems they pose, as well as the striking challenge they hold out:

- To be *aware* means to be given all kinds of information that one might need, even, at the appropriate time, information on the possibly bad influences of one's own early training, and of the beliefs of his society.

- To be *skeptical* means to be encouraged to be critical of any authority or tradition that is no longer serviceable.

- To be *employed* means everything that Paul Goodman—that courageous critic of the smug society—says that a truly man's work means.

- To be *identified, responsible, and tense* means that the youth may have to be encouraged to *actively seek* things that are radically wrong with his society and with his world. He may consequently need to be asked to offer his own original criticisms and solutions to what is wrong, to offer his own active powers, and be allowed to use them; and, not least, perhaps to propose the kind of world he might like to live in. Democratic education, ideally conceived, would, in effect, train children *to take over and reshape the world* rather than live tranquilly in it as it is handed down.

When reconstructionist educators urge us to educate for living in the modern world, to me this means that we should take our children seriously—train them to take over society partly on their own terms, instead of wholly on ours. Certainly this is what Otto Rank adumbrated when he said that "it almost seems in the meaning of our pedagogic ideas of reform that the child itself must be left to construct a new educational ideology, must be forced, so to say, *into the role of the leader.*" Of course we would have to do some unaccustomed things in this kind of effort: we should have to have the courage to tell our youth, in effect, that we are not presenting them with the best of all possible worlds; that enormous problems remain to be tackled; that their energies, ideas, solutions are what is needed; that since it will be their world soon, then it is partly up to them to put it into shape. Only in this way can true awareness be fostered; it would become a continuous training, from elementary

school on, in a continuing hierarchy of problems—problems ranging from self probing to probing the whole array of adult motives and established behaviors. It is
against the backdrop of the challenge of educating for true awareness that we see in
clear focus the answer to Bestor's criticism of progressive education: contrary to his
views, the school *must* be inseparable from the community and social life; learning
can only be by doing; but we must face the fact that learning and social living that
cheat the child of real, toothsome problems are perhaps indeed worse than the old
faculty learning. Yes, we may well have to do what others have suggested—burden
children with the hard facts about such things as anxious racial problems. After all,
they are going to have to live with them long after we are tranquilly fertilizing the
earth. Children must have the opportunity to be . . . their own social engineers. And
social engineering in a democracy means that the child must learn to take a strong
stand on democratic, moral values. The pseudo-neutrality that we now encourage, in
order to spare the child 'emotional upset,' can only result—as Karl Mannheim saw—
in really crippling restrictions on individual awareness.

Social Science and Psychiatry (1963)*

DEMOCRACY, IT IS SAID, DEPENDS UPON THE INTELLIGENT layman:
specifically, upon his access to correct information. We have long since learned that
in our age we have the greatest cause to fear; expertise is rampant. It's an old story.
The in-group knows, but, because knowledge is snowballing in complexity, it is difficult to impart. We have also learned to trust these experts—largely out of necessity:
somebody has to be depended on in a chaotic world. So we have experts within
experts, puzzles within enigmas, cages within cages. And the expert who doesn't
know has to trust others who do, like the shaman who assured the anthropologist that
although his shamanistic powers were fraudulent, he could always count on the
authentic powers of other shamans.

Take the problem of mental illness. If ever there was a booming field for experts,
mental illness is it. The public demands that somebody get to the bottom of this, and
the researchers have been enthusiastic in response. After all, we are building the good
society and want to spare no effort to iron out the irksome kinks—if only the viruses
would stay put and the brain chemicals remain in balance. It is annoying enough that
nature put such capacities for hope and joy into such ridiculously fragile bodies. It is
doubly annoying when we seem to be in possession of the 'good life' and have so
many who are prevented from enjoying it.

Psychiatric experts are not a particularly reticent group—few Americans are.
This is both fortunate and unfortunate, as we have learned from our space-rocketry
experts: fortunate when the information imparted is dependable, unfortunate when it

*Original, full text: E. Becker, "Social science and psychiatry: The coming challenge." *Antioch Review,* 23:
353-366 (1963). Copyright © 1963 by the Antioch Review, Inc. First appeared in the Antioch Review, Vol.
23, no. 3. Reprinted by permission of the Editors.

is not. Psychiatrists assure us that gigantic progress is being made, drug research is closing in on sure formulas for rebalancing the unbalanced. It is true, they say, that we do not know exactly what mental illness is, but we are nevertheless on our way: the sufferers who crowd our mental hospitals find relief, for the most part; after some chemical and electric manipulations, most of them are able to join their loved ones and carry on as before. The medical message is clear, confident, hopeful. We have learned to expect this from the medical expert; the trail of his successful discoveries has so far spoken for itself.

But the medical expert is in trouble—real trouble; he is being crowded in his expertise. He is reaching out for help beyond the confines of the traditional medical areas: more and more medical schools are employing behavioral scientists from sociology, anthropology, social psychology. Psychiatry is turning to behavioral science precisely because the chemical approach to such syndromes as schizophrenia and depression (the major ones) has delivered nothing—nothing in the way of discovering their cause or prevention. Chemical and electrical treatments provide mere alleviation or, at best, a purely chance cure for causes unknown. Not to know the causes of things is, to say the least, an uncomfortable posture for scientist or shaman.

The behavioral scientist is a strange bird in the glittering medical cage, and he is demonstrating both his strangeness and his unexpected value. The new, combined onslaught on the problem of mental illness brings to mind Dewey's cautious hope: Once we start thinking, there's no telling where we'll come out. The fact is that the influx of social scientists into psychiatric research is causing something of a major stir in psychiatry. For one thing, many of these new experts do not believe in a physiochemical approach to human unhappiness. The idea of a 'schizophrenic serum secretion' strikes them as possibly true but etiologically trivial. They have been trained to see life in the broad, in the round, to see man as a growing, groping, cognitive animal who differs from others precisely in that he is motivated by fears, hopes, and thoughts, and not by chemicals.

Surely (they are willing to admit) chemistry is 'part' of thought, but how much is it a part of the abysmal human misery that we call 'mental illness'? Put in unscientific terms, the question would read like this: Does a wayward amino acid wrench a wife's insides as decisively as a husband's scowl? The sophisticated behavioral scientist thinks that the medical approach to human problems is a mere fraction of the attack that is needed. He holds that medicine is to mental illness somewhat as a scarecrow is to farming: a stage prop added to awe outsiders, to preserve the field without changing it. For medicine, this means the preservation of its age-old prerogatives over human ills; for the public at large it means a sheepish trust that they need not bother their heads over the means and ends of human well-being: the men in the white coats will carry the burden.

The question we have asked is whether the behavioral scientist's opinions are too strong-headed, exaggerated, or, better, factually uninformed. Specifically, does the behavioral scientist's hard-nosed cynicism about microscopic approaches to human happiness lead us into any sounder understanding of mental illness? There are excellent reasons for believing that it does. Perhaps an examination of the phenomenon of menopausal depression will demonstrate why.

Here is indeed an enigma. Why does a woman, who to all appearances has led a satisfying life, suddenly break down at menopause and decide that her life is not worth living? There is a medical explanation for this—a direct one which holds physio-chemical changes as somehow responsible for a change in mood and tone. There is a quasi-medical psychiatric explanation which holds that the woman, now seeing concrete evidence of the passing of her biological prime, sees herself in the perspective of death and eternity and develops acute melancholy—an existential melancholy.

The traditional psychoanalytic explanation is hardly a medical one, but it is graphic: the woman re-experiences the psychological loss that she once felt in her early childhood, when she compared her body to a boy's for the first time and imagined that she had been castrated. Very neat.

What are we to make of these various explanations? A good case can be made out for each of them, of that there is no doubt. These explanations have been the rule for quite some time now. But let there be no doubt either about the far-reaching implications of the explanation we choose.

If we choose the first explanation, the medical one, we can comfortably continue to assign the search for human failure to the cloistered chemical research laboratories. If we choose the second, the quasi-medical psychiatric one, we can continue to nod, wisely and wearily, our assent to the timeless vicissitudes of the human condition.

If we choose the third, the psychoanalytic explanation, we can look pityingly and cynically upon the human animal as a contrary child who never grows up, who is always prepared to relapse into a vain longing for the innocent animal paradise that he was forced by his parents to give up. This eternal child never accepts his body, nor the world to which he was forced to submit by virtue of it.

It is easy to see that if the expert accepts any one or any combination of these explanations (as we do in our psychiatric hospitals) he can leave work at five and eat a peaceful (even stoic) supper. If everything is not right with the world, it can be righted. And if it cannot be completely righted, then that too is in the 'nature of things.' But happily, the sophisticated behavioral scientist cannot accept any of these explanations. His most provocative trait is that he does not believe in the untroubled 'good society' or the present version of the 'good life'—nor does he accept the idea that the 'nature of things' applies to the realm of human action, where man is the maker and doer. I say 'happily,' because in the long run the behavioral science approach to mental illness holds revolutionary implications for the way we conceive our lives. There is a fourth possible explanation for menopausal depression. . . .

The modern view of human conduct was so long in the making because we had to wait for the general theory of evolution. This gave the possibility of seeing man in proper perspective. We had to find out that man was an animal, and this discovery did not come with full force until the nineteenth century. Why was it so important? Simply because it eliminated two age-old hurdles which had been distorting our vision of man.

The first hurdle was the idealistic view of man, the notion that there was some special soul, substance, spirit, peculiar divine force that animated his action. The theory of evolution showed very persuasively that man was indeed an animal. It followed from this that he was not essentially different from other animals: he was a striving organism seeking to move, act, survive, and reproduce in a particular environment. Ideas of spirit and soul were not necessarily shown to be untrue, they were merely seen to be not helpful to a scientific description of man as he lived and acted in the world. We had to find out what man was about on this earth, and not what God and Nature were about in the universe. Science had to limit its scope to come to grips with its subject matter.

If the idealistic notions of soul and substance were not helpful in clarifying man's nature, neither was the materialistic notion that man was merely an aggregate of deterministic atoms moving blindly and mechanistically under fixed laws. Instead, it became obvious that man was an organism, moving under his own powers and acting with certain ends in view. *He was a biological entity, and not merely a physical one.* He was a composite of chemicals, cells, and organs, and not simply atoms and ether. If anything, the materialist version of man's nature was more harmful than the idealist, because it closed our search to the unmistakable differences in levels of life.

By eliminating these two misconceptions, then, man was placed squarely within the animal kingdom. He was seen to be neither god nor thing. But he was still different from other animals: he spoke, hoped, planned, and pined, cried and dreamed. The idealistic versions of his nature were not based on pure hopeful fancy; they were attempts to account for these real and observed differences from the lower animals. It remained, in sum, to explain these differences: In what way had man become a special kind of animal?

The answer was remarkably simple: he possessed language. The mechanism of the voice box coupled with a large, retentive nervous system permitted him to push out word sounds and to remember what they stand for. Simple sounds like 'ma-ma,' for example, made dependable connection with something in the environment that could be counted on for warm, soft comfort. Other objects too were gradually named and controlled. The result of this was to build up an action map of the world, based on words and memory: "Tomorrow I will go to New York and see Mom." Words and the images they call forth not only give memory; they also sketch out a future, permit one to plan, to hope, to expect. The edifice of word-expectancies becomes a structure of meaning. Our word-world is the only world we can count on, the only one we have earned, and the only one we know. Our life-meaning is a conglomerate of word-sounds and the memories and images they call up. We are all like Othello in that words seal our fate.

This, then, in simplest terms, is the special kind of animal man is. He has taken control of the world because he ranges freer and further than other animals. The reason he can do this is because he has been able to name objects for his attention and use—language alone has made his world broader and richer. But this has not been an unmitigated blessing, and we can easily see the reason why. If to gain words is to gain a world full of named objects, then, conversely, to lose words is to lose the world. The person who can put more words together in more varied combinations has, theoretically, a larger world in which to move. But to be tongue-tied is to be hog-tied. If words make man human, to lack words is to be sub-human.

How do these abstract introductory remarks apply to something as concrete as menopausal depression? The answer is not self-evident, but neither is it far to seek. To introduce it, let us preview our discussion with a straightforward statement of the main thesis: Women become depressed at menopause because they have based their lives on too narrow a range of words. They do not have enough reasons for satisfying action, and when they lose the one apparent reason upon which they predicated their lives—their femininity—their whole action world caves in. Let us be brutally direct: Menopausal depression is the consequence of confining woman to a too narrow range of life choices or opportunities. It is a social and cultural phenomenon, for which the 'designers' of social roles are to blame. We create menopausal depression by not seeing to it that women in their forties are armed with more than one justification for their lives.

If this direct and rather simple explanation for a crushing human failure holds true, the reader may well wonder: Why have psychiatrists and psychoanalysts not seized upon it sooner and used it to propagandize and direct our attention to the way we design our lives? But we saw above the three alternative formulations that our mind healers put forth: chemistry, biology, childishness. Let us look further at their reasons for not coming to grips with the issue in its stark and yet ominous simplicity. . . . Psychoanalysis, in effect, in order to explain man, reduced him to manageable proportions: greed, lust, hunger, frustration, aggression. A tidy picture of primal strivings over which reason somehow governed.

But human action, peculiarly human action, is based on language. Freud did not seem to understand that human life was governed by a search for words, for meaning, and not a search for the expression of antisocial urges. This point is so crucial that it sums up the last half century of argument that has raged around Freud and his formulations. One of Freud's famous cases, used to illustrate the correctness of his views, makes all of this quite clear; at the same time, it permits us to probe more deeply into our discussion of menopausal depression.

A fifty-three-year-old woman sought out Freud's help because suddenly her life was flooded by an insane jealousy. She imagined that her husband was having an affair with a young career girl employed in his factory; and, although she knew her jealousy accusations to be without real foundation, she found herself curiously powerless to put them out of her mind. Freud saw this woman for two short hours and, demonstrating the 'unbelievable' clinical acumen for which he became noted, he got right to the heart of the matter as he saw it.

For Freud it was quite simple. During the interview, the woman had let fall 'certain remarks' which hinted that she felt her attractiveness to men waning. Also, Freud seems to have brought out that she felt this waning particularly with reference to her young son-in-law. No mystery here for any believer in man's basically salacious nature, that of a poor creature victimized by forces beyond his control. Freud concluded that the woman's delusional accusations of unfaithfulness directed to her husband were merely a cover for her own unconscious desires to commit adultery with a younger man. That was that, for Freud and for genuflecting psychoanalysts ever since. The master had again penetrated unfailingly to the core of human motivation.

Now the fact is that the whole matter is much richer and more complex than Freud supposed. One cannot make out, in his account, any evidence for the woman's infatuation with her son-in-law, the secret urge to infidelity that Freud claims he detected. Indeed, he says it was 'unconscious,' which is just another way of saying, "It is there, upon my word; no point in trying to prove otherwise." Of course, it is possible that this woman sensed the attractiveness of this young man; it is likely too that she assayed her own possible appeal to him—a human dialogue that not only women are prone to. Perhaps this was the hint that Freud seized upon in the interview and then elaborated out of all proportion. It is possible too that at fifty-three this woman sensed the decline of her only value to men—her physical charm. After all, society tells woman that this is her only interpersonally marketable quality in a man's world.

Even more to the point is the patient's status as compared to the young girl whom she imagined involved in the affair with her husband. The young career girl had done something most unusual for that time: she was of low social status and, instead of going into domestic work, had defied convention and entered a man's world. She took business training, got a position at the factory, and became a social equal of the men, even being addressed honorifically as Fraulein. The jealous wife, on the other hand, had played the social game according to all the conventional rules, but something had gone wrong. Something had happened that threatened her whole position in the world. As we read the account, we get a full picture of her dilemma. Her children were now grown up and married. Her husband, instead of retiring and joining her at home, as she expected, had decided instead to continue operating his factory. He had chosen not to retire, but she had no such choice. Now she was no longer attractive to men nor could she ever have any active place in her husband's world. The world belonged to men, and to certain courageous women who hoped for a career in that world. She was alone, without usable skills, no longer with children, without her accustomed beauty.

And, what is more important to our understanding of this ordinary human dilemma, she was without words in which to frame her protest. Her whole reason for being in the world was to play the role of loving mother, devoted wife, capable housewife, and now this had all vanished. She had been trained to live in a certain kind of world and to accept it dumbly. But now the curtain had closed on this world, and there was no question of beginning life anew, or of joining her husband at the factory. Not only is there no question of it, but the question does not even arise. The only thing that arises is an inchoate female protest against inequality and a threat to her own feeling of value in a man's world. This cry against helplessness and potential meaninglessness takes the form of jealousy accusations; it is a protest against personal and social injustice: *"I am being cheated!"*

In saying "I am jealous of you," she is actually protesting something much more involved: "My world is caving in, and I can't pin the trouble down anywhere; but it seems to me that you are right on top of things as always, and this doesn't seem fair. I have no reason for knowing that it is unfair, since society has never formulated this idea in words that I might use. With a bit of ingenuity, though, I seem to get my feeling across by using jealousy language."

Freud, it seems, did not understand jealousy-language. Instead of conceiving it as a mask for human failure, he thought it was a diabolic veneer over animal urges. But he demonstrated in his own life, in his actions toward his wife Martha, that he had no idea of female social inequality, of a woman's need to protest her own sense of value in a man's world. Thus, he could reduce a still-born cry to supposed instincts, and thereby keep up the appearance and the conviction that the social world we have designed is ethical and right. Freud sacrificed a real understanding of a complex human situation to the smug interpretations of a fanciful theory and to the morality of a Victorian world.

But we do not have to dig back to turn-of-the-century Vienna for case materials on how we keep people childish and then call them naughty when they protest. Take the woman in our society who helps her husband through college but has to give up her own long-cherished career plans in order to do it. As the years go by, she may find that her husband, increasingly successful in the career she helped launch by working, say, in Woolworth's, spends less and less time at home. He may take her less and less into his confidence, since many years of attention to the details of running a house have not permitted her to keep up with the outside world or the technicalities of his career. She finds herself growing old, her children married, her husband increasingly independent and disturbingly distant.

It is at this point that she may begin a serious search for a language in which to phrase the gradual undermining of her sense of human value. Again, jealousy language can fill the need. It may be the closest she can come to formulating the idea that he is not upholding his end of the original marriage bargain. If her thoughts could take definite shape, they might be voiced as follows: "I gave up a career to help you, and now you are leaving me in the lurch. While your life is rich with meaning, I feel that I am living in a ghost world." By accusing him, say, of adultery, she comes as close as she can to adumbrating that he is cheating her. There is no other way she can give voice to the feeling of being cheated, and this for one very good reason: Our society does not put into words the idea that the frustrated career wife of a successful businessman should feel cheated. After all, hasn't she 'had children' and thereby realized her 'true nature'? Hasn't she been well provided for, had a house in the 'better part' of town, a new car regularly, and so on, and so on?

In her search for a vocabulary of protest, she may expand her jealousy-language. She may strive to make it credible to herself. She may go to any lengths to imagine adulterous affairs of her husband, even in her own home while she sleeps upstairs. She senses that her world has been undermined and this is her way of conveying the idea that she is being 'defiled' literally at her very doorstep. Nor can she be convinced by any calm reasoning that she is wrong. If her ingenious jealousy-language were to fail, she would be struck dumb.

These illustrations of jealousy-language have nothing directly to do with the physiological fact of menopause, but they do help us see how the biological changes can serve as a symbolic sign of a greater threat to one's life-meaning. A more common language in menopausal depression is what we might call guilt-language. Not only does the depressed woman lose her zest for life, but also, for no apparent reason, she takes on her shoulders the total blame for her failure. And this shouldering of blame achieves, sometimes, grotesque proportions: Everyone is good, supremely good, kind, considerate, self-sacrificing; only the depressed woman alone is guilty, evil, foul, conniving, sinning, worthless. The self-accusations are sometimes so merciless that it is obvious that only a rare human being could possibly merit them. Yet the depressed, mild, plodding, everyday housewife insists that she does deserve them, and deserves even far worse epithets if these could be found.

At this point we realize that we cannot ask: Why does this person feel so humiliatingly guilty?—but rather: What is she trying to accomplish with this particular language? The personal reasons for depression will vary in each individual case; yet, in all of them, it is obvious that the individual is groping for a language with which to supply a meaning to a life that has somehow bogged down. Action has become unsatisfying, devotion is no longer automatically possible, things do not 'stack up' with the same jigsaw fit: the meaningful world is somehow edging away, slipping out of one's free and easy grasp. A whole lifetime of training and practice for a particular role suddenly threatens to become senseless. The cozy self-justification that infuses every little act is no longer there. And yet there is no explanation that the woman herself can give. Everything and everyone around her urge her that she should be content. The outward trappings of the good life are apparent to all: home, husband, children, grandchildren; the mirror-reflected image of the faithful wife and patient mother—it is all there. But it doesn't send back the instantly warm feeling of self-righteousness. The objects are cold, the world a pale gray, the insides deep, empty, yet heavy with an unexplainable, massive frustration.

Guilt-language is the perfect formula for justifying failure, a failure in which the woman forfeits all claims of her own. The reason she forfeits these claims is simple: she has no idea that she is entitled to any. . . . This portrait of human failure is so pitiful that for a long time the obvious explanation that we are considering seemed too benign. It did not seem possible that self-accusation of guilt was merely an ingenious attempt to hold one's world together. For this reason, psychoanalysts, especially, were fond of dredging up their favorite 'hidden aggressive instinct' that everyone is thought to possess. Psychoanalysts postulated that the 'normal hate' which we direct toward others had somehow 'gone awry' and was instead deflected toward the person themselves. This radar-model of human striving robs the person even of his minimum of ingenuity, that is, the invention of a guilt-language that unblocks the hopeless situation.

But this much must be said, and it must be said loudly and clearly—in fact, we must begin seriously to allow it to take full hold on our minds: the psychiatric and psychoanalytic explanations for human failure let us off easy. If we accept these explanations and act on them, as we do in our psychiatric clinics and hospitals and private doctors' offices, then our task is delightfully simple: we need only probe around inside individuals. We are spared the task of coming to grips with the full range of human and social problems that exist outside the patient. . . . We see this every day in our psychiatric 'treatment' facilities. When the woman who uses jealousy language or guilt language makes her protests a bit too discomfiting for others, she usually finds herself recommended for psychiatric care. She then becomes another test case for the miracle of drug cure, or for the correctness of Freud's smug theories. If Freud insults our intelligence by reducing the richness of human aspiration to the fornication motif, then modern psychiatry insults us equally by reducing it to chemical charts. Of course the woman can be admitted to a psychiatric hospital and pumped full of drugs. She may even be wrenched around on a table by electroshock, and her painful adumbration of failure temporarily effaced thereby. She may have the ultimate benefit of 'personal' discussion with a psychiatrist, who will show her how unreasonable she is to feel jealous toward her obviously devoted and exemplary family. In short, she may be so well 'cured' by the miracles of modem medicine and mature mind healing, that she can take her rightful place again in society, solidly beside her loved ones in rededication to the good life.

And so we see that the obvious explanation is hardly the easy one. It cuts ever so deeply into the very fabric of our legal, social, ethical, and moral lives. People use stupidity-languages like jealousy and guilt when they have not been given the cognitive tools (the words, ideas, reasons) with which to examine the plan of their lives. The ingenuity that the depressed woman demonstrates at menopause is a reflection of social tyranny. And this tyranny is the most telling in a democracy where free information is the highest goal; where life should be under continued scrutiny of reason; where tradition is to be examined to see if it fits human needs; where 'old ways' are not necessarily the best ways. And above all, where the individual good stands on the same footing of importance as the common good—where the one is not sacrificed to the many.

In the phenomenon of menopausal depression we see the effects of denying people the education that each rightfully deserves: the education for choice, the training in alternatives, the awareness that comes with the broad, critical perspective. We see democracy subverted at the base: in denying to the unique individual the knowledge that permits him to choose, to cultivate and exercise his very uniqueness. We see instead that the individual is kept stupid for the sake of everyone else's equanimity. As in Freud's Vienna, women are given their status in the social structure as a matter of course, as a matter of right, and they should not question otherwise. People in close and loving identification with others are taught that they should derive all their life satisfactions from the quality of these relations and from the pattern of rights and obligations they entail.

In democracy, informed communication is the one and only hope. Only by means of it can we gain the ability and the confidence to plan our lives in intelligent unison. In a democracy, experts and kings share a quality: we need not take their clothes for granted. Even more, in an informed democracy, the intelligent public does the dressing of its heroes. Now that the broad scrutiny of behavioral scientists has penetrated the previously sacrosanct domain of medical psychiatry and psychoanalysis, we are beginning to see the full reach of life designs—and, more painfully and soberingly, the broad responsibility that we all share for these designs.

PART TWO
TOWARD AN INTEGRATED SOCIAL SCIENCE OF BEHAVIOR
(1964-1971)

The chapters in this section present selections that were written during the time Becker was a nomadic scholar, working on short-term contracts at various institutions in departments of education, sociology, and social psychology. During this time, Becker cut back on the output of journal articles, but continued to publish book after book. He was consumed with a couple of Big Ideas in these years. One of these grew out of his earlier work in criticism of psychoanalysis. Becker's psychosocial understanding of mental health and illness implied that improving and maintaining mental health required change not only in the individual, but also in the social environment. Psychoanalysis was by its very nature, given the time and expense involved in the psychoanalytic process, an elitist treatment for the very few. But, thought Becker, if it were true, as he was convinced it was, that unconscious human behavior is more or less habitual, for good or ill, and was based on early social learning and experience, then it could be changed by insight into the process of how these behaviors were formed, and by new learning and experience. In short, Becker saw that learning and experience were the keys to changing behavior. And what is learning and experience but the process of education? Drawing especially on the experimental educational theories of John Dewey, therefore, Becker became animated by the idea that public education could be conceived, in this sense, as psychoanalysis for the masses. Were public education to be guided by the right kind of philosophy, the same sorts of insights and behavioral changes that occur on a small scale in psychoanalysis could occur on a social scale as a result of progressive public education.

Becker's second Big Idea during these years is closely related. As he tried to understand how and why progressive education had failed or produced only very mixed results, he found himself again exploring the impact of larger social forces on the educational system, and how again and again these forces diluted and undermined our best human intentions for social learning. This led him to conclude that in the final analysis, all learning was related, and if we cannot easily agree on what is good for human beings, we certainly can find wide agreement on what is bad for human beings. This Becker subsumed under the category of 'alienation.' His educational project, which he dubbed the 'Unified Science of Man,' was essentially that of allowing each discipline to contribute its part in outlining how and why human beings become sidetracked from achieving their fullest development.

These were exciting and optimistic years for Becker, despite the precariousness of his situation in the academy. He was convinced that he had had a glimpse of the original Enlightenment vision, which was the very spirit of democratic humanism, and also a deep understanding of why this vision got off the tracks. In his concentrated reading of the founding literature of the Enlightenment, and of his own disciplines of anthropology and sociology, he was convinced that the same struggles between production of critical knowledge for social transformation and production of a complacent knowledge for institutional prestige and gain were a recurring theme. Becker's only interest was in production of knowledge that would form the basis for transforming social criticism, even criticism of the very social institutions that fund the research. Becker was eventually deeply sobered, as he observed the American university system, far from taking the vanguard in promoting human freedom and progressive social change, sink ever more deeply into entanglement in the alienating forces of capitalist consumerism and the funding largesse of the military industrial complex.

Chapter 4

ALIENATION

The Great Historical Convergence on the Problem of Alienation (1964)*

IF WE HAD TO SUM UP THE MAIN PROBLEM of modern social psychology, I think it would be this: We know that man is an historical actor; we also know that he is a more or less integral personality. How do we theoretically reconcile the two into one comprehensive system? . . .

The Problem of Motivation. . . . [C. Wright] Mills faced the basic problem of human motivation. If man is an historical actor, a symbolic creation, then he must be pulled ahead expansively by words and images, rather than pushed forward narrowly by innate drives. At the top of the animal hierarchy, man performs on a level of his own. His conduct, then, is steered by symbols rather than driven from below. How can the forward momentum of conduct be explained? A pseudo-problem, says Mills, following [John] Dewey. The organism is *active by definition of organism.* We do not have to explain why animals move, any more than why the universe is in motion; it is a fact we can easily accept, and, indeed, must accept. The problem for a social psychology is not to divine purpose in nature, as [Sigmund] Freud and [Sandor] Ferenczi tried, but merely to describe and explain what is peculiar about human action. And for this, word-motives suffice. If the problem of action no longer resides in meeting the demands of inner drives, then it must reside in meeting the problems of external situations. Thus, Mills borrowed [Charles] Peirce's and Dewey's pragmatic notion that the prime task of the moving organism is to overcome problematic situations in its field. Word-motives are supreme for man because they help the individual navigate in his social field. Motivation was thus no problem for Mills, and he used the familiar concept of role as a superordinate performance category by means of which the individual is led on. Roles tell the individual how to act for maximum self-satisfaction and facilitation of conduct. They provide prescriptions for choice in situations that present alternatives, and they guarantee public approval

*Original, full text: E. Becker, "Mills' social psychology and the great historical convergence on the problem of alienation," in I. Horowitz (ed.), *The New Sociology: Essays on Social Theory and Social Values in Honor of C. Wright Mills* (pp. 108-133). New York: Oxford University Press (1964). Reprinted by permission.

for the choice. Man earns, via social roles, the two things he needs most: the animal possibility of moving safely forward in his environment; and also the distinctively human need for the reflected appraisals of others, the image of himself as a creature of value in a world of evaluations.

   The Problem of Perception. With the concept of role the problem of motivation is not resolved; it is merely shifted. It is shifted, furthermore, into a far more difficult area of theory and research, that of perception. Mills narrowed his focus down very expertly, but one senses that he felt himself on more difficult ground. . . . He saw that the problem of perception had to be, at the same time, the problem of personality and the problem of social role. To achieve this unity, nothing less than a fully transactional theory of perception would do, and this is what Mills used. . . . [An] organism organizes, constructs a world out of its perception and action. The human organism is not born into the world ready-made; rather, it comes into being as it transacts with the social world around it. Raw feelings must be shaped into proper emotions. Brute sensations must be organized into clear perceptions. Random impulses must become guiding purpose. Since, for the human animal, this shaping takes place in a social world, we can see the fundamental importance of a transactional theory of perception: *the very biological organism is socially formed.* The world it sees and the world it feels and moves in grows up together with the seeing, feeling, and movement.

   Mills used the concept 'psychic structure' to cover the feeling, sensation, and impulse that are socially converted into emotion, perception, and purpose. If the animal is thus socially fused in its basic responsiveness to the world, it is obvious that social roles penetrate literally to the core of the organism. With the concept of psychic structure, Mills was able to maintain that man is an historical creation, even while he remains basically a biological organism. The psychic structure and the organism are fused into the 'person' or role-player. In order to have a coherent theory of personality, Mills adopted the further term 'character structure,' to refer to the stabilized aspect of the integration of psychic structure and social roles. . . .

   The Problem of Strain in the Human Personality. . . . Now, an adequate theory of personality must show man pulling and straining against himself; it must reveal a man who is somehow less than fully socialized, or who is idiosyncratically socialized, which amounts to the same thing. Does this mean that man has an 'unconscious'? Does it imply that there are inner stirrings in the human animal that are not amenable to socialization? Is it necessary, in other words, for the sociologist to go into the enemy camp, so to speak, in order to fill out a picture of human complexity? Mills' social psychology indeed reflects some standard borrowings from psychoanalysis, which are counterbalanced by unfinished attempts to do without these borrowings. Let us look at this cognitive embarrassment of Mills a bit more closely.

   In order to get a personality theory of adequate complexity, Mills had to deal with the problem of strain or fragmentation—although I prefer to use the word strain, or even more broadly, dialectic of individual striving. There are two major poles or dimensions on which these strains or dialectics take place. Both of these poles fall under the more generic problem of perception and action, so that, by considering them, Mills was actually filling out the bare framework of the psychic structure.

First, there is *the dimension of individual action in time*. . . . This dimension carries the basic strain in human striving . . . a sharp conceptualization of the strain between early training and later adult experience. This dimension is the primary dialectic in human action. The child is trained for certain choices (perceptions) which he learns to handle with a sense of adequacy and well-being. When his parents approve his choices (perceptions), he earns a necessary self-esteem; when they disapprove, he feels anxiety. As he grows up, the individual is confronted with choices which cannot fall in the same clear-cut fashion into the earlier patterns of perception and action. He has to continually learn to overcome anxiety in new ways, and to earn self-esteem in new ways. The kind of early training he had, as well as the kind of opportunities which present themselves to him as an adult, will determine his flexibility in making new choices. This is a simplified way of viewing what Freud conveyed so well by the idea of 'neurosis'—the fact that later adult choices will be frustrated and undermined by constricting early learning. The equanimity of the human animal is thus subverted by the carrying-over of old learning, of antiquities unrelated to new problems. . . .

Next there is *the dimension of individual action in space*. This dimension reflects the basic strain between self and objects. It contains the problem of moving about in a world of things which must be labeled verbally in order to be controlled. The dilemma arises when words are not available to describe and make one critically aware of problematic situations. If we do not have the words, we are unable adequately to frame the problem. On the other hand, the dilemma can arise where we have too many words, too many vocabularies, and no behavioral order in our world. In this case, problems are manufactured where they need not exist.

Again, this is an axis of strain that derives directly from perception and learning. Mills dealt with this axis beautifully. It is here that his vocabulary-of-motives thesis provides rich insights, and it is here, too, that Mills makes the attempt to do without borrowings from psychoanalysis: human confusions and fragmentations, the tortuous complexity of personality, he tried to frame largely in terms of conflicting vocabularies of motive. His attempt remained unfinished, as we shall see.

A role is a vocabulary of motives suited to a performance part; it makes interpersonal action possible. What happens when there are several vocabularies for the same part? This is the dilemma that Mills underscored for man in complex, industrial society: man has lost the easy integrity of role performance that existed in simpler, more homogeneous societies. In primitive society, for example, roles are relatively integrated. On a hypothetical primitive level, a woman may be associated with the motives represented, say, by the words 'wife,' 'children,' 'family obligation,' and so on. But society sustains her in all these identities, and the unity of her personality is assured. In modern, commercial industrial society, on the other hand, a woman's designations may be more subtle; she becomes a possibility of 'romantic love,' 'career,' 'wealth,' 'clever children with good heredity,' 'winter house in Key West,' 'appreciation of Bach in common,' *ad infinitum*. In itself this would not be confusing, but society does not sustain her in the unity and integrity of all these performances. Without this kind of support, social performance becomes mechanical, and the individual gets lost in the artificiality of his roles.

In addition to this, there is another kind of confusion and fragmentation in complex society, which Mills called attention to as a 'segmentalization of conduct.' In simpler societies the world views of the individual actors would be somewhat more homogeneous; people would tend to share similar definitions of role performances. But in modern society many contradictory perspectives can be brought to bear on the single role, depending on who is looking at the role. Thus modern man often has to adjust his vocabulary to his interlocutor, and change it each time. He might not use the same vocabulary of motives in talking about marriage, say, to his wife, as he would in talking about it to a friend—or even to his own mother. There is no consistent self-image reflected in the many perspectives, and the individual's 'real self' tends to become inextricably lost in vocabularies and sub-vocabularies. Religion, business, family—all tear in different directions. Innumerable and interchangeable perspectives for self-justification undermine a firm identity.

Thus, the dialectic of individual action in space comes down to this: how sufficient and how many vocabularies of motive can the individual bring to bear on a particular situation, and what kind of self-satisfying action can be undertaken? He may be limited as well by poverty as by a plethora of word-motives. . . .

Depression: A Brief Sketch of the Theory. The phenomenon that we call depression, for example, seems to be best explained by the most Spartan model of personality functioning. We seem to be able to approach it adequately as primarily a dialectic of individual action in the dimensions of space and time. For a long time psychiatrists were baffled by the two outstanding characteristics of the depressive syndrome: the sudden surrender to despair, the opting out of life; and the unbelievably self-depreciating accusations, which the depressed person brought against himself. Why should people whose lives have been normal and even exemplary suddenly give up? And why should they be so merciless in denouncing themselves, when it is obvious that they cannot possibly be as bad or as guilty as they paint themselves?

The answer to these two questions, which arose as a *medical* problem only with the development of modern psychiatry, is simple—even astonishingly simple. It goes something like this: The depressed person had, like everyone else, the principal life task of keeping action moving forward in relation to those around him. He did this in the way most of us do it—by accepting to perform with ready-made vocabularies that we inherit from those others around us. The depressed person accepts to earn a reflected image of his own worth, in sum, by a more or less uncritical performance in a few tightly tailored cultural roles. Then suddenly, or gradually, a crisis develops. The crisis can take any number of forms: the individual may find himself threatened with divorce; a woman may find herself at menopause, deprived of her female role, and deprived at the same time of the only satisfying predication of her identity in a masculine world; a mother may find herself approaching old age, with the last of her children suddenly married, and herself suddenly deprived of her accustomed self-justifying action; a celibate, who has been sacrificing all rights and practice of personal decision only to earn his parents' approval, may suddenly find them dead, and, in one blow, be deprived of the only performance audience he has learned to appeal to. All of these examples have one common thread: life has suddenly been sapped of significance, and the individual does not know exactly why. He has been performing uncritically, with a limited range of vocabularies of motive, in a narrow circle of people who have significance for him. These three interlocking ingredients make up the formula for depressive breakdown: uncritical perceptions, poor vocabularies in which to frame choices, narrow range of people to whom one can appeal for his identity.

Why does action bog down into a passive surrender that we call depression? Simply because accustomed performance parts no longer serve to reflect a satisfying self-image; and the individual does not know any other kinds of parts, or cannot begin, within the time left to his life, to undertake to learn them.

What about the baffling self-accusation of guilt? This is the keystone in the new theoretical explanation of the phenomenon of depression. The self-accusation of guilt is exactly what we would expect from someone who is poor in vocabularies of motive, limited in words with which to frame the problematic situation, shallow in his critical perceptions. The guilt language, in other words, serves as the perfect justification for failure, where this failure cannot be otherwise understood. With this language the depressed individual takes cognitive command of a situation that is undermining him, and with it he also attempts to unblock his action. That is to say, if he can make himself into the most blameworthy person within his narrow circle, then he need not focus critically on it and thereby perhaps risk losing it entirely. In his surrender to his circumstances he can at least take his own fate into his hands, and work out his destiny in daily expiation. Historically, the phenomenon of self-accusation of guilt as a form of positive control is not new, but in depression we see it in microcosm. . . .

Schizophrenia: The Need for a Complete Social Psychology. If the simple model applies so well in the theory of depression, does it apply equally to schizophrenia? No, it will not suffice simply to tally the linguistic and perceptual repertory in order to explain this rather complex behavioral phenomenon. *If depression is the microcosm of poverty in vocabularies, schizophrenia is the microcosm of the whole human condition.* And in order to understand this phenomenon we have to pick up one historical current that was not elaborated in Mills' social psychology. This permits us to evaluate Mills' social psychology from still another point of view, that of phenomenology. . . .

Man operates in two modes; he possesses both thing-objects, like all other animals; and, uniquely, symbol-objects, given in full only to the symbol-using animal. Consciousness proceeds to two spheres to make contact with the world, and two kinds of human powers are brought into play: active organismic powers and more passive cognitive powers. Fortunately, this line of reasoning was lifted out of the confines of philosophy and applied to human development by James Mark Baldwin. . . . Baldwin postulated that the sense of the dualism of mind and body is something that develops as the child learns that he has an inside, a thought process, that is separate from the outer world of things. For example, there is something the child wants to control. He puts together a few memory images of how he controlled this object in the recent past, and then reaches out for the object. But suppose he finds that the object acts differently than he expected on the basis of the memory images he had put together: say, it turns out to be an unfriendly dog instead of the expected tame rabbit? In this way, the child is forced to build and alter conceptual categories, refashion generalizations, and clarify specific details, to make them accord with the outer world of things. This teaches him that his memory images and thoughts are not the same as the world of hard and unpredictable things—that his 'insides' (thoughts) have an existence 'all their own' that may or may not permit easy control of the outer world.

Now, this self-body dualism, as we would expect, is not uniform in everyone. That is to say, some of us pay more attention to the external world, act in it more, test ourselves with the outside of our bodies. Others among us act less in the external world, shrink up more within ourselves, feed ourselves on thought and fantasy, take refuge from the demands of the outside, expand our inner life, and nourish ourselves on it. Our 'self,' in this case, our 'sense of being,' takes root more in what we feel inside, in what we think and imagine, than in what we actually do. In addressing ourselves to a different kind of opposing object, in order to come into being, *we become different kinds of organisms*. The idealistic Hegelian dialectic has now been worked out as an explanation of worldly character-types, in terms of individual preferences for ranges of objects and experience.

This is a considerable achievement. Having broached the basic dualism, Baldwin went on to build up the following view of the development of the individual. The self-body dualism, he saw, was not primarily a liability for man. Far from it. By means of memory, reflection, and judgment, the individual uses the process of thought to control the external world. As an animal, man alone could dependably stop the flow of experience, recombine its salient elements in his imagination, and propose new solutions to external problems. With the rise of thought as a means of control of the outer world, man established his dominion over nature. The matter only becomes a liability when thought turns in upon itself, when the individual uses thought and fantasy to seek justification from within, rather than by testing himself in action. Baldwin concluded, then, that one becomes an individual by overcoming problems, by making successful decisions in trial-and-error action. One gains experience as he successfully combines the inner modes of thought with the outer mode of action.

What concept could serve to convey the unity of the individual, the fusion of the duality in the acting person? Baldwin, along with Dewey and W. M. Urban, borrowed a term from the Austrian psychologists—the word 'funded.' Baldwin used 'funded' to describe the synthesis of inner and outer, the unity that is forged in successful action.

As the inner thoughts meet the outer problem and help the individual to overcome it, the organism forms a coherent link with its object, and closes the gap between itself and the world. Every gap successfully closed is a satisfactory experience. Hence, in Baldwin's view, the organism 'funds' experiences by overcoming the inner-outer dualism, by using the mind and body in one active, outer-directed unity. The organism then possesses a fund of experience, deposited in its very structure. Individual development takes the form of an equation: the synthesis of inner thoughts and outer acts = unity = the well-funded person = satisfactory experience = individuation.

Now, as we are finding out in the theory of schizophrenia, the schizophrenic is precisely the one who lacks this unity, this funded fusion earned through outer-directed experience. He takes refuge in the world of symbol-objects, and forfeits trial-and-error experience in the external world. It was Dewey who saw very clearly the trick that nature plays on the human animal. He stressed the difference between the two kinds of experience—the experience that is lived by the flesh, and the experience that is recaptured only in hollow words. Words mean little to the development of our total personality unless we connect them up with some kind of lived experience. . . .

We can sum up this whole section, then, by adding an indispensable third dimension to the two we have already described. *The dimension of individual action of seemingly disparate phenomenal kinds.* This is the strain between self and body; it is reflected in the difference between experience available in words, versus the experience which is funded in the total organism, the lived experience that forges a unity in the individual. Schizophrenia is the microcosm of the failure to forge this unity, the failure of the self to come into being substantially in a hard world of things. Man is basically a body . . . subserved by a mind, but the schizophrenic makes heroic efforts to reverse this formulation. If Mills had worked with this mind-body dialectic, he would have been able to complete what he left unfinished with his thesis of vocabularies of motivation: the plethora of role vocabularies of motivation, the profuse symbol-world that the dweller in modern complex society cannot control in any self-satisfying manner, is precisely the problem of schizophrenia. The confusion of the city-dweller that [George] Simmel so beautifully described in *The Metropolis and Mental Life* is the schizophrenic's confusion: a profuse world of words, images, and objects, sensations which cannot be controlled, or ordered. Why not? Simply because the active organism has not developed the habit of taking a firm stance toward the external world; the individual has not learned the secure development of his initiatory powers in relation to ranges of external problems. The depressed person is, as we saw, poor in vocabularies of motive. The schizophrenic is overly rich, but this is a plenty which is unmatched by sure behavioral powers. . . .

A complete social psychology must, then, comprise our three dimensions of individual action. It must include, indispensably, a phenomenology of object relations and organismic powers. . . . We know that [Karl] Marx touched on this problem with his concept of alienation. But the fact that he did not develop it in full has produced two results: the continued strong appeal of his tantalizing hints and the frustration we experience when we try to put the unfinished concept to use. . . .

Marx's early writings on alienation can be summed up directly and simply: they describe what we sketched above—the organism's need for objects in order fully to come into being. Self powers grow only as they meet resistance. As Marx put it, in order to be, in order to have a nature, it is necessary that there be an object outside oneself. In other words, each organism must relate to some kind of object in order to substantiate itself in the world. This is the basic phenomenology of alienation: the failure to develop self-powers by transacting with the world of things. . . .

Alienation as the Forfeiting of Self-Powers. Marx, quite correctly, and from the start, put the burden of coming into being upon the active development of one's powers. For him, alienation meant, first and foremost, the overshadowing of the organism by the object. And this is exactly what we see in schizophrenia, where the individual cannot navigate securely in a threatening world of things, simply because he has failed to develop sure powers for coping with them. Marx leaves no doubt about his meaning when he singles out for criticism the traditional philosopher, who is "himself an abstract form of alienated man. . . . The whole *history of alienation* . . . is therefore only *the history of the production of abstract thought,* i.e., of absolute, logical, speculative thought." In other words, the philosopher is, par excellence, the individual who relates to symbol-objects rather than to person-objects, for the development of his self. What exactly is Marx driving at here? Simply, that any thought that divorces one from action, and separates itself from involvement of the total individual, is alienated. Marx makes this clear: alienation exists when man "objectifies himself by distinction from and in opposition to abstract thought, which constitutes alienation as it exists and as it has to be transcended." In the language of the new theory of schizophrenia, this would read: The individual who strives to develop a sense of self merely in opposition to symbol-objects sentences himself to the danger of the loss of the real world of external things. He sentences himself to a fantasy existence divorced from and unworthy of human powers.

By living in the fantasy world of symbol-objects, and renouncing action in the external world, the individual seems forced logically to abandon his commitment to the external world. Marx, in attacking German idealism, accused the traditional philosopher of this very failing. When one abandons commitment to the external world, one attempts to justify himself in fantasy, since he can no longer do so by his acts. The groundwork for a false morality is laid, whereby the individual divorces himself from commitment to his acts. He no longer feels that he has a stake in anything he does. This kind of fantasy justification of oneself has the direst of consequences, for it leads to the renunciation of any further stake in his own active initiatory powers. . . . [Marx] saw that the renouncing of commitment to the consequences of ones own acts leads logically and inevitably to something more: divorce from the community of fellow men.

Marx described this process in terms of alienation of the producer from his product. When the producer renounces active control in the shaping of his object, his work becomes unrelated to his own powers. The objects he produces, therefore, do not confront him as his own. This means that the world of his creation is not his own world. So, says Marx, if man is estranged from his own products, from his own life activity, he is also estranged from others. Anything that confronts him is then alien to him. He has no responsibility for the free creation of it, or involvement in it. To lose self-powers is to lose community. . . . *All objects in their field confront them as alien objects, for which they are not morally responsible.* When labor is coerced, man is separated from his fellows, because he is no longer committed to the consequences of his active powers. . . .

Marx understood alienation also in a second sense, which is too familiar to need expansion: the individual skews his perceptions by orienting to objects in terms of their use-value and commodity-value. This prevents him from throwing fresh perceptions on the object. It is just this automaticity, in fact, which the best efforts of modern psychotherapy try to remedy.

Alienation as an Empirical Problem. Thus, the history of the concept of alienation is now about to enter a new phase. . . . But the central problem in this historic development remained: how to unite the individual-phenomenological with the social dimensions of the problem of alienation? This means uniting early (phenomenological) Marx with late (social) Marx; and, more comprehensively, uniting Mills' social psychology with his social criticism. I hope we have demonstrated that this could only be done effectively by a fully cross-disciplinary approach to human breakdown. . . . In the modern theory of mental illness, the phenomenological aspects of individual action merge with the social role aspects. We have sketched out both syndromes, and it is obvious from these sketches that they can be understood basically as problems in action and perception. This understanding did not spring full blown, as we noted, nor did it come from medical psychiatry. Simmel had spoken of the dispersal of self-identity, attendant upon role fragmentation in complex, industrial, urban society; and Mills also put heavy stress on the problems of multiple role vocabularies and conflicting allegiances between the institutions of religion, family, state, and occupation.

The circle can only really be closed by providing empirical substantiation for alienation. In order to do this we had to show that alienated individuals really break down, as they do in the two major syndromes of modern psychiatry. And, we had to find in the causes of their breakdown the same factors at work as in the hypothetical problem of alienation.

Finally, one more clarification remains. In order to find in the early Marx the basis for a radical critique of society, we must show how individual breakdown is related to the full social field. Is mental illness due to some peculiarly alienated conditions of society? There seems to be every indication that it is. Let us briefly recapitulate the outstanding features of the two major syndromes.

First, depression is characterized by an inhibition in perception and action. The depressed person is too uncritically committed to a narrow range of objects and role-behaviors. When something occurs to undermine role-behavior that was previously satisfying, the new problematic situation becomes overwhelmingly threatening. The individual, lacking the vocabularies and perceptions with which to move ahead, bogs down in futile self-accusation and surrender. Likewise, schizophrenia is characterized by an inhibition in the possibilities of action. A precarious self-body integration, the foundation for which is laid in childhood, leads the individual to a dangerous separation from active engagement in the real external world. Action takes place largely in fantasy, and the self that is developed lacks a firm foundation in lived experience.

In both these behavioral phenomena, we can see clearly that the individual needs the possibilities for self-satisfying action in a world of rich experience. When the possibilities for this action bog down, and the individual is not armed with dependable behavioral alternatives, there is either temporary or permanent surrender of self-powers. But what are the social needs? How is society responsible in terms of the roles it makes available? If man contains no essence, how is society responsible for the kind of human nature he develops? There are any number of exciting glimpses of the social burden of individual failure. We are beginning to see some striking differences in the bogging down of action: differences by social class; differences by the type of society and social structure. We are beginning to understand that menopausal depression is a problem in availability of alternate cultural roles; that hysteria is a problem in level of awareness and communication; that, more broadly, both schizophrenia and depression are problems in early training and life experience. Along with this, we are learning that the physio-chemical, reductive approach to behavioral malfunction offers comfort only to researchers seeking prestigious grants, and to those who are already sick. A preventive attack on mental illness must focus on the total social situation: kinds of family and early training, kinds of social structure, kinds of opportunities available to the adult.

Alienation, Illness, and Contemporary Society. Surely, however, even the society that we call 'alienated' is building for a better, healthier, more intelligent environment for its citizens. The fight for mental health, for instance, is undertaken by social workers as well as laboratory chemists. This is just the point: we are having recourse to conventional solutions. If there is anywhere that a piecemeal approach to alienation is bound to fall hopelessly short, it is in the problem of mental illness. There must be instead a full-scale critique of the institutions of contemporary society. Alienation, as we now understand it, boils down to this: Self-powers grow up and are maintained in an increasing hierarchy of actions that overcome problematic situations. *The typical syndromes that we see are failures to carry through self-satisfying action.* The basis of this failure is, in every non-organic case, a kind of stupidity—a behavioral stupidity in the face of challenge, choice, and problems. The schizophrenic simply cannot cope with the pluralistic world of uncontrolled situations and objects; the depressed person simply cannot or will not understand the elements that make up his failure; the hysteric cannot formulate an essential cognitive grasp of the frustrating situation. In other words, *people break down when they are not 'doing'—when the world about them does not reflect the active involvement of their own creative powers.* It has thus taken us a century and a quarter to return, with empirical support, to Marx's concept of alienation. Mental illness is itself the strongest possible critique of the owning society: man is a doing animal, primarily, and not an owning one. We cannot keep people immersed in the miasma of unreason represented by mass-consumer society and expect that they will fashion for themselves that commanding view which is the basis for health. *We are so fond of talking about 'emotional' problems precisely because it relieves us of the need of talking about cognitive problems.* People must be given information, knowledge, and the ability to command choices in difficult situations. This is exactly what we are not giving them. We have undertaken a mass-media brainwashing on the largest scale; we will not heed the most obvious criticism of our way of life; we are clinging to our institutions with a mechanicalness that is terrifying. We are stubbornly objecting that the good life is here—that all we need do is tidy up the ramshackle neighborhoods and remedy the adolescent and traffic problems. And in all this, we have sacrificed the primary task in man's search for himself: the championing of the fullest development of his own responsible initiatory powers. . . .

With his insistence on the centrality of the concept of role, Mills saw that personality is transcended by society. . . . [The human being] is not an animal like all the rest, who are already built firmly into their world. Alienation, in other words, is ultimately related partly to what man has not yet dared. It is related to still unformulated grand designs and as yet unknown powers. To forfeit executive powers is to forfeit humanity. Nothing could be clearer or simpler.

Nor could we, as a culture, be further from realizing this simple truth. Our most ambitious gropings aim at turning our entire society into docile consumers and uncritical bipartisan voters on really crucial issues. But we can no longer aim at mere complacency, at consecrating the smug society. When [Pierre-Joseph] Proudhon had urged equality of wages, Marx replied that this would only mean that society would become the capitalist. Now we see fully that the historical problem of alienation from one's executive powers would still remain. Perhaps at last, with mounting evidence from the theory of mental illness, we will not be able to avoid coming to grips with our social problems. We may yet be obliged, however painfully, reluctantly, and deviously, to opt for man over things.

A Theory of Alienation as a Philosophy of Education (1967)*

IT IS TIME TO TAKE A LINGERING LOOK OVER OUR SHOULDER to see exactly the way we have come. We began . . . our study with the great historian [Jacob] Burckhardt, and his patient waiting for that something—whatever it was— that would liberate the human spirit in the modern world. It was a something that would have to work in opposition to the world that the nineteenth century left us: that

*Original, full text: *Beyond Alienation: A Philosophy of Education for the Crisis of Democracy* by Ernest Becker. Copyright © 1967 by Ernest Becker. Reprinted by permission of George Braziller, Inc.

bare and efficient world that was crushing the human spirit, and that would soon try to mash it to a pulp with World War I, II, and if necessary, III. What a world it was! It was intent on forgetting completely the mystery of the cosmic process, the presence of divine purpose in human destiny. . . . Could there be any solution to this incredible world-picture of the twentieth century? The passage of time seems to aggravate it impossibly. Especially today, with the immense growth of population, the problem of feeding the sheer numbers of men seems to forbid the development of the human spirit. . . . Is there something that can work against the death grip of both commercial and communist ideology, and mechanistic science, and maybe even history itself? One thing, perhaps—one thing alone. It was the thing supplied by the depths of the human spirit itself, and it found its expression through man's mind: a theory of alienation, a broad and compelling theory, which showed what man was, what he was striving for, and what hindered this striving—in himself, in society, in nature. We needed a theory of alienation that was composed of the best knowledge in psychology, sociology, ontology, and theology, and this is what the hard-pressed human spirit itself supplied. . . . Alienation was the strangled cry of modern man, the key word of our times, the epigraph to our whole age; and as the eighteenth century responded to the deep urge for Liberty by finding a way to translate that urge into law and action, the twentieth responded to its helpless feeling of alienation by translating that feeling into a compelling prescription for education and social reconstruction. . . .

1. The Natural Solution of the Problem of Liberal Education

[This . . .] general theory of alienation is what I have elsewhere called it—an *anthropodicy*. It is an explanation for the evil in the world that is caused by manmade arrangements; and as such, it points out those evils which could be ameliorated by human effort. We can see how splendidly it answers the problem. . . . What is a 'liberal' education? A general theory of alienation, an anthropodicy. It features a body of knowledge that teaches man how his human freedom and responsible choice is constricted. It teaches him the 'good' by showing him the causes of evil. And what can good and evil mean for man except in terms of the liberation of responsible human powers? This is what [Ralph Waldo] Emerson understood when he laid down the challenge of self-reliance as the keynote of American democracy: whatever limits self-reliance works against man. And the great historical task, since Emerson's enjoinder, was to develop a comprehensive theory of the limitations of self-reliance. If we could get this, we would answer the problem of education in a democracy.

We saw that in order to get it, the nineteenth century had to find out what man was striving for, what was distinctive about his action; and it found out that man was peculiarly the animal who strived after meaning, and the creation of meaning. The problem of self-reliance, the problem of human liberation, was how to permit the self-creation of meaning. Then we saw that as each discipline reached maturity, it was able to deal with a dimension of the restriction of meaning. Sociology was able to study the whole social system as a dramatic social fiction; psychiatry could understand mental illness as the constriction of action and meaning; ontology allowed us to deduce a critical individual and social aesthetics which showed that man needed integral meaning and intensity of conviction for his meanings; theology confirmed psychiatry, and showed us that man cannot stand alone with his meanings; but theology also showed us something more: that the truly free man will reach for free fellow men, and ultimately for a theonomy on which to base his highest strivings. In this way, from all fields, we could understand all the dimensions of human striving as a search for rich and secure meanings; and we could see that evil was not due to 'inborn' hates and aggressions, but that it resulted from the natural use of one's fellow men to satisfy one's urge for meaning. And one thing we could see above all: that if weakness was greater, evil was greater; and weakness for man means shallow and narrow meanings, and lack of critical awareness of who one is, and what he is striving for. . . .

The Solution of the New Humanist Contradiction

We can now understand better how right the critics of the New Humanism were. . . . Commercial society created the herd opinion, frustrated self-criticism and self-mastery, by making man a puppet in search of consumer satisfactions. No wonder C. H. Grattan, in his evaluation of the New Humanists, said that the burden of all sensible critiques of modern society must be against its economic structure. Otherwise, how can we begin the retreat from mechanization of the person, quantification of the human soul, the separation of man from man in the individual search for shallow satisfactions? How can we overcome fetishization of sex and commodities, reorient our earth-bent strivings to higher and nobler visions and ideals, to greater intimacies with meanings that transcend our own petty lives? The New Humanists, for all their worthwhile idealism, failed to see that education had to be education for intelligent social criticism. . . . And it was only when we saw that man was not Practical Man, but aesthetic man, that we could see how far commercial industrialism fell from satisfying truly human strivings; and it was not until post-Freudian psychology that we could see man uncompromisingly as a striver after meanings, and not as a creature of instincts. The critique of commercialism does not rest on any counter-ideology, but rests on a mature understanding of man himself. And this understanding the New Humanists did not yet have. They gave us classical ideals, but what could we do with them? We needed to judge the forces that kept us from realizing those ideals; we needed a science of self-study . . . and we needed a standard for scientific evaluation of the institutional panorama of a given society: How does the social fiction constrict and hobble man's search for ever *more life?* . . .

The Solution of the Progressives' Dilemma

[The Progressives] wanted truly *liberal* education, a liberating education worthy of man; an education that would make new men, Promethean men, capable of carrying on the dangerous venture of democracy. Not education for indoctrination, not education for servitude, not education for the status quo, but the education of men who will bring needed change into the world; the kind of education that was championed by . . . Emerson above all, who wanted a 'manworthy' education; Everett Dean Martin, who wanted an education that would emancipate the student from herd opinion and vulgar self-interests; A. D. Henderson, who wanted a student who had a critical understanding of social dynamics; Theodore M. Greene, who wanted a mind that can function powerfully, creatively, and wisely under its own steam; Kenneth Burke, who asked for an education that would expose the motives of secular ambition, cut through the uncritical use of symbols with which each society brainwashes each generation; C. Wright Mills, who wanted an education to produce a mind that would not be overwhelmed by events; and Horace Kallen, finally, who called for an education that would set the world into transforming perspectives.

How would we make this kind of education, . . . the kind that would give us the social leadership we need? . . . It would have to be an education based on the unity of knowledge from within the imperatives of knowledge itself—exactly as Dewey wanted. Knowledge would grow by seeing the interrelationships of subject matters; the student would no longer be able to say that he 'has had' a course, over and done with a meaningless segment of fact. He would not have to resort to petty grade-seeking, because he would not be cowed by meaninglessness. . . .

This is the world-historical significance of our anthropodicy. It has filled the frame in, as Dewey wanted; and it has filled it in both in society at large, and in its significance for education. The frame is *democracy*—democracy as an ideal of the maximum liberation of free human subjectivity. No longer dim as Dewey lamented in 1937; but clear—compellingly clear.

Compelling? Yes—there is the problem. . . . [N]o theory is ever finished, because truth itself is never finished. Scientists accept a unified theoretical framework because it is compelling. In the science of man, this problem is especially aggravated, because the theory deals with man himself; and we are burdened with tons of prejudice, which hinder our agreement on even the most basic facts. Just as we do not 'see' under a microscope without training, so too are we blind to man, until the scales have been painfully pulled from our eyes. But when we deal with man, the scales cling tenaciously. This is one of the reasons that we have been so relatively long in getting agreement on the facts of human alienation: our own deep-grained ideologies keep us from seeing clearly. But the anthropodicy is there—starkly there—no matter how we may at first hedge. . . . It is the true Public Philosophy of our democracy—of any democracy. . . . It would not be difficult to get agreement among men of good will on the theoretical principles of alienation, simply because we have seen in the laboratory of history what they have caused, the evil that they have unleashed upon man. We know that when freedom is equated with the right to buy and sell goods it fosters a nation of sheep under the control of the mass media, just the opposite of the self-reliant man that Emerson hoped for; we know that when revolutions make success their only criterion, and when they lose their guiding humanistic ideals, then they make societies of new consumer puppets . . . or of well-fed, obedient citizens. . . .

[W]e know what fetishization means; we know that scapegoating by empty-headed masses could consume the entire world in gas ovens; we know that most mental-illness is not caused by brain chemicals gone astray, or by microbes in the nervous system: it is caused by social arrangements that constrain man, that deprive him of a broad, critical command of his life and experience; we know that atheism is the last barrier to true freedom, because it turns man in upon himself, makes him slavishly dependent on others, separates him from contact with the great cosmic mystery; we know that it narrows his life, and so deprives him of the highest purpose, the deepest and most lasting possibility for self-realization and self-transcendence. We know all these things: They are our national propositions of alienation for which we would turn for agreement to our fellow men. They are natural, empirical, historical data, which allow us to design a new ideal of human freedom, and work together to realize it.

2. The Natural Solution of the Problem of Education Versus the State

This, then, is the solution to the problem of liberal education, seen from both sides—from the side of the conservatives, and from the side of the progressives who criticized them, and yet who themselves could offer no true solution of their own in their time. But wait. What about that other great problem . . . the problem of education versus the State? The chief enemy of education, said Horace Kallen, is the "economic-industrial-financial-political powers that happen to be." The State itself is thus the enemy of academic freedom, said Bernard Iddings Bell; this freedom is threatened "by no other source as it is by organized secular government." This is what keeps education from effectively changing the society; this is what prevents our experimental democracy from being truly experimental; as each new generation is brainwashed anew into the shared social fiction, our best educative efforts are subverted. Education is little else than indoctrination, said Kallen, and the reason is that the "democratic ideal of education for democracy never quite broke away from the authoritarianism which has pertained to education from its beginnings." The problem, then, is how to permit education to work actively against the prevailing ideology, how to get it out from under the heavy hand of the political and economic powers that control it. . . .

We also saw that Condorcet proposed the great solution to this problem, the logical and necessary solution: The answer to the control of education by Church and State must be the establishment of a truly autonomous, self-governing community of scholars, protected from encroachments from all outside authorities. Only in this way would we prevent the citizens from becoming docile instruments in the hands of those who seek to use and control them. And this could only be done by placing education under a supreme body for the direction of science and education, who would thus be custodians of progress and human liberation. . . . H. G. Wells's proposal for a 'World Brain' or 'World Encyclopedia' was a similarly inspired vision. It would achieve much the same thing as a superordinate and independent 'Faculty of Culture.' It would be a true synthesis of knowledge that "would hold the world together mentally." It would provide the mental background of every intelligent person in the world. As a true synthesis, it would unite scientific facts and moral facts; in this way, it would act as a clearinghouse of misunderstandings. It "would compel men to come to terms with one another," said Wells. This common world vision would provide a scientific solution to the problem of social and moral order. It would be a 'super-university' that pointed the way out of social confusion: it would be the standard, superordinate overall education throughout the world. . . .

Now the temperate voice of caution breaks in, and blunts our jubilation: 'Not so fast,' it urges. . . . Are we suggesting a State within a State? An authority unbounded within an authority unbounded? Irresponsibility enclosed within irresponsibility? Is this our 'great historical solution' to the Enlightenment problem? What about the danger from within? What about the human greed and passion for power of the scientists and educators themselves? Here, surely, is the Trojan Horse in our midst. . . . We have seen the world that scientists helped bring to birth: a world armed with weapons that they fathered—thermonuclear weapons, bacteriological weapons—the 'gifts' of science to man! If they made them so willingly for the ideology of their national politicians, what would stop them from making these weapons to protect their own scientific elite? . . .

So concludes the voice of caution. What are we to reply? It is all too true. Science has betrayed us in all branches of knowledge because it became an end in itself, and forgot that it was to serve man. But the science we hoped for was one that would be interested in something quite different: one that would be occupied in promoting the free human spirit, one that would further the development of the life force in its highest embodiment—in man; a science that would seek to help the unfolding of the comic mystery, even if that meant willingly limiting its power to know and control man. The science we wanted was one that would serve the growth of the individual subjectivity, serve the birth of mystery. But, then, we have our reply to the voice of caution. Science is not Antichrist; we have seen through the false vision of mechanistic, quantifying science—and we have seen through it in our time. We have seen that Condorcet's vision of science was erroneous because it was based on mathematics as the queen. . . . In other words, in our time we have seen that false science failed because it sought its unity in a false principle, in the principle of mathematics and quantification. Mathematics was a false unity, because it forced qualitative nature into its own constrictive mold. Thereby it constricted the human spirit, and thereby it has progressively effaced and objectified man. In its place, we wanted a science based on true unity, on the natural unification of knowledge. And by natural unification, we mean a unification stemming from the nature of the knowledge itself, and not from any principle or model imposed from the outside. In a word, we needed a unified science that would stem from what was unique about man, that would stem from quality and value, . . . based firmly on man's urge for the free creation of subjective meaning. . . .

The Orientation

But suppose that we go back and reanimate the Enlightenment vision of science, the one that was proposed by [Denis] Diderot and [Jean-Jacques] Rousseau. Suppose that we understand the science of man as an ideal type of science: a science that postulates an ideal toward which men might strive, and then seeks to help realize that ideal. And suppose that we put the idea of progress at the basis of this ideal, and that we understand progress as the progressive liberation of human energies, of free subjectivity on the part of the greater masses of citizens. If we do reorient our science around this ideal, then we have to say that the Enlightenment vision was the correct one, even if history did not turn out that way. We can agree that man has not yet shown that he has made progress; that progress since the nineteenth century is a myth. But we have to add very quickly that the reason we have made no progress is that we have not consciously tried to realize a rational ideal of man in society. We have not put forth a design of man, nor have we tried to shape man in its image. No wonder the idea of progress dropped dead: We left it to evolution, and not to our own energies! . . . Once we realize that progress is an ideal that we have to help shape and achieve, we can restate the Enlightenment vision of the panorama of history. It is not that man has progressed, *but that he could progress.* And he could progress only if he understood the forces that hold him in bondage. So that, our *tableau de l'esprit humain,* our panoramic view of the development of the human spirit, is actually a picture of the present constraints on that spirit. . . .

What, then, is the basic orientation for our curriculum? . . . the principle of 'self-esteem maintenance.' It unites all the various kinds of behavior . . . all the various types of aesthetic striving, of the striving for meaning on both individual and total social levels. It declares that man's behavior is neutral, by the desire to 'feel maximally good' about himself. . . . [O]ur general theory of alienation explains the full field of evil that is caused by man to man, but it explains it on the principle that man is basically good. It is this great paradox that has taken us over a century and a half to solve. . . .

But isn't this proposal itself a visionary dream? Isn't it farfetched to imagine that we could get compelling agreement on this thesis as a basic orientation for education? It seems like the myth to end all myths. Yes, it is . . . a myth in the true meaning of the word: myth as creative and generative; myth as providing a new and unmistakable guide for a whole world view; myth as an adumbration of a new reality that marshals our feelings and strivings; myth as an image with endless facets, ramifications, richness—yet, an image that is simple and clear; an image that calls up our highest yearnings, yet that gives the most immediate and deep-seated satisfaction. . . .

It should not be difficult to get compelling agreement on this myth. It was in Rousseau's time, but it is no longer so today; we now have the compelling body of knowledge on just how society causes human evil; and we could teach it in the three different dimensions which explain it.

1) The history of alienation in one's own life. How evil arises as a result of
    the law of individual development.

2) The history of alienation in society. How evil arises as a result of the
    workings of society, and of the evolution of society in history.

3) The total problem of alienation under the conditions of existence.
    How evil arises as a result of the condition of life itself.

This third dimension is, of course, the theological one; and as I hope we have
fully seen, it is the indispensable crown to any education. Without it, the science of
society is foredoomed to failure. Thus, the eighteenth-century thesis that man is
good is no longer an argument against the theological view of man: It is perfectly
compatible with this view. Only, the theological view has to be nondogmatic; it has
to understand 'sin' as springing naturalistically from the conditions of existence.
In this way, the theological view of man's condition should be compelling. . . . A
society of atheists is possible, but it is not desirable for the fullest development of
the human spirit. . . .

1. The Individual Dimension of Alienation

The first thing that would have to be taught, in order for the new university to
dawn, is the law of the individual's unfolding. This means several things, many of
which are now covered in our college curricula. We would learn how man is basically an animal, and how he developed from the other animals; we would study the
growth of perception and language; the development of the self—those things, in
sum, which are now roughly included under courses on 'Human Development,'
'Developmental Psychology,' 'Personality,' 'Social Psychology,' 'Culture and
Personality.' They would show how every human being is born into his cultural world,
and is molded by it into a social actor. They would show how man forfeits his place
in the animal kingdom, in order to become a self-conscious human being whose life
is directed by values and meanings. They would show that there is nothing absolute
about these values or meanings, that they are relative to the society in which one
grows up—what the anthropologists call 'cultural relativity.'

But we have called this particular nucleus of the curriculum 'the individual dimension of alienation.' It is supposed to show the individual the history of his estrangement
from himself, from reliance on his own powers. But as our curriculum stands today, it
does not show this. We teach all about human development, all about growing up in
society, in the variety of courses that we just noted. But now we may ask: Why does
each specialty have to have 'its own' distinctive say, when they are all saying pretty
much the same thing—psychology, sociology, anthropology, social psychology? Why
this needless overlap and luxuriant redundancy, why so many offerings on the same
subject? The reason, we know, is largely the fantastic specialization in our time: the
urge of each department to its own area of power, the cloak of special competence, the
greedy hoarding of the label of scientific respectability for one's own discipline. But

within each department of this Tower of Babel, the same ineluctable disease of modern science is at work. We do not have any clear agreement on what is important for man to know about the child's early training period. Consequently, each discipline bloats itself on its own esoteric and special problems, on the elaboration of details, the examination of empirical studies, of models, and so on, and on, and on. The student is buried under science, and instead of finding out about himself, he finds out how vastly knowledgeable scientists are, and how difficult the study of man is.

There is only one way to cut through this miasma, . . . to make the knowledge self-critical. For this, we need our ideal model, the standard against which to measure the knowledge, a standard that infuses it with life and relevance, a standard that leads the individual to apply the knowledge to his own life and fate. The standard is, of course, the Socratic and Emersonian one: *Know thyself,* know what prevents you from being 'self-reliant.' Know how you were deprived of the ability to make your own judgments; know how the world view of your society was built into your perceptions; know how those who trained you to see and think, literally placed themselves into your mind; know how they became the self upon your self, the 'superego' upon your 'ego,' the voice of conscience whispering behind your voice.

This means that courses on human development will have to be oriented around its fundamental law—the law of the Oedipus Complex, or, as I prefer to call it, the *Oedipal Transition.* It will highlight above all how the individual becomes human by forfeiting the aegis over his powers. It will show how conscience is built into each child on the basis of his need for affection, and his anxiety over object-loss. It will teach him how his own animal sensitivities and need for survival cause him to shape himself to the design of his parents. It will show him how the social fiction is built into his primate body, and how he comes to strive for meanings that he never knew he had chosen. It will show, in sum, . . . how man is born into a world that he has not made, and that he is not permitted to remake. It will show how his lifelong habit was laid down, for the most part, during his early years, and how it has prevented him from making new and independent choices, from meeting new challenges and opportunities—in a word, from exercising and developing his own unique meanings.

In this way, courses on human development will be courses in the brainwashing that takes place in each society; they will give the person the knowledge and the impetus he needs to take his own life into his own hands—if this is what he wants. They will help him, 'see through' his own Oedipus Complex, the accidents of his birth and place, the relativity of the meanings that infuse his life. The insights of psychoanalysis will thus become the basic property of a free science of man, taught in the university to all students. No more esotericism of the medical profession; no more unaired dogma; no more exorbitant fees charged for sessions in closed rooms. No more 'psychoanalysis' so-called, but instead, a free development of all our knowledge about what makes people act the way they do. Students would learn how different life styles are developed, and they would learn the full range of social and historical influences that shape these styles. No more futile reductionist research into brain cells and chemistry—no more alchemy to learn the 'secrets' of human behavior. The students would study man in his social world, and would come to understand easily how the mental illnesses develop; how they too are life styles that the person resorts to in order to try to keep his world convincing and meaningful.

They would learn . . . that evil is a result of weakness, of narrow, inflexible, frightened, clumsy, ineffective life styles; that only the strong person can perform the ethical act. Why only the strong? Because it takes strength to take the responsibility for one's own unique meanings; it takes strength to allow the world to be peopled with others whose meanings are unique and unexpected, who introduce in their very person an element of danger into the social encounter. The student would learn that man needs self-esteem, and that he seeks it in the manifold performances of his social roles; and hence he would learn that the constrictions on the life force, the constrictions on the free development of human energies, stem from the way we bring children up, and the kind of social roles we provide for them.

As the students learn what blunts and twists the free expression of life energies, they would also know how the life force itself is frustrated by society, by the codes for behavior prescribed by man, the unexamined conventions of our social world. They would be encouraged to think about themselves in terms of all these insights and knowledge, to help each other with their problems, if that is what they wanted to do, in free exchange. A new generation taught in the arts of self-criticism and self-discovery would unfold, while the university would truly be a seat of knowledge. It would seek to unfold the universal man, the man free from the automatic constraints of his own culture and times. The university would thus be the handmaiden of life itself, entrusted with the care of the most sublime mystery, entrusted with breaking the cultural mold that constricts evolution.

2. The Social and Historical Dimension of Alienation

The individual level blends, of course, very naturally into the social level. As the student learns how he is trained to function in a social role, he understands the social fiction. He sees how he earns his feeling of value by filling the status available to him in each society; in a word, he sees through himself as a performer on the grander social scene. His early child training shapes him to be a cultural performer, and from here it is but a step to analyzing the whole social system as a dramatic social fiction. The individual life history becomes an inexorable part of the social plot, and the individual destiny becomes the fate of man in society, in a particular society in history.

Now this part of the curriculum, as we know, is the domain of social psychology, sociology, anthropology, and history. And just as in our courses on human development, here too there is tremendous luxuriance and overlap: how social groups function, what a society is, how societies came to be historically, how civilizations succeeded each other, how classes function and are formed, how social change takes place, what happened in pre-history, what is happening now in small social groups and large ones — and so on, and on. Political science and economics also move in here, to stake out areas of special study, as do departments of Romance languages and English, and Germanic studies, and literature. But here there is not only overlap and duplication; there is actually a truly great amount of diverse and important knowledge that one discipline alone cannot handle. What are we to do with this crushing mountain of knowledge, of fact and more fact, of a world that defeats the student before he can even begin to get under way? How are we to extricate him from all this, give him a firm footing in the face of the library stacks, rows and rows of books which mock his best efforts, choke his budding initiative, attack his very existence and personhood with their silent integrity and aloofness? We have the problem of giving the student a bearing in the face of all this, making it meaningful in his life, in the most forceful way possible. We must bring the human person up front, put him back in the center, establish him as a locus of control; he must have reverence for books, but for more than their volume of ink and paper; he must be beholden to mankind's accumulated wisdom, but an independent and rightful heir to that wisdom — someone who can take command of it, and shape it to his life.

Again, just as with the knowledge on human development, there is only one way to handle this problem, and that is to make the knowledge self-critical. Only here, in order to make it self-critical, it has to be made frankly social-critical, historical-critical: This is the social and historical dimension of alienation. The mountain of knowledge here is so great, what standard could we possibly apply that would make it directly personally relevant, that would organize it in some coherent and meaningful way? What standard could we apply without losing the breadth and richness of the data, without sacrificing the probing of experts, without slighting what is good in all the branches of knowledge about man in society? What standard would allow the student to make sense out of the whole panorama of history, out of the whole social system in time and space, without losing the breathtaking vista, and without sacrificing the rich detail? What standard would allow each student to learn that society is a joint human adaptation to the hard facts of material survival, in all its dimensions; what standard would allow at the same time the understanding that the social system is a vast social fiction, a dream staged by man for man, a splendid creation of life meaning on the level of the total society? What standard would allow man to understand the growth of knowledge and ideas, the development of the human spirit, as well as the foibles, weaknesses, and impermanence of the symbolic structures elaborated by man?

The standard . . . can be nothing else than the ideal of communal equalitarianism under God, the ideal of the Stoics, and of the Biblical Hebrew and Christian community. It is the ideal that shows every social system to be a social fiction, and that shows civilization to be the uncritical style of social life across the face of recorded history. It is the standard that passes judgment on the default of two to five thousand years of Western history: the default of community, the failure to create a social system worthy of free and equal men. . . .

The History and Sociology of the State

The student would have to understand two major things: what happened in history that led to the great unequal scramble that we call the 'civilized State'; and how the social system functions as an interrelated dramatic fiction. He will thus have a basic general framework with which to understand how evil arises in society; specifically, how man has been prevented from achieving self-reliance in a community of men. He will see history as the development of inequality, exactly as the ancients had already seen it, and as the nineteenth-century scholars thunderously reminded us: the saga of war, greed, acquisition, social classes, fragmentation, the exploitation of man by man. He will see the social system as . . . a great dramatic fictional staging of life, on the level of the total society. In this way, he will learn that the failure to reconstruct society is itself the source of social evil; he will learn that man's failure to take hold rationally of his social institutions is a type of stupidity. And that this social stupidity is the abrogation by man of the responsible power over his own destiny; it is merely an extension, then, of the automatic early learning that we call the Oedipus Complex—an extension of the unexamined life into the whole social arena.

The curriculum would be composed of courses that show human society on its most basic, simple, and 'primitive' levels: the life of a community of equals, celebrating their social meanings with a maximum of dramatic intensity. It would study the rise of the State as the breakup of traditional community, the full development of classes and their struggles, of the pursuit of money and private gain, and so on. . . . All in all, the student would learn to analyze the panorama of history as the history of alienation from community; he would learn to analyze the various ideologies of the modern world as failures to establish the most liberating type of community; he would learn how the human spirit has been trapped in history, and how it is kept bottled in the modern ideological State. All this would be his education as a future shaper of his own society, as a mature hand in the process of experimental democracy and continued social reconstruction. . . .

Historical Psychology

[I]t was only when we could truly understand what hindered self-reliance on the level of the individual personality that we could begin a mature historical psychology; it was only when we advanced beyond the narrow Freudian formulations on human behavior that we could see man in the full dimensions of society and history. We stopped seeing him as a creature of narrow instinctual drives and biological satisfactions, and could understand him as a groper after meanings; and when we speak of meanings, we speak of the whole range of social and historical possibilities open to human action. It allows us to talk about meanings realized and realizable, about meanings latent in the potential of man's social world; it allows us, in a word, to talk about . . . the full relationship of human values to the state of a society in which man is born. It is the final crown on the Enlightenment scrutiny of history and society, and it is the latest gift of post-Freudian psychology. Instead of talking about how nature baffles man, we can . . . talk about how society, in all its interrelationships, causes human 'stupidity,' causes a constriction on available meanings and values.

This is not the place to expand on the possibilities of historical psychology; it is better saved for a separate work. But we have already had several glimpses. . . . We know how social groups seek for unity, intensity of meaning, highest conviction for those meanings; and we know that this seeking for maximum meaning is intimately linked with what society allows at a given point of history and with a given type of social organization. Thus, we can talk about historical opportunity, and 'social stupidity'; but not 'social stupidity' in the sense that the eighteenth century liked to talk about it: as superstition, outmoded beliefs, rudimentary stages of human awareness; rather, we can talk about it in terms of the physical organization and of the social fiction of each society—even the most supposedly 'advanced.' This allows us to understand not only the fetishism of commodities, but any fetishization of the human world, sex fetishization, self-fetishization, and so on. Fetishization is a word that shows us how man narrows down his meanings when his society does not educate for, nor make possible, broader ranges of self-rewarding experiences. It is not an absolute concept—none of our concepts are—but it is the perfect 'ideal-typical' concept; it helps us to focus on what is broader and richer in comparison to the way things actually are.

We can understand other types of social stupidity with a richness that has not before been possible: Scapegoating, for example, is, as we saw, a clumsy and easy way to achieve the unity of one's own group, to reaffirm one's own values and meanings, to exercise firm control over one's social world by offering up the sacrifice of the evil stranger. We can also understand why it takes an even heavier toll in the modern world perhaps than it ever did; today man has been fully emptied of the quality of his individuality; he has become finally a fully quantified thing, to be tallied like any commodity. At a time when we thought we were becoming 'civilized' and outgrowing 'irrational' conduct, we can understand that man never outgrows his need for intense and unified meanings; if anything, then, he is bound to become more vicious, as his ability to satisfy this need is more and more restricted under the shallow conditions of modern life. Potlatch for potlatch, we are more dangerous than the Assyrians and the Romans.

But most of all, we are coming to understand mental illness itself as a general problem of social stupidity, as a problem of constricted action and meaning, for which education and social structure are directly responsible. This means that we understand the significance of the great manias that seize social groups, and we can relate these manias and hysterias to the state of their society in its historical period. . . .

Our curriculum, then, will offer all this rich knowledge in its study of the sociology of the State. And specialized or interested students will be able to go deeply into the problem of how a particular society elicits mental illness—just as we now understand how our own society fosters menopausal depression by limiting the roles available to women after menopause. In this way, they will have the fullest possible view of the dynamics of alienation in society and history.

3. The Theological Dimension of Alienation

Finally, our alienation curriculum would be crowned by the theological dimension. Just as our individual, social, and historical dimensions teach us how alienation comes about in the individual life and in society, so our theological dimension naturally completes the picture by teaching the law of the limitations of human satisfaction under the conditions of existence.

There was a time when the proposal that a theological dimension be required in a core college curriculum would have met strong protest. Unhappily, that time is not yet past: secularists, scientists, sectarian religionists—all might find reasons for keeping a theological dimension out of a required course program. Their protest is a natural and justified one, if it means that we should not introduce a particular theological point of view as a required belief; or, if it means that we should not require any body of knowledge that is not subject to the critical requirements of all universal knowledge: empirical control, examination and discussion, full and free debate aiming at potential refutation.

What can we answer? If we required of students that they study a body of knowledge that did not meet these universal criteria, we would indeed be subverting the aims of the university in a democracy. But there is no longer any problem; we need no longer make a dogmatic defense of theology. For the first time in history, we seem able to introduce a fully mature theological dimension into our education that meets the most rigorous critical criteria. This is truly an event of great historical importance. Not only are we able to do so, but we must do so, if we are to carry what we know to its fullest point of analysis and synthesis.

[Theology] is the natural complement and continuation of our best knowledge about man. We saw that we cannot talk meaningfully about human striving unless we introduce descriptive ontology; and we saw further that if we talk about descriptive ontology, then we must proceed to its logical conclusion, which is the perspective of theonomy, as [Paul] Tillich calls it. This means that the insights from Tillich's great Systematic Theology would form an integral part of our naturalistic study of man. The empirical study of man would be continued into descriptive ontology, or the full study of 'being' in the dimensions of existence. . . . Only by studying all the ambiguities of existence would the student come to understand fully how evil is inevitable in life. He would then see that man can achieve sporadic and fragmentary healing of the ruptures of life only by a perspective of theonomy on all the dualisms that characterize human striving. He would learn how to give life the dimension of ultimate meaning, the dimension which alone pulls our world together in an unconditional way. This would show him the one thing man needs above all to know: the direction in which he can experience the maximum exercise of his freedom. And as we saw . . . this is the freedom to contribute our own energies to the eternal meaning of the cosmos, the freedom to bathe our daily life in the highest possible intensity and scope of meanings; and these must be divine, self-transcendent meanings.

Thus, we see how theology is the logical complement to a science of man based on an ideal vision of man. . . . If we allow society as it stands to tell us what man needs to use, then we can continue with our present fragmented curriculum, which holds together only because it turns out people who fit into their society as it stands. It is a professionally and vocationally oriented curriculum—and that is a kind of unity. But if we want a unity that is aimed at the release of unknown human energies, then only an alienation curriculum can give it; and an alienation curriculum is not complete without required courses on the limitations of human satisfaction under the conditions in the of existence itself. If the secularist and the scientist accept this, then they need have no qualms about Tillich's theology . . . it allows a relentless criticism of any social fiction that constricts human energies, no matter what institutions are empowered under that social fiction, be they even the Church itself, in any of its forms.

Finally, we must understand that the science of man must be crowned by theology, in order fully to design a standard that transcends pragmatic relativism. And that standard, as we saw, is the standard of the life forces themselves, as they develop in the individual person. Our theology, like our science, opts squarely for the human person, against any social fictions which constrain the free development of his personhood. And these constraints cannot be fully understood without a theonomous perspective on human ambiguities. . . . In this way, the theological part of our curriculum gives the fullest support to the communitarian ideal, by showing further how a true community differs from a mere collective of empty individuals. The student would understand that the theonomous perspective can only be realized in a free community of equal men, devoted to the self-transcendent creation of meaning. The Biblical ideal of religious socialism is thus the natural complement to the science of man . . . it is an objective measure of the inadequacies of any social fiction. . . .

Why did it take so long to bring theology naturally into science? We saw one reason: We had to wait until the science of man itself matured; we had to wait for it to rejoin its own neglected Enlightenment vision, and we had to wait for it truly to crown the Enlightenment beginnings on the problem of human nature. And this was not achieved until very recently. We had to understand man fully as an animal who strived after meanings; we had to see history as the problem of the decline of community; and we had to understand personal failure and social failure as both due to the constrictions on responsible action. When we understood this, we could naturally merge the scientific and the theological perspectives because both of them gave us the ideal of fully developed personhood in equalitarian community; the Biblical model and the Socratic model were natural partners. This is nowhere better understood than in the historical problem of 'sin.' Sin . . . can only be understood in relation to the problem of autonomy. It is almost impossibly difficult for the individual to assume the responsibility for his own meanings; he must, by his very nature as a creature immersed in the infinite, try to ground his acts in superordinate authority, in self-transcendence of some kind. The weight of sin, then, is the weight of meanings that are not related to a broad and self-transcending framework; they are meanings that do not justify the individual in the light of the eternal significance of the universe. With sin, man is cut off, he stands alone with meaning, separate from the ground of things, uprooted in his own finitude. This is what gives sin its deep anxiety. As [Blaise] Pascal and [Soren] Kierkegaard so well knew, sin is existential anxiety, because it is man standing alone with the full burden for the meaning of life. Few men can stand this; and if even these men would stand truly erect, they could not stand it. Man can only stand sin by limiting his perspective, by narrowing his questions, by bending his gaze. Even those who would be strong—say, a Sartre or a Camus—take refuge from the burden of private meanings by claiming that life is 'absurd.' It is only absurd because it is absurd for them to be alone with their trivial meanings. This is the logical outcome of the revolt against the theological dimension of life. When men said that the idea of sin was absurd, they were right: sin is absurd because it means that man alone is responsible for the meaning of life. And it is this absurdity which must drive modern man back to a theonomous perspective on his existence.

When we understand this, we can also understand 'sin' as an historical and social problem. . . . We know that it arose as a cumulative problem in the ancient world; it arose when the integral primitive communities began their inevitable breakup. It was then that daily life became more and more separated from the cover of divine meanings, from an integral pattern of myth and ritual that consecrated most of the important acts of the individual in community. With this breakup, man lost his firm rooting in the divine ground, his daily life became increasingly secular—which means increasingly narrow and shallow, increasingly pragmatic, increasingly autonomous. And it was here that the cumulative 'terror of history' began to make itself felt. Man had lost his contact with continual natural cosmic rhythms; he ceased to be nourished in the feeling that his life was transcendentally significant; the anxious burden of 'sin' thus pervaded more and more of his daily cares. . . .

This is the great lesson we have learned after twenty-five hundred years of wandering across the face of 'civilized' history: We need to combine Socratic self-reliance with a new life-giving myth in a new community. So we now see fully how our naturalistic understanding of man's problems makes the theological perspective the perfect complement of our curriculum. It pulls together the individual, social, and historical perspectives, and makes alienation a problem that ideally can be solved. Without the theological dimension, we could not understand how man could ever experience a true resolution of his anxieties, how he would ever discover a proper direction for his full freedom. We know that he needs nothing less than a true community of free men living a theonomous life. We have a fully sketched ideal of what experimental democracy must mean. Only with this ideal can man design the highest vision of the good; only in this way can he see the good as the evolution of the unknown forces that take root in his being; only in this way can the entire college experience be forged into a unity for the highest development of life itself.

Chapter 5

A Plea for Social Scientific Synthesis

A Design for Ethical Man (1968)*

I F [OUR GENERAL THEORY OF ALIENATION] IS A GOOD THEORY, it will allow us to design an ideal of man that would defeat historical alienation. It would show us how to achieve the integration and rich creativity of primitive societies, but now on a new basis, with the fullest possible liberation of individual energies and freedom. . . . [We] must try to achieve *maximum individuality within maximum community*. [P]hrased this way, the ideal is an unattainable paradox, and this too is proper for an ideal. . . . [T]he only things worth working toward are those which are unattainable: the ideal is the 'un-real' by necessary definition; it leads man ever onward. . . . The problem is, simply, that we have found no way of controlling scientific and artistic meanings without smothering them.

This is another way of saying that the ideal of the innovator must remain pure; this pole of the paradox must remain undiluted. We cannot compromise on an ideal of maximum individuality. What would happen to the creative, innovative spirit if it could not counter all present meanings, scientific as well as artistic? We noted earlier that [Henri] Bergson saw the innovator as the instrument of evolution itself, nature working against encrusted social forms. Max Weber too held a similar view, and assigned a very important place in his thought to the charismatic person, the radical innovator who reworks all meanings and cuts through the 'routinized' cultural forms. Weber built a whole philosophy of history on the alternation of periods of standardization of meanings and periods of charismatic innovation and shattering of accepted meanings. Like Bergson, he saw charisma as one of the few hopes for mankind.

When the Enlightenment thinkers called for the discovery and promotion of genius, they wanted a similar thing: to release the pure forces of nature embodied in the individual spirit. It is an age-old belief and hope of mankind, this quest to release the forces of nature in their pure state. And where else to look except in the subjectivity of the most flexible animal in evolution? Hence the awe and fear that surround

*Original, full text: *The Structure of Evil by Ernest Becker*. Copyright © 1968 by Ernest Becker. Reprinted by permission of George Braziller, Inc.

charisma, as well as the hope. Today we are less superstitious about the matter than our ancestors were because we understand a lot of what goes into making a genius.

As we saw earlier, man's groping for meaning stems from the most idiosyncratic individual needs. This is another way of saying that each individual derives his feeling of self-value in a way that is bound to be a little different from that of all others. What he is doing is resolving his own esthetic tensions in a way proper to his own organism and its own unique and accidental history. The genius is the one who has reworked meanings into a product that the whole culture can share: that is to say, he has made a personal resolution, which can be utilized by others. What is so marvelous about the genius and why are we so taken with him? We are carried forward with him, and so we experience the triumph of the total organism, moving forward, over the conventional systems of culture. The genius has tensions of his whole organism, his whole 'life situation,' which cannot be resolved by the standard world view. This is another way of saying that the total organism can no longer take its sustenance from the partial symbol systems offered to it at an accidental historical time and place. Culture, in sum, has failed to do its universal job, to give the organism what it needs most—a sentiment of self-value derived from standardized symbol systems and the action they direct. Therefore, we can say that with the genius nature triumphs over the constraints of culture by 'declaring' that it cannot be nourished in its need for satisfying organismic self-feeling by the particular meaning games being played at that time. The genius carries nature forward, renews the common pool of meaning by organismically breaking out of the narrowing constraints of the old meaning. Hence, he embodies the triumph of the organic life process over the stilted symbolisms of culture.

This is the dialectic of human freedom, the tension between an animal who needs a symbolically constituted sense of self-value and a society which—by granting it to him—reduces him to the slavery of habit and a narrow world view. [Jean-Paul] Sartre understands this very well when he says that genius is not a gift, but a creative solution of the problem of meaning, a liberation from cultural automaticity. And so we see why society 'needs' the genius, even though it fights him, and will usually not be ready for his vision until after his death: his supremely private achievement is always potentially of the highest public good; and it is of the highest good precisely because it is made over and against habitual social meanings.

But, in order to have this high public value, the creative privatization of the genius must be convertible into general currency. In other words, there is the broadest possible leeway for private products in human society, but not all of them can be legitimate. This is the test of paranoia, for example. The paranoiac makes a resolution of meanings that sustains his self-esteem, by a very creative act. . . . But it suffers precisely because it is a privacy that is not generalizable. . . . The whole thing, then, depends on the degree to which the creative catharsis of meanings is generalizable. Baudelaire's poetic catharsis and his forgiving God were part of a very private affair, but they did make poetry that appealed to others. . . .

Man feels that he must reach outside himself in order to be himself. We discussed this earlier, and made a point of noting that the problem is complicated in modern times, especially for the truly radical innovator. In the Middle Ages every man could delegate responsibility for choices that were not his accustomed ones. It is not just a coincidence that the existential consciousness of man's inner emptiness arose in history precisely at the time that man was thrown back on his own meanings: Pascal marks the crucial turning point in postmedieval man's consciousness of his aloneness, and his famous wager on the existence of God still haunts us today. . . . Our question now is, what kind of an ideal of individual freedom can we design for an empty animal who cannot believe that he has the right to fabricate his own insides? Put thus baldly, we can see how central this problem is to any social vision.

The Problem of Autonomous Meanings

The great fact that we must be clear about before we attempt any kind of solution to this problem is that for the individual it is insoluble. Let us pause and emphasize this one final time. Man simply cannot believe in and accept his own meanings in the face of all the other meanings that existed before him and that transcend him. We might call this one of the fundamental phenomenological facts of human existence. It has its basis, as we saw, in the very nature of man's immersion in a transcendent world; it is rooted in human psychology. . . . To attempt to offer up new meanings is to give birth, to bring the unknown into the world. In the process, the individual gives birth to a new self, and the anxiety that floods him is a reflection of the gravity of what is at stake: the birth or death of a new person, one who has broken away from the old, common world. It is as if the individual were choosing to create himself as a god. How is one to accept this role? How justify the unique act, the unique choice, over and against all other acts and choices? Where, in a word, is the moral standard by which to justify the act that does not conform to any moral standard? Truly, the situation borders on the divine. And the rub is that man does not feel entitled to the arbitrariness of a god. . . .

The whole problem of neurosis and anxiety is basically a problem of cognition: we cannot be anxious about that which we truly understand. To say that one is 'neurotically constricted' is simply to say that one lacks understanding of himself in relation to a situation in which new choices are demanded. Looked at in this way, we can say that there are always two basic things that the individual has to find out about himself in order to earn more freedom of action: (1) Why do I not feel that I have the right to my own meanings? (2) Why do I not have strength to sustain that right?

This formula may seem overly simple, but the basic problem of neurosis and individual freedom is contained in it. What the individual wants to know, and needs to know, is what is depriving him of the right to act on his own. Why does he not feel that he has the right, as an organism, to do what he has to do? In terms of self-analysis, one would have to try to find out what has happened in his past, and is happening in his present, that influences the way he sees the world, the way he feels about himself, that prevents him from moving forward under his own power. This is what the Oedipus complex really means, as [Alfred] Adler knew long ago, and as [Erich] Fromm has repeated more recently: neurosis is a problem of the authority over one's life. . . . The Oedipus complex, as we saw, is better called the Oedipal phase of learning. It is here that one builds up a mode of perception that is more or less automatic and habitual: all of one's action potential is influenced by an a priori definition of the situation. Perception, after all, is action: it is the movement of the organism in a situation; thus, to limit perception is to limit action.

On the individual level, then, the problem of courage is clear. Man must try to frame problems in ever-more-explicit, cognitive terms, because this alone unblocks action. One can convert a situation in which there was no choice to one in which there are new choices. And this way, man liberates himself by *creating indeterminacy*. . . . [Yet] . . . strength can never be an individual problem entirely; it overlaps fully into the social world. In our design for ethical man, we need a program that will support the individual in sustaining the most original meaning and since it is the individual who needs to be sustained the program will have to be a social one. A good part of the answer to the burden of individual choice, in a word, lies in society. . . . Our ideal would have to be one that merges the problems of the individual innovator with those of society. We would have to have a design for man that gave the individual maximum support, but that at the same time gave society the maximum celebration of life . . . . [W]e would have to give full play to the cabalistic passion in a way that would be maximally satisfying to the individual and maximally beneficial to the community. [Martin] Buber gave us the key to the solution of this paradox by reminding us that any ideal vision for man must be built upon the basic human encounter. Whatever else man may reach for, in order to celebrate his existence and get support for himself, his basic dialogue is with his fellows. . . . Using the basic idealist ontology, Buber understood that man can only come into being by relating himself creatively to an external world; the important thing is transaction, without which there can be no knowledge, no testing of powers, no heightening of being. But from everything that the external world offers to man, he can find the greatest enhancement of his being in the encounter with his fellows. The reason for this is strikingly simple: man is the only animal in nature who has a self, and the self can be developed only in transacting with other selves. Man exists in a fourfold field of relations, a field unique in all of nature: man relates to the world and to things; he relates to other men; he relates to the mystery of being; and he relates to his own self. Buber concluded that man can know himself, come to feel his own deep powers, heighten his own being, only by establishing a transaction between his own being and that of another. In other words, we would say, in terms of our discussion, that since man is an instinct-free animal he has to get back into a segment of reality in a most convincing manner. And Buber has shown that the problem of conviction for man is one of trying to get into contact with the full mystery and vitality of being. Only in this way can the world he discovers seem ultimately real, since it is this very vital reality, from which his lack of natural instinctiveness has cut him off. Furthermore, since man is the only animal who has a self, he is, as we just noted, further 'inverted' from a direct natural dialogue. Man is the only self-reflexive animal. Buber helps us see that the only recourse is to turn this inversion to good account, and to use the self to relate to other selves. Instead of potential poverty, he has the possibility of finding infinite richness. In this way man can experience ultimate reality. . . . Maximum meaning for man, as Buber holds, thus lies in the interpersonal realm, in the realm of the 'I and Thou.' In this way man best goes beyond the feeling of his own determinacy and isolation, the sense of feebleness of his own meanings.

In briefest possible compass, then, this is Buber's basic view of the interpersonal nature of meaning and human becoming. Man needs man in order to discover and validate his own inner powers, in order to unfold himself; and man needs to see and experience man in order to be convinced that there is absolute value, absolute meaning, in nature. It is quite fitting for man to have to address himself to the highest organism in nature in order to achieve the highest consciousness of life—both his own life, and that of the world around him. It is this community of the interpersonal that is thus our best and most natural place to seek for ethical man.

This discovery is important because not only does it fully naturalize idealism in the interpersonal realm, but it also allows us to see what we need to know about agonism: that this competitive motive is basically neutral, essentially innocuous. Historically, agonism has had its vicious forms, but the urge to agonism is merely the urge to find the really real in the validating encounter with another self. . . . Buber brought the tradition right up to our time by a further naturalistic refining of the union of idealist esthetics and self-psychology. Moreover, he could be very explicit about the political implications of this whole tradition; as he says, the discovery of reality as essentially interpersonal can lead us to a science of man that goes beyond narrow individualism and constricting collectivism. . . .

The Enlightenment thinkers, down to Lester Ward, meant the same thing when they called for the promotion of human potential to its highest reaches, and wanted the full subsidization of genius in all its forms. Thus, when we talk about the holy in man, we are talking about it in 'hard' scientific terms—it is almost a sheer matter of common sense when put into the framework fashioned by the people we are discussing. But when science opted out of life and, objectivized man, scientists of course lost the possibility of seeing any mystery at all in man, of seeing any heightening of being, even in secular terms. The rich and vital tradition that we are sketching here was forgotten, and life itself was trivialized in the service of mechanistic, managerial science. We have seen this tragic fact crop up again and again. . . .

And it is precisely in the wholeness of his essential relationships that man is infinite, infinite in terms of the possibility of unfolding and becoming. . . . By holding up the ideal vision of the freest possible individual, working in the most equalitarian social community and subserving the unfolding of the cosmic process, we have answered a question with which so many thinkers have grappled and argued: can human association take the place of worship of the divine? . . . . But now we know that the [pro and con] positions are not really opposed, but that they are indeed compatible: the best way to gain an intimacy with the cosmic process, the best way to find support for man's efforts in the universe, is to trust to some divine purpose trying to work itself out in nature. But the most effective way of establishing and maintaining this intimacy, support, and trust is by the joint efforts of men in a free society: celebrating human meanings together, in a devotion to higher ideal ends. . . .

So much, then, for our design for ethical man. If there were any need to be apologetic about Leibnitzian words like *soul, God,* or *cosmic community,* we can now see that they have a proper place in our understanding of man. They are naturalistic scientific words that describe the situation and the relationships of man in society. It may take us some time (it has already taken us over a century and a half) to feel comfortable with insights that both poets and scientists share. The contemporary scientist must object (almost reflexively) against the kind of constructs we are proposing here. At most, he might tolerate them as peripheral to the 'hard' business of science. But we are not proposing mere toleration. Far from it. We are now in a position to see that these kinds of constructs—meaning, conviction, sense of intimacy with the cosmic process—must be at the very center of a science of man in society. They are part of the human situation, and a science of man in society cannot permit itself to overlook what is typical of the human situation. . . .

But freedom means nothing unless it means championing the fuller play on the powers that each unique organism brings into nature. It can hardly mean freedom to do what everyone else is doing, freedom to follow in the preset cultural design. . . . [W]e know that man can never be man unless he is the locus of his powers . . . this is what alienation means, the forfeiting of responsibility for one's own action. Whether it takes the form of mental illness—of action constricted to the narrowest possible range—or whether it takes the form of mindless collective action, the basic problem is the same: the failure to exercise one's own powers within a unified, critical framework. The phenomena of fascism and collectivism in our time are all part of a logical piece with our destruction of the interhuman, with the sacrifice of the whole man to further the empty forms of commercial society. . . .

Collective action and uncritical devotion to unscrupulous leaders have been a problem all through history. But there is no doubt that in modern times it is peculiarly aggravated by the institutions of contemporary society. We have created a quintessential mass man by failing to value concrete living organisms as sacred centers of life. And we have paid the proper toll: The destruction of the human has led logically to the destruction of the interhuman, and ultimately to the unthinking destruction of other humans.

The Ethical Society (1968)*

AT TIMES THE NINETEENTH CENTURY SEEMS a truly Biblical epoch, in which passionate visions sprang up on a hostile soil, and there was nothing to do but wait. The great difference is that the nineteenth-century soil was not arid; the great wheels of industrial plenty had begun their relentless grind. For the first time in history, grand Utopian visions were being obtrusively accompanied by the proper means for their realization.

Fortunately, nature does not grant the wishes of men who want to see the promised land. . . . Today we have so lost the Faustian promise that we are even afraid to fulfill it. What will happen, we lament, when the wage-work day is abolished, when the automated factories grind out their plenty, and distribute it to all, when annual salaries are guaranteed, regardless of work—what will man do with his leisure; how will he keep from running wild?

The question betrays the whole failure of our time: the failure of the science of man to put forth an agreed, synthetic theory of human nature; the failure of society to see beyond the kind of monster that it has created with its commercial-industrial madness. Of course social welfare dampens public interest in a society in which there is no public interest, no agreed purpose. Why should the individual design larger, self-transcending social ends when the society as a whole frowns on it? Each person is bent on his own security, his own future; as a result, there is no social future, no future for men in common.

All of this is commonplace enough, but it explains why mass man is so impotent. He lacks a basic human dimension—control over the future; in a word, he has no 'social ego.' . . . What happens when the society lacks an ego? The very same thing that happens when the individual has very weak control over his destiny: he fetishizes. He begins to look for control in narrow areas, areas that have nothing really basic to do with his problems. And society does the same: if it cannot handle the principal problem of adaptation by intelligently harnessing the future to its purposes, it tries to exercise firm control over areas where it does have power. . . . Today we are witnessing our society trying to gain some kind of control over the national life and some kind of meaningful national design by forging what we might call a *military social ego*. This kind of adaptation is old enough and it has often been necessary for the survival of free communities—e.g., at the time of the Greeks. But the question that is critical today is whether a military social ego any longer represents an intelligent adaptation to the problems of morality in the modern world. We know that this kind of ego defeats dictatorships and today our best scientists are warning us that it will defeat commercial-industrial democracy.

Our fetish social ego and our 'futuristic living' are all of a piece: they represent

*Original, full text: *The Structure of Evil* by Ernest Becker. Copyright © 1968 by Ernest Becker. Reprinted by permission of George Braziller, Inc.

a pious wish that everything will turn out well if we feverishly and uncritically play the game of our society. But there is a real difference between this naive and clumsy attempt to influence the future and the creative design of a new future horizon; and it is the one that [John] Dewey outlined, namely, the difference between mechanical action and real action, the difference between external, coerced means, and individually controlled means. It boils down to the question: is the individual a free source of action, does he have aegis over the kinds of means he will use to achieve the desired end? This was the whole basis of Dewey's pragmatism. It summed up his entire social philosophy and justified his theory of education and his vision of a truly sane society. . . . Ordinarily, man is burdened by designs inherited from tradition that impose means and ends upon him. He barters his free energies in uncritical acceptance of the life the elders impose. Pragmatism sought to overcome this by making means relevant to ever-new problems, changing as the real problem changed. The free man, like the free society, would be one who could continually re-adapt his means to ever-new ends, and would not follow slavishly in the footsteps of tradition and habit. Or, put in terms that are now familiar to us, we would say that the free man is the true genius who creates new meanings and continually cuts through old forms. . . .

In our definition of alienation, we said that it could only mean exile from the free and responsible aegis over one's own initiatory powers. We also noted that alienation, mental illness, the 'unconscious,' are all synonymous. They refer to the results of an early learning process in which the natural ability to learn by trial and error is paralyzed in some ways and in certain areas of awareness. As a result, in the face of new choices the individual will experience great anxiety, and will distrust his powers of independent judgment; he will have a greater or lesser 'unconscious,' depending on the ways and the length of time which his self-powers have been crippled. Thus, we said that the 'unconscious' was not a problem in 'depth,' but rather that it was a problem in the range of behaviors and in the richness and flexibility of the cognitive grasp of problematic action situations. Man's alienation, in other words, is not a phylogenetic problem, not a question of man being shackled by instincts. . . . Man is alienated when he is not 'doing,' and in order for the symbolic animal to 'do,' he must command an effective cognitive grasp of a problematic situation. This means that he must not only 'know' what is wrong, but he must also feel and believe that he has the powers to act on what he knows.

Psychoanalytic theory helped to clarify immensely the basic dichotomy that exists in human experience between the early training that man is subject to and the adult choices that will later present themselves. It is this dichotomy, as we saw, which deprives man of a belief in his own powers. He does not make new choices—create new meanings—without awakening the anxiety he learned in his early training. By thus discovering this dichotomy, and tracing how it comes into being as an interplay of ego and anxiety, psychoanalysis also outlined the problem of neurosis. We might say, then, that neurosis can be understood as the avoidance of self-created meaning. . . . Progressive education, ethics, and cognition are intimately related. . . .

Dewey . . . saw that the educator could never cede his place to the psychoanalyst, that the critical educator antedated him historically, and that the problem of individual maladjustment and liberation really belonged to him. Progressive education itself, as Dewey understood it, proposed to overcome neurosis. And the progressive educator's understanding of neurosis is the same as the vaunted 'clinical' one; he could rephrase it in terms of two basic and related deficits: (1) The paralysis of the ability to learn by natural trial and error; and (2) The distrust of one's powers of independent judgment, throughout life. Both of these deficits are a result of the early learning process. . . . Hence, as Dewey saw, true democracy is the only atmosphere in which man can grow because it is against nonreflective action at all times. It is geared to meeting with the full force of cognition continually new, problematic situations. . . .

Today we can see that education for social living in a democracy was not an inevitable stumbling block for progressive education. The stumbling block was in our definition of democracy. We have utterly lost the pragmatic, Jeffersonian understanding of it. We have made a wholly false definition of democracy as the freedom to buy and sell goods and to perpetuate the ideology of commerce. We understood democracy as just another *ideology*. Instead, we should have seen that democracy is an *ideal*. As an *ideology*, democracy differed little from Stalinism—it treated the individual as a means and not as an end. As an *ideal*, democracy would treat the individual as an end. The ideology is culture-centered and constricting; the ideal is man-centered and liberating. The word *democracy* simply cannot stand for any social system which treats individuals as means. How can we be induced to realize this? When we see the implications of this false definition of democracy, we can understand something very crucial for our whole discussion, namely, that democracy, aiming for the ideal liberation of the individual from constrictions on his powers, would have to aim for what seemed to be a fantasy: it would have to pose, as its ideal, the 'maximum unconstriction' of individual capacities. *And it would have to do this despite the fact that this threatens the going cultural belief system.* In other words, democracy, like liberty, normality, progress, cognitive or ethical man, is an *ideal-type*. This implies, furthermore, that in order for the ideal of 'maximum unconstriction' not to get immediately bogged down in ongoing cultural forms, the accepted routines of the society must allow for continual change and progress toward the ideal-type. Democracy cannot mean—can never mean—institutions which are already formed. Again, this is what Jefferson so perfectly understood when he wanted to allow for a new Constitution every nineteen years. He understood the ideal-typical nature of democracy and human freedom. . . . As long as democracy was an ideology, and not an ideal, it used the person as a means, not as an end: it did not permit him to surpass himself (ethically). It abased man by defining equality as equal right to consumer goods—equal right to self-seeking within the national grab bag. This is another way of saying that democracy was defined as the free pursuit of self-interest. It is only when we define democracy as an ideal that self-interest can be transcended. Democracy then becomes a superordinate ideal toward which all members work. If this ideal has as an aim the treating of all individuals as ends, then all members will work toward the ideal of treating all others as ends. In other words, creative community and altruism become socially standardized under the ideal-type. . . . The most fluid and changeable ethics, then, becomes morally defensible and desirable because it aims at all times at treating individuals as ends. Pragmatist ethics is thus fully vindicated even in its most extreme tentativeness, and in its protean morality it is the most steadily moral of all. It carries out the great promise of Kant's categorical imperative.

The Vision of the Science of Man (1968)*

THE NATURAL INTEGRATION OF THOUGHT has been a deep hope of thinkers ever since mankind passed out of the stage of mythology. The truly broad thinkers have always aimed for it, but up to now the integration has been forced—it did not proceed from empirical knowledge, from the world as it was, but instead from the world as the various thinkers hoped it might be. This led many to turn away from integration as an idle pastime of speculative philosophy; it led others to attempt an integration around mathematical, logical, or physical principles—which is another way of saying that they tried to integrate thought in the same way as speculative philosophers: by forcing it into an artificial mold with which alone they were comfortable. Yet the problem remained. For at least two thousand years Western man has wanted to grasp the world as a whole, as a totality which would give meaning to all experience, no matter from where it was drawn. But except for theological interludes like the Middle Ages this unity has escaped us.

When we see what the Middle Ages attempted, we can also understand one very important thing about the unity of thought, namely, that it is not an idle pastime. It goes to the very heart of the human condition, because without a unitary, critical world view, human dignity and social order are impossible. This was the great discovery of the nineteenth century, whose thinkers could see what man had lost with the downfall of traditional society. Man no longer had a view of the togetherness of things and of his place in the center of them. It fell to the twentieth century to reap all the bitter fruits of the dispersal of a unitary conception of experience: science in the service of destruction; mankind converted into mindless consumer masses, rocked this way and that by sensational news items and by strong demagogues. What else? Man had no grip on the manifold of experience, could no longer imagine himself at the center, and so he quite naturally had a very poor opinion of himself. The whole phenomenon is summed up in the words 'mass culture,' words which mean that man has lost the sense of his own significance; he has become a plaything rather than a player.

*Original, full text: *The Structure of Evil* by Ernest Becker. Copyright © 1968 by Ernest Becker. Reprinted by permission of George Braziller, Inc.

Yet many thinkers in the nineteenth century did not despair; they saw that something truly new was at hand in the history of thought. They saw that philosophy could only achieve the unity it wanted in one way: it would have to settle for working within questions that were truly soluble, seek answers that man could find; it would have to focus on the human condition as it is lived on this planet—it would have to study man and his works. . . .

But this kind of anthropodicy was bound to fail, as [David] Hume had already understood: he knew that history could never be a direct key to a new anthropodicy, that its chief use is only to help find the 'constant and universal principle of human nature.' Hume ferreted out all subjective bias in man's approach to experience, and history, above all, is a highly subjective enterprise. One reconstructs the past largely according to present purposes. How can we base a compelling anthropodicy on a reading of history alone? Nearly everyone would have his own, according to his beliefs and sentiments. We see this very clearly in the nineteenth-century arguments between the socialists and the free enterprisers: they could even agree that history is the saga of the exploitation of man by man, but the believers in free enterprise felt that the benefits of this saga far outweighed the injustices, and that things were getting better all the time anyway.

What we need instead is to find recurrent features of our subject matter, the 'laws' of 'human nature.' The burden of our anthropodicy would rest on these while history would be used to round out and support our vision of human suffering. It would help give us a more compelling and comprehensive picture. [Franz] Oppenheimer's theory of the origin of the state in conflict could never give the 'objective standard of justice' that he sought, no matter how graphic and dependable the facts. And the reason is that men generally do not become outraged, morally, about what happened in the past—especially if the present—seems comfortable and promising. Man needs compelling proof that something is wrong in the present, and will continue to be wrong if present circumstances continue. After all, an anthropodicy is just that; it has to muster moral indignation; and it can only do this by being based on a full scientific theory of the human condition in and of the present time. When we understand this, we can see that the nineteenth-century venture into history and evolution temporarily sidetracked and delayed the establishment of a mature social science. . . .

Perhaps the most direct way of summing up this whole problem is this: that in order to show the dependence of private troubles on social issues, one had to develop a thoroughgoing theory of the nature of the social bond. And this is exactly what the whole nineteenth century set itself to do. In order to give . . . a clear directive for morality by showing the social correlates of private ills, a full-field theory of alienation had to be developed. It could not be enough to show historically that human intelligence was insufficiently developed. What was needed, in other words, was a comprehensive social psychology. . . .

After Darwin, all scientific conceptions had to be naturalistic. And it was just this that posed an enormous conceptual problem for the science of man. An anthropodicy, by definition, had to reveal the source of evil in the world, and provide for directives for overcoming it. In other words, the naturalistic anthropodicy had to be scientifically objective; and yet, at the very same time, it had to be suffused with value. There did not seem to be any way over this hurdle within the ordinary conceptualization of science. The nineteenth century then had to find a principle which would break through scientific objectivity and would permit a judgment of higher and lower in a neutral naturalistic world. . . . The importance of this complete social psychology of human valuing was that it got at human experience from within, emphasized its utter neutrality with a breadth and subtlety that would have astounded Rousseau, and thus could allow us to see how evil in society arose. It got to the heart of action in its necessary ontological dimensions, where we could see man's search for meaning. Nothing less than this would do. The Benthamites forfeited their chance for a social psychology by having to have recourse to a legalistic principle of individual responsibility. Thus they were embarrassed by the notion of social sympathy, because it was not individualistically reducible. Up to now, most modern social scientists have forfeited the possibility of a social psychology in another—but related—way. They have been embarrassed by the individual subjectivity, and, not being able to deal with it in any objective way, they have overlooked the heart of human action.

Only by getting at human experience from within would we be able to give what the Enlightenment wanted—a science of man in society that was an anthropodicy and an ethical design. But, in order to provide substance for the ethical design, a complete social psychology had to be able to answer two basic and related questions, namely, what did man want and how did the feeling of right and wrong and good and bad grow up? And, in order for this answer to be achieved, there had to be a union of three things: phenomenological psychology, a naturalistic ontology of organismic striving in a neutral world of nature, and a complete genetic theory of the development of the sense of self, self-consciousness, or conscience. In other words, we had to have a naturalistic morality that would be under man's control, and not a theological morality under Divine control; neither could we have that curious, grotesque compromise: a naturalistic morality under control of unconscious natural forces. So neither the idealists nor [Herbert] Spencer would do for a mature social-psychological theory of the social bond. This theory had to approach action simultaneously from inside and outside, from science and philosophy, and it had to define where nature transcended human powers and where it did not. It had to place the control of ethical action into human hands, and it had to delineate that control scientifically. . . .

The unique result was the complete secularization of human meaning, achieved without belittling man. The inevitable could be accepted: the ideal, or the 'really real,' is the *human creation of meaning*. It grows up in the transactional interplay with the material, everyday world. Its ideality can be no more than the continual fabrication of new meanings. By these meanings man enhances his life, and actually quickens the real in the material world. Not only are man's meanings not cheapened by being attached to things. On the contrary, this is the only way that the ideal can unfold. With esthetic mergers, with science and art, man fuses his meanings into the world of things. In this way he is led on to a revelation of his own ideal gropings, at the same time that the external world is increasingly unfolded for his use. . . .

These lines of inquiry were given great critical weight and sharpness by the small handful of sociologists who still insisted on doing meaningful work. Thus, [Thorstein] Veblen and [C. Wright] Mills could show us how society, under certain kinds of distributional systems, leads individuals to constrict their behavior to certain hollow forms of self-display. Perhaps most important for our time, Mills could show further how a society devoted to the ideology of dignity and freedom could actually severely limit these things, and flirt with global war, in the interest of maintaining its unexamined and irrational economic-distributional prestige system. This took the basic problem of economics that Marx had raised and broadened it to an understanding of how the social forces function in a total social system; it allowed us to take the broadly descriptive ontology of human striving, and give it critical weight for our historical period.

Once this was accomplished, there was nothing to prevent us from appropriating the ideal-real framework fashioned by the nineteenth century, from linking up with the earlier tradition of the science of man. We can answer the question What does man want? And with this answer we have at the same time laid the basis for our anthropodicy and our ethical ideal.

As we promised earlier, by providing an answer to this basic question, a large part of the problem of the nature of the social bond was solved. But in order to have a truly complete picture, a really mature social psychology, we had to answer another question: how does the feeling of right and wrong grow up, and why is it so ingrained in the human spirit? Only by answering this second question would we be able to give full substance to an ethical idea. . . .

Furthermore, Freud helped us see the great gulf that could exist between early learning and the demands of adult experience. By focusing on the dichotomy we could see how early training in the cultural ideology actually constricted cognition and behavior. This revelation could then be coupled with the work of the critics of society and culture, and the larger-scale analysts of society, that we sketched above. In sum, when we had supplied a complete theory of the nature of the social bond, we had at the same time a full-field theory of human alienation, a theory which we can now see united several levels of explanation: the phenomenological, the social-psychological, the historical-institutional, and the individual-genetic. All the currents flowed into one, and we could understand man's striving in its fullest, most neutral terms, and see clearly all the various constrictions on human choice. It was as complete an anthropodicy as the Enlightenment could have hoped for, and one for which we had been groping with increasing intensity these past decades. It showed . . . the fullest possible correlates of the dependence of private troubles on social issues.

Perhaps most important of all, the ethic of this new anthropodicy shined through as clearly as day. The problem for all the thinkers of the Enlightenment, and especially for [Auguste] Comte, was how to get social interest to predominate over selfish private interest. The new theory of alienation showed that ethical action could not be possible where man was not supplied with self-critical and socially critical knowledge, and with the possibilities of broad and responsible choices. Recurrent evils like sadism, militant hate, competitive greed, narrow pride, calculating self-interest that takes a nonchalant view of others' lives, mental illness in its extreme forms—all stem from constrictions on behavior and from shallowness of meaning; and these could be laid in the lap of society, specifically, in the nature and type of education to which it submits its young; and to the kinds of choices and cognition which its institutions encourage and permit. Man could only be ethical if he was strong, and he could only be strong if he was given fullest possible cognition, and responsible control over his own powers. The only possible ethics was one which took man as a center and which provided him with the conditions that permitted him to try to be moral. The antidote to evil was not to impose a crushing sense of supernatural sanction, or unthinking obligation, or automatic beliefs of any kind—no matter how 'cheerful' they seem. For the first time in history it had become transparently clear that the real antidote to evil in society was to supply the possibility of depth and wholeness of experience. Evil was a problem of esthetics—that is, esthetics understood in its broad sense as the free creation of human meanings, and the acceptance of responsibility for them. It had never been so well understood that goodness and human nature were potentially synonymous terms; and evil was a complex reflex of the coercion of human powers.

The Enlightenment Paradox (1968)*

ONE OF THE REASONS THE POLITICIAN SCORNS the academic intellectual is that he knows that to work things out in elegant theory is not to work them out at all. The theoretical problem of a science of society is a case in point. How do we finally establish a synthetic science of man? The answer is now common intellectual property: we establish this synthetic science when the diverse analytic activity of the various disciplines has given us enough knowledge of our human subject matter to make the new synthesis compelling. We establish it, in other words, by agreeing on the rationally compelling nature of the new anthropodicy, of what makes people act the way they act, and why they are unhappy. . . .

At this point we come up against an uncomfortable realization. When does a paradigm for a new anthropodicy become compelling enough, so compelling that the scientific world uses it actively to champion the institution of a socially experimental science of man? *We realize that the answer to this question can be never. . . .* [W]hat can 'fully developed' mean in science? Here is the rub. Science is never 'fully developed.' Thomas Kuhn . . . has shown that science is not only a cumulative activity, as we had always thought. On the contrary, it can also be a saltatory and radically changeable

*Original, full text: *The Structure of Evil* by Ernest Becker. Copyright © 1968 by Ernest Becker. Reprinted by permission of George Braziller, Inc.

activity. . . . From Kuhn's history we can see strikingly how much a matter of conventional agreement science is, how much it depends on commanding loyalty, on its historical appropriateness, on active personal choice. Hence, no science is ever 'fully developed'—nor can it be. Its claim to maturity rests only on the fact that it has offered up an agreed paradigm which is compelling enough to group the loyalties of a majority of workers in the discipline. It then becomes *the theory,* and everyone proceeds *to do science* on its mode. . . .

In the human sciences the problem of gaining wide loyalty to a paradigm is no different than in any of the other sciences. . . . Only, a subtle new factor magnifies the problem immensely, and gives it entirely new proportions: *in the human sciences it is sharpened to an extreme degree, because the agreement cannot be disguised as an objective scientific problem.* That is to say, in the natural and physical sciences, paradigm agreement looks like a disinterested matter of option for an objectively compelling theory. It does not look like an active social and historical (moral) problem. In the human sciences, on the other hand, *the same kind of option for a compelling theory looks unashamedly like a wholly moral option,* because of the frankly moral nature of its subject matter. The physical sciences, when they opt for an attack on reality, also set in motion massive social and institutional changes of a moral nature. Only, there is a difference between this kind of change and that projected by the human sciences: the process of change is indirect; it does not call immediately into play the deep-seated reaction to the habitual human world. This helps physical science assume the disguise of a spurious kind of detachment since its reality is removed from immediate repercussions on the human realm.

And so we can see that we would have every reason to use the same language as the other sciences, and insist that paradigm agreement in the human sciences is just as much a conventional agreement based on compelling rational grounds as the paradigm agreement is in the physical and natural sciences. Paradigm choice, in sum, in the human sciences differs in no way from that of the other sciences except that the willful, moral nature of the option cannot be disguised. The human sciences, just like the others, read nature in the Enlightenment tradition and vision: in order to find compelling reasons for agreed action. The reading can never be complete, hence the action must always be willful. All of science, as the Enlightenment understood, is thus a moral problem.

If this is so, we can understand how important the historical context is in determining the shape of a science. Scientists will choose only those theoretical paradigms for which they are historically ready: it is never merely a matter of abstract, objective, rational compellingness. In the science of man the problem is infinitely sharpened: since the paradigm in the science of man is in effect an anthropodicy which enjoins a new morality, an option for it will be almost wholly influenced by the historical context in which the new anthropodicy would be set to work. . . .

We are now in a position to appreciate fully what we noted earlier, that the unity of science is a social problem, as Dewey so well understood. Furthermore, we can see with complete clarity that the science of man began as a moral problem, and that it must always remain one. Rare thinkers have seen this, that 'the supreme unity of social science' cannot be sought in the widest law of causal sequence, but must rather come about by getting agreement on ultimate social ends.

We can see, then, the question we must ask of a science: 'Is the theoretical picture offered by it enough, at a particular stage in history, to gain support for its active moral implementation?' 'Or are the socially (or scientifically) conservative forces so strong that even the most compelling paradigm will fail to rally support?' In the case of this failure, we would have to say, paraphrasing Comte, that the positive theory has not 'sufficiently succeeded' in dispelling the 'previous metaphysics,' that there is still a need for 'more complete' knowledge. We can always judge whether this is so, post facto, by seeing whether the various professional disciplines withdraw into their shells of 'further research.' Indeed, this is the only way we can judge.

This, then, is the continuing *Enlightenment paradox* in science, the creative moral dynamic of all the sciences, sharpened acutely in the science of man. We can now rephrase the paradox in terms of two necessary contradictions:

We must have an abstract, full-field theory of human nature in order to compel agreement on a new science of man in society, a new anthropodicy. But we cannot wait for such a theory, since it will never be 'full.'

(And)

We must use our reading of nature as a guide to the paradigm which will be offered up for option, but we cannot continually lean on a passive reading of nature: we must make a willful option that is at all times based on incomplete knowledge.

Put this starkly, we can well understand that the Enlightenment paradox is like a haunting curse over social science. When we talk about the 'alienation' of the intellectual in modern society, we are really referring back to the basic paradox that has dogged him since he emerged from the medieval time with his bright new hopes. The philosophers of the Enlightenment were in the same isolated and heroic position as was Erasmus earlier: they were budding scientists in a pre-paradigm age. Hence they had to look both heroic and pathetic: heroic personally, like Condorcet, Diderot, Rousseau; pathetic scientifically, with a trust in reason that has provided succeeding generations with much cause for scoffing. On a flimsy basis they had to lean to a social activism that makes them look naive to the present generation of social scientists.

But today's intellectual is alienated exactly as was his Enlightenment prototype: he is caught in the identical bind between abstruse analyses of his subject matter and the impotence of his active powers. Unless we understand this acute similarity between the Enlightenment intellectual and today's social scientist, we will not be able to understand today's drama in social science. In fact, we are still continuing the Enlightenment today so it is small wonder that we are plagued with its problems. The recent bitter disputes in sociology reflected a re-enactment of the Enlightenment struggle, and issued in the same Enlightenment paradox…

But, if I accomplish nothing else with the present work, I hope at least to have pulled the mask down, or to have left a piece of writing that shows how the mask can be pulled down. Sociologists should no longer imagine that it suffices *to do science;* that in order to have a science of man, they need only work piling up data, and trying to 'tease out' (horrid positivist word) social laws for eventual use. They may turn their backs on a paradigm; they may shun a theory that seems only to reflect historical accident, but they cannot shun an active option for man as an end. If they continue to do so, they will not have any science. The reason is, simply, that the science of man is an ideal-typical science, or there is no science of man. This must be grasped wholly and digested once and for all. An ideal-typical science is an inseparable *union of liberty, progress, and a scientifically etched ideal-type*. This means that all social scientists must work toward a projective vision of the good life, which the whole society works toward in unison. This was the nineteenth century understanding of social science, and it is the same one that will have to be recaptured today. . . . The nineteenth century, decidedly, was the century of grand visions which we have since lost. But today we have the material for the vision, material which the nineteenth century did not have; we are able to provide a solid scientific structure for the indispensable Utopian method of an ideal-typical science.

What does an ideal-typical science mean for us today? It means that we have to recognize three essential things in order for us to have a science. In the first place, we must actively opt for furthering the ideal-type projected by the science. In the second place, we must realize that such a science deals on superordinate levels. It is a science of human meanings, human becoming. It is not and cannot be a reductionist science, except to derive data that will be used to serve free human development. Finally, and inseparably, the science is characterized by a natural fusion of fact and value, which will repair the split that was begun by the decline of the medieval cosmology and was intellectually justified by Kant. Let us consider each of these questions briefly, as a conclusion to our retrospective discussion.

The ideal-type projected by the science of man is the vision of the kind of man we would have if we could banish evil in the social realm. It is thus an ideal-type designed by the science of man as anthropodicy. We have learned that alienation means the constriction of individual, responsible self-powers. Our ideal-type, therefore, is an autonomous, ethical man, who would represent the increasing development of human powers. Thus, there can be no 'autonomous man,' or 'ethical man,' or 'normal man,' as a finished product; he represents a value option, an ideal-type toward which we must continually aim. If we accepted any definition of 'normal' as a finished product, we would be without a science since we would be deprived of a man-centered ideal-type. This makes it very clear why we cannot tolerate any fear of the human subject matter. We have to choose man as an indeterminate end, and opt for the furthering of his powers on the basis of scientific knowledge about what is constricting them.

By the same token, we cannot tolerate any theoretical approaches to man which take a dim view of human nature; nor can we avoid planning society to absorb the changes that would take place by the fuller release of individual human energies.

Democracy and liberty, in other words, are also ideal-typical, along with the image of man. Alienation, neurosis, democracy, autonomy, and so on, are always relative terms, terms about which the science must at all times be valuational. The reason is that it approaches man from within his behavior primarily, and only secondarily does it approach him objectively. The purpose of the science is to provide conditions for man's development, and to trust in the limitlessness of that development. It cannot seek to 'adjust' man to any fixed forms, either scientific or institutional.

Here we understand why a pan-reductionist approach has utterly failed to produce a science of man. Pan-reductionism has been beside the point, first, because man operates on superordinate levels, and microscopic data do not reflect what is truly characteristic about human action. A second reason why pan-reductionism has failed to produce a science of man is that its option is always for a continued 'reading' of nature. It looks forward to an unlimited future of scientific research, with an ever more precise approach to a smaller and smaller segment of reality. Now both of these emphases are fallacious enough, but there is a still more powerful reason that pan-reductionism misses the science of man. By objectivizing man, and seeking to reduce him to deterministic laws, pan-reductionism fouls the entire nature of an ideal-typical science. This has been one of the outstanding fallacies in social science since the early Newtonian mechanical philosophers. . . . They wanted a science of man that would draw its laws and principles from a knowledge of human nature, a knowledge of man achieved once and for all. They simply did not see clearly that the subject matter of such a science would then be a determinate thing. There would be no science of man in society, but rather a parceling out of man to the physical and natural sciences. Many, even most, scientists and philosophers of science still envisage this today as a desired goal of science.

But this is to fail utterly to think through the implications of such a program. Granted that the deterministic and pan-reductionist study of man should succeed beyond the fondest hopes, and that all levels of behavior are firmly linked into causal laws. Granted that science, working diligently, comes into possession of the knowledge to control and determine man, to do what it will with him. The next question is the crucial one: when this knowledge for controlling man is finally in, when we can manipulate him by physical, chemical, and genetic means—who is going to exercise this control, and in the name of what? What 'democracy' is going to use this knowledge? Obviously none; we should have to renounce the knowledge, and the science that accumulated it, and keep the scientists themselves under close surveillance. A fine end to the Enlightenment venture, and to the billions of research hours and dollars. Charles Beard foresaw and lamented this very thing: he said that even if narrow scientific method were to reach its impossible goal, its victory would be defeat for mankind. In other words, the pan-reductionists, and those who fear man and want to control him, would subvert two out of the three interdependent and indispensable elements of an ideal-typical science, namely, liberty and the ideal-type. They imagine that the third element, progress, can have some kind of meaning particular to itself. But without liberty (democracy) and the ideal-type, there can be no progress that could possibly have any humanly desirable meanings. With no ideal that seeks to further man's own inner freedom and development, and no liberty by which to do it, how would progress be determined? We can thus see how vital this triad is, and how it is fouled at the base when man is not taken as a free, indeterminate center of the science. . . .

The third and final thing which an ideal-typical science means for us today is the fusion of fact and value. This fusion obviously follows from the entire structure of the science. The problem dates from the decline of the medieval cosmology, thus, from the rise of the science of man. What was needed was a science, which hopefully would fuse fact and value in a new way, and not in the theological synthesis which had declined. Fact and value had to split, so that science could proceed unfettered in its investigations. But the split was a temporary one, pending the discovery by the Enlightenment of a new scientific structure, which could reinstate the fusion of fact and value in an entirely new way. Kant was the pivotal figure here: he wanted to keep a predominant place for morality, and also for science; and thus he intellectually legitimated the separation of fact and value by marking off the internal world of morality from the external world of the senses. This is the crucial problem that we are still hung up on today. It led Dewey to criticize Kant for closing off the realm of nature and experience as a guide to moral action. In Kant's system, said Dewey, "Every attempt to find freedom, to locate ideals, to draw support for man's moral aspirations in nature, is predoomed to failure." We continue to pay the price of this artificial separation, since we have neither Enlightenment science nor Christian morality.

But it must be added that Kant was the tragic figure here, as well as the pivotal one. One can argue that the criticism of Dewey and others are not fair to the whole body of Kant's work, and the thrust of his thought: that Kant did not leave man separate from nature or condemn the moral world to remain empty of precepts drawn from experience. Kant proposed that we can read nature up to a certain point, and that point is the one at which we decide that moral action is justified by the facts at hand; moral action thus becomes an empirically supported ideal. Kant's dilemma, as we mentioned earlier, reflected that of the whole Enlightenment: he outlined a program of empirical study of man, a true anthropology, which would be used to buttress a moral ideal; but at that time the program was only at its beginning, and consequently his moral enjoinders had to remain merely formalistic and 'empty.'

Of course the fusion of fact and value is very troubling; it weakens the authority of both science and traditional morality. Science becomes more human and indeterminate, and morality becomes more humanly determinate. Little wonder that so many have held on so tenaciously to the separation of fact and value. Without this separation, man is thrown back on his own decisions. But we must realize that there is no alternative to this; we must begin again to trust man, as the early Enlightenment did. And this will mean learning to live with a tentativeness in both ethics and science. This would be a secularized ethics . . . it would go beyond all absolutisms toward a true human freedom. And this relativist ethics would keep the best of Kant—it would be tentative and transactional; it would keep the best of Hegel—the emphasis on process and historical changeability that he so timidly put forth. Surely this is as compelling a picture as we need to show how distinctive the science of man is, and how resolute we must be to insist on its radically different structure. . . .

With the curse of our Enlightenment paradox, and with the ponderous problem of giving reason half a chance in our staggeringly irrational world, we have cause to feel wistful over the prospects of a science of man as anthropodicy. We might well echo Erasmus's complaint: "Although I am aware that this custom is too long accepted for one to hope to be able to uproot it, yet I thought it best to give my advice in case things should turn out beyond my hopes." But today there is no one man who is giving advice, or hoping beyond hope that the habits of centuries be uprooted. The whole Enlightenment speaks potentially through the voice of every social scientist, trying fumblingly to praise man. This is the soul, as Durkheim so well put it, that lives in the conscience of scholars, the soul of a science that has long been ignorant of itself.

The Second Great Step in Human Evolution (1968)*

WE ARE NOT SURE WHEN IT HAPPENED—a million or many millions of years ago—but we know that somewhere in the deep of prehistory, man developed out of an apelike animal. We know too that this development came about through the acquisition of word symbols, or language. It seems probable that language grew up in group hunting and scavenging in open grasslands: as the apelike animals pursued their search for game they developed increasingly more complex signals and calls. In the process they perfected their weapons; their brains developed as the versatile new word sounds came into use; their consciousness of one another sharpened as their perception of the environment became more rich and systematic. Finally, with the development of nouns, proper names, and pronouns they came to have a consciousness of themselves, of their careers and destinies on this planet. And so, where once there had been only an animal-like blind and reflexive following out of instinctive drives, there now emerged a self-conscious, self-objective type of existence. ... [It] represented not only a change in modes of dealing with the environment, but a change in the basic structure of humanoid animals.

None of the subsequent great 'revolutions' achieved a change in structure—neither the agricultural, nor the scientific, nor the industrial; nor the political revolutions of our time. I insist on the importance of this fact, because it was not until modern times that the second great crisis in basic structural change made itself felt, presenting itself as the next challenge of evolution. In other words, some tens of millions of years elapsed before a new evolutionary problem arose, one which had to be negotiated by the emergence of a new type of human animal. . . . [D]evelopment of the symbolic

*Original, full text: E. Becker, "The second great step in human evolution. *Christian Century,* January 31: 135-139 (1968). Copyright © 1968 The Christian Century Foundation. Reprinted with permission from the January 31, 1968 issue of *The Christian Century.*

modes of behavior that marked the first great advance was an ambiguous achievement. For the symbolic modes were built into the human animal—a highly sensitive, emotional, anxious, group-living animal; one whose greatest fear in infancy was separation from the mother; one whose greatest need was for care and love and approval by the group. The human animal was characterized by his utter inability to stand alone. The symbols and words that enabled him to meet his physical needs, the pronouns and proper names that gave him his vital sense of self, represented at the same time a claim laid upon him by the group. His actions, his sense of self, his security were achieved by uncritical performance according to the world view in which he had literally been programmed.

This, too, is well enough known; but again recognition of the deeper level of what was at stake in the achievement must be insisted on. *The symbolic mode was not a real step in attainment of freedom from the natural order: man had abandoned instinctive behavior only to be symbolically reinstinctivized.* That phrase is clumsy, but use of it seems to be the only way to conceptualize what actually happened. The anxiety-prone higher primate overcame animal instincts only to fall slave to the symbol-reflexes of his trainers and his group. His conceptions of the world, of nature, of himself; his emotions, his sense of right and wrong—all these he arrives at as reflexively and uncritically as a cat tenses to pounce on a bird. In this fact lies the meaning of the great Freudian revolution in modern thought, of the *Oedipus complex* that Freud discovered.

The achievement of post-Freudian thought has been to strip the Oedipus complex of the narrow sexual connotations with which Freud surrounded it. We now understand that complex as a synonym for the early conditioning process to which each child is subject, for the world view which is implanted in him, for the unknowing barter that each child makes when he exchanges his promise of independent thought and action for the security that comes with functioning as his trainers have mapped the course. . . .

It was Alfred Adler who saw more truly what the basic dynamic of the Oedipus complex was—that it was a problem of authority and power, not of sex. Recently, Erich Fromm has reiterated this more true and sober thesis. Adler taught us the real secret of man's slavery, and the origin of it, more straightforwardly than did Freud. As I have written elsewhere, according to Adler, the basic situation of the child is one of natural inferiority in the face of an overwhelming and superordinate world. In order to overcome this inferiority, the child plunges ahead, trying to fashion his own distinctive powers. But since the child has no cognitive grasp of what his life-style is, he is actually deriving his sense of power uncritically. Or, put another way, he is deriving his sense of power vicariously, from a way of being in the world that is not his own, since it is not under his control. The result is tragic, and puts the stamp on man's fate: the adult finds himself rooted in a source of power that literally controls him; he is determined by his unknowing choice of a *model of power.* The tragic paradox, then, is that instead of overcoming his early inferiority, the child merely exchanges it for a semblance of power, a power that is not his own, but that is delegated to him by the models that he uncritically follows. The struggle of man against man, the terrible evil that men will unleash on their fellows, stems from this unconscious rooting of their own felt powers: they will fight to the death to protect the models of power on which their lives are predicated. To lose the ground of their delegated powers is to lose what they feel to be the right of their own lives.

When we phrase the second great crisis in evolution in these sober terms, we not only express essence of the achievement of modern psychology but we also bind together 2000 years of Western thought. We know that derivations of power and authority are not limited to models of men that we might uncritically follow, but extend to ways of life and to things: to the acquisition of money and goods, to technical manipulations and the worship of quantity and speed, to reliance on arms and uniformed ranks of men—in a word, to any fetishized ordering of the world that has a superordinancy over our own feeble and finite selves.

After Augustine, the Reformation spiritualists, the nineteenth-century ontologists, and a purified modern psychology, it has become clear what is at stake is the second great crisis of evolution. The dialogue of nature is one between the unknown energies that emerge from the subjectivity of human organisms and the social-historical structures that contain and constrain that energy. The depths of nature alone contain the possibilities of renewal and freedom. These depths are present in human beings par excellence—but only in those human beings who become open to the widest possible spectrum of action and meaning. The symbolic instinctivization that we call the Oedipus complex is thus plainly the second great hurdle life must overcome in order to give the freest possible expression of itself. Men must throw off the shackles of the automatic ways, action, the constrictions on originality and unique personhood—bonds that society has perpetuated since remotest times. Judeo-Christianity and evolutionary scientific naturalism have posed identical tasks.

The evil that man has unleashed on himself and on his world stems not from a wickedness in his breast but from his uncritical allegiance to the program for action which his society has fumblingly and blindly mapped out. Man earns his feeling of worth by following in the lines of authority and power internalized in his particular family, social group and nation. In [Paul] Tillich's terms, we can say that man is part of an objectified structure instead of a free center, so that the renewing forces of nature herself are choked off and sacrificed to the daily signs of frantic action, smug security, empty-headed complicity. Each human slave nods to the next, each earns his feeling of worth by doing the unquestioned good. And so the best and most 'natural' intentions work the greatest historical and evolutionary evil. 'I only followed orders!' is the phrase that rankles in the breast of modern man.

If we accept the framing of the problem in these terms, the task of education becomes clear, and we can see how momentous it is, how vital its promise. We can also see how colossal is education's 'loss of nerve.' . . . As we can now understand it, this was actually a program for achieving the second step in human evolution. The modern ideal of democracy emerged at the same time and went hand in hand with that program: democracy was the form of government that promised to develop free, independent, self-reliant individuals who would live tentatively and experimentally, changing their institutions to provide a channel for the new energies of each generation. Ideally, the United States Constitution would, as Jefferson saw it, be revised every eighteen years or so to facilitate the activation of those new energies. Democracy and the 'free university' would work together in an unprecedented and inspired task, giving expression to nothing less than the depths of nature.

The failure in both France and Germany of the Enlightenment ideal of knowledge represented a loss of nerve that took a twofold form. The safe and facile pursuit of the fetish of scientific specialism destroyed the synthetic nature of vital knowledge; without such a synthesis, there is no possibility of holding up to society a moral-critical ideal by means of which to guide its struggles. So the university failed both scientifically and morally. Fascism filled the vacuum left by that failure—after all, what is characteristic of fascism is not so much the presence of unscrupulous leaders as the uninformed moral gropings of a slavish and uncritical populace.

The potentially liberating, deeply courageous question for our time, then, is this: What is the moral-critical world view that the universities will impart if they are to provide an island of guiding sanity in the midst of social madness? What is the nature of the nerve we need to save our world, to rejuvenate our society, to give purpose and direction to the stirring idealism of our youth?

The answer, it would seem, lies in imitation of a new, unified, morally informed curriculum based on a natural synthesis of the specialized scientific and philosophical knowledge that has been accumulating since the early Enlightenment. It would be a curriculum that would show man the nature of his alienation, his powerlessness; one that would reveal the constrictions on his freedom, on the full development of his individuality—what I have elsewhere called an 'alienation curriculum.' This is the only synthetic principle that is natural and vital to human knowledge.

The curriculum would explore the dimensions of alienation in the three areas where it exists: (1) The alienation that results from one's early training and indoctrination—the Oedipus complex broadly conceived; (2) the alienation that results from the blind and uncritical functioning of the social institutions—the fetishized games that are played in each society, that bind men's loyalties and work to unman each new generation before it has even a chance to discover its own new designs and purposes; (3) the alienation that results from the conditions of earthly life itself—man's finitude and his ambiguities, as Tillich in particular has detailed them.

The aim of this curriculum, taken as a whole, would be to overcome fetishization of human powers and human consciousness, so that the greatest possible number of people could develop new meanings, could expand the horizon of the human quest to embrace questioning of the purposes of creation. Only such a curriculum would suffice to breathe life back into the universities and hold out hope for social rejuvenation. It would give young people a sense of their own significance, a chance for true heroism and dedication, by bringing them to a thorough understanding of what is wrong with their lives and their world and of where they must look for improvement, for the broadest possible spectrum of meaning. The university would become the locus of the most informed and responsible criticism of the nation itself. It would become the source of design for the nation's deeper ideals. . . .

Nothing less than this will do if we are not to go the way of German education and society in the 1920s and 1930s. Nor does such a program reflect the sin of *gnosis* that Eric Voegelin and others have held up as the real failure of our time. The Enlightenment ideal of the liberation of human subjectivity through the pursuit of reason did not fail because it was false, but because it was never really used. Our sin has been rather one of uncritical *gnosis*, of value-free *gnosis*. . . .

We know that we cannot bring into being a world in which sanity can reign unchallenged and in which self-expansive pleasure can be assured for the masses of men. At least the lesson of our age seems to be that the social arena is one of struggle, inequality and irrationality. And there seems to be no way to overcome this situation except by revolution, which in turn leads to a centralized statism that itself crushes the human spirit. But this does not mean that a utopian stance by the universities is unrealistic or unseemly. On the contrary, we must believe more strongly than ever in the 'instrumental utopianism' that stems from 2,500 years of Western thought—the conviction that we must become as rational as we can, as critical as possible of our social arrangements; that we must continue to design, rework, and uphold a synthetic ideal as a vision for masses of men.

We know that this will not achieve the great community of man under God; we realize that it is only an instrumental utopianism that can avoid disaster, that can prevent the death of mankind. And this is its great potential benefit. A moral-critical ideal based on our most vital knowledge then becomes a way of transacting dialectically with a fundamentally irrational and evil world; it helps to hold that world somewhat in balance—to 'save it from itself,' from its own plunge toward destruction.

Reason, then, is not the dream of utopia; what we strive for is rather a *utopian holding action* to help assure continuation of a social pluralism of incompatible forces. Man's reason then would have a role suited to its true powers in the face of the infinity and multiplicity of the universe. It would not order that universe once and for all for the benefit of man, but it would fulfill the more modest task of sustaining man in the face of overwhelming and unmanageable forces, while God and nature continue their unfathomable work. In this way, the Western dream of reason would eventuate in a natural merger with the great Judeo-Christian and Eastern philosophies of history. . . .

What is really at stake, as I hope the greatest possible number of people will come to realize, is nothing less than the question of evolution itself: either we will succeed in bringing new meanings out of the subjectivities of human organisms as they now are, or this animal himself will be sacrificed to a new surge of destruction and creation. In theological language, he will be driven out of the body of sin, rather than saved through it.

Chapter 6

THE END OF OPTIMISM

The Perspective of the Present Time (1971)*

WHEN WE LOOK BACK OVER THE DISCIPLINE OF [American] sociology since [Albion] Small began it at the turn of the century, we are left with an astonishing realization. Whatever Small's alternating misgivings . . . the discipline nonetheless succeeded in becoming what Small wanted most of all, the objective study of social life. We can appreciate the extent of this success by citing the most astonishing demonstration of objectivity possible for man, an objectivity that sociology achieved when it uncovered for man the social-fictional nature of his own life-meanings. What *Homo sapiens* needed as much as the air he breathes—the symbolically contrived meanings that keep his action moving forward and give him an imagined sense of his own worth—was revealed to him in all its social, historical, and cultural artificiality. The eighteenth century began the conquest of this last and most complex constraint on the human spirit by showing the relativity of social customs. The twentieth century completed it by showing exactly how an artificial world view became the very heart of the acting self. This is a conquest that science had to snatch almost literally from the heart of the human spirit. . . . This is actually the unraveling of the riddle of the 'social forces' with which American sociology began and with which it was so plagued in its beginnings. And here again Small was right when he said in 1910 that it would take all the disciplines to converge on the central core of human conduct, and that sociology could not do it alone. . . .

Are we saying that this is what sociology should be, that all research should focus only on what Small called 'radical problems,' that sociology should be social criticism? No, hardly that. We know how many odd and seemingly inverted kinds of scientific work it takes to know the social reality, how the idiosyncratic scholar's preoccupations one day turn out to be meaningful in a larger theoretical scheme. Above all, we are not forgetting the great historical paradox of social science, the main lesson that we have drawn from Small's career. Our omission seems to be that we have overlooked the paradox almost entirely, and this at a time when national and world events should be causing us to live more in the teeth of it than ever before. In the final analysis, only the community of scientists can decide what form their science shall take. But the lesson of Small's life is that in the social sciences today we must go back to history to find the controlling facts for these kinds of decisions; these facts do not emerge from the day-to-day disciplinary work.

If social scientists were to clarify the shape of their science, using historical bearings, perhaps we would achieve what Victor Branford called for: group consciousness of a heritage and trust around which a political party of social scientists might be formed, and which would include their supporters in other sciences and the intelligent public at large. It would advocate legislation based on the best agreed social theory. (To judge by recent editorials in the journals of the 'hard' sciences, one could expect a considerable rally of support from the other sciences to a social-science political group. Many physical and natural scientists are literally pleading for a healing of the perennial rupture between science and society, and they know that somehow only social science can provide it.)

In the U.S. today, we are able to judge the extent of the default of social scientists, who do not group themselves professionally and organizationally around certain principles and programs of social action. Our leaders and lawmakers consequently see no responsible scientific opposition group whose principles and programs they might want to take into account. This failure of the sprawling organizations of social scientists to support their own best-considered knowledge means that when catastrophes do come, our society will be deprived even of the recourse that primitives had. As we noted earlier, they turned to their seers for advice on which of the old ways to change and what policies to adopt. Our social scientists have gracefully avoided the only role proper to them, that of repositories of scientific wisdom in social affairs.

We can come to at least one conclusion without equivocation: a unified social science in the Enlightenment vision, or a national university in the vision of Jefferson, would have plenty of copies of Veblen's, Small's, and Mills's studies in 'functional political science,' and it would pass these copies around for urgent reading to government officials at all levels. And we are certainly saying that in a truly experimental democracy, as envisioned by Jefferson and his heirs up to Dewey, the legislators and executive branch would be eager to read and digest these facts, eager to study their interrelations, and eager to apply them to the ongoing formulation of law and the pursuit of social justice.

President Eisenhower's famous warning to watch out for the military-industrial complex was an intimation, however faint, of the original role of social science in government. But instead of being a fleeting afterthought to a military-diplomatic career, it would be a central preoccupation of a whole body of people in Washington, continually studying and advising on the national condition. Then we would not have to lament with Veblen that we know what is wrong but can do nothing, or with Mills that our best enjoinders and programs are swallowed up in silence as the nation spins on in its uncritical career.

Finally, we can say without any fear of contradiction that a society which is willing to apply social science in the active process of changing its own vested-interest institutions has never yet been seen on the face of this planet. It would be a true democracy, and it would eagerly offer its highest rewards to men like Albion Small who would radically question every single thing, except the sanctity of the individual human spirit.

The Road Back to the Science of Man (1971)*

THE SCIENCE OF MAN GREW OUT OF THE CRISIS of the eighteenth century, and the nineteenth century inherited the crisis. It was a moral crisis. The medieval world view had loosened its hold on society, and now there was nothing to replace it. Whereas the Church had offered the one thing that man needs as much as the air he breathes—a dependable code of behavior for himself and his fellow man—it was precisely this that was now wanting. Society was headed for the kind of chaos that *Homo sapiens* fears most: the chaos of undependable and immoral behavior in his fellow men, the chaos of unregulated, irresponsible social life.

The science of man, let it be emphasized once and for all, had the solution of this moral crisis as its central and abiding purpose. Why build a science of man in society? In order to have a sound basis for a new moral creed, an agreed, factual body of knowledge that men of good will could use to lay down laws for a new social order. When we get a more or less reliable and reasonably rich knowledge of what man is and how things came to be as they are, we will have the basis for a new morality. Not a supernatural morality, like the defunct one of the Church, but a positive morality based on empirically demonstrated facts. This was Comte's vision, and his whole raison-d'etre, and Comte was merely carrying out the mandate of the eighteenth century. . . .

The Twofold Approach to the Problem of Freedom

We have been able to answer simply the question, 'What is the larger theoretical critical framework to which we must turn to get back to the fundamental questions on which the science of man began?' It is the answer to . . . the whole contemporary failure of the various disciplines to be humanly relevant in our time, or in any time. When we ask what caused things to develop as they are now, how man in society got to be as he is, the only relevant principle must be the principle of human freedom; the only possible synthetic framework must be one that explains differences in human freedom in society and history.

*Original, full text: *The Lost Science of Man* by Ernest Becker. Copyright © 1971 by Ernest Becker. Reprinted by permission of George Braziller, Inc.

A. The Origins of Inequality

Whenever we turn to a truly significant question—one that illuminates for us a clear path through the maze of scholarly accumulated work, through the subtleties of philosophical logic, through the vested interests and narrow visions of any group—we sense the great presence of Jean-Jacques Rousseau. It is truly amazing how he had conceptualized what is basic in our social scientific dilemmas. Do we want to know how to read history for a moral enjoinder? Very simple, answers Rousseau. Read history as the saga of the origin and evolution of human inequalities. Read history as the development of the exploitation of man by man.

In his famous *Discourse on the Origins of Inequality,* Rousseau postulated a primitive state of man, in which there existed no exploitation or unhappiness. The inequality began when one man laid claim to a piece of land and called it 'mine,' and the whole mad tourbillion of history began. Man is born pure and innocent, said Rousseau, but he is corrupted by what he learns in society. The primitive state, the state of nature, should thus be held up as an ideal to measure the whole gamut of vicissitudes that man undergoes in the artificial world of so-called civilized life.

We can have no true idea—unless we have given long thought and study to the problem—how world-shaking this simple speculation of Rousseau's was. It gave rise to endless speculations and an incredibly voluminous and long tradition of empirical work, which stretched through the whole nineteenth century up to the present day. It influenced Kant to make his own speculations about the origin of things; it influenced Marx in his reading of history as the history of economic exploitation; it influenced Proudhon when he pronounced, 'Property is theft'; it influenced the Scottish philosophers to study and speculate on the problem; it actually determines the nature of Russian anthropology today. And, finally, it may help us to reorient ourselves, at least in part, to the proper framework of synthesis for the science of man.

Let us try to hit some of the high points in this extremely rich and complex tradition and so make some sense out of it. Naturally, I must limit myself to a very small part of all the work that this tradition encompasses, partly to keep my essay manageable, and partly through sheer ignorance and helplessness in the face of it. It literally crams our library stacks and would take a lifetime to go through.

One of the thorniest and continuing debates on Rousseau's speculation on the state of nature has been over just what he meant by it, how seriously he took it. . . . [James B.] Monboddo in 1784 had a correct understanding, which must today still be ours, that Rousseau meant the *state of nature* to be an ideal model of the elemental condition of man. . . . The eighteenth century began with a search for the primitive and used him as a standard to show up the corruptions of effete, civilized life. The debate raged in the philosophes around Rousseau, and he immortalized it by giving it literary and scientific form. He sent voyagers looking for the state of nature and for the original nature of man, which he had pronounced innocent. As we noted earlier, Kant agreed that such a voyage was properly called an 'anthropological' one. Perhaps the most recent noted anthropologist to make such a voyage was Claude Levi-Strauss, who went to the Amazon. But the major problem of which we are now speaking was the one of the precise origins of inequality, and this is the tableau that we promised to sketch in vague outline. . . .

The question we set out with was the search for a critical model by which to measure the differences in human freedom in society and history. And in order to get a grip on this problem we began with Rousseau's own answer in his idea of the origin of inequality through private ownership of land. We are interested in those writers whose work was aimed at this question and who wanted to study the origin of inequality for a moral purpose, namely, as a critique of the contemporary rule of private property over the lives of men and the oppressive effect and consequences of class differences. This is the vital tradition, and from it we must of course leave out the names of all the optimistic unilinear evolutionists, all the apologists for Western, *laissez-faire,* economic man. Thus we must stop and note that there are two distinct currents in the nineteenth-century search for the origins of civilized society:

1. The current stemming from Rousseau, which saw civilization as an evil based largely on economic exploitation and class differences established by coercion to maintain privilege.

2. The current stemming from [Adam] Ferguson, [John] Millar, Adam Smith, through [Herbert] Spencer, [Edward B.] Tylor, and the rest, who understood how inequality got started but who concluded that it did not matter once it had begun, since its fruit—Western civilization—was worth all the evil that came out of it. Thus Ferguson said that primitive equality was fine, but man had to blur it out in order to progress, and property is the progress. Kant belongs in this current too, since he reckoned that on the whole the evil of inequality is outbalanced by the good that resulted from it. Man had achieved too much to bemoan the price he had to pay. This was, in a sense, the precursor to Hegel's whole philosophy of history as the unfolding of human freedom.

I do not mean to imply that this second current comprised only rosy optimists and empty-headed apologists for property and its inequalities. This would be far from the truth. Adam Smith's vision called for reforms and deep-going economic measures—for example, the idea of a tax on land value that was later made famous by Henry George and his followers. The intent of this tax was precisely to do away with historical injustices in a gradual, legal, nonviolent way. Alas, it was already too radical and threatening to the mad, scrambling new society in the nineteenth century; today it would place Smith among the ultra-leftists. Smith's heirs failed to carry through an intelligent program of political economy and instead put their trust in the institutions they already had, hoping these would magically assure the development of freedom through plenty.

Today we know that human freedom has not at all 'unfolded,' rather that what little there is risks 'folding up' entirely. The radical element in Smith's vision has remained a museum piece, and it fell to people like Fourier, de Laveleye, Engels,

Marx, Oppenheimer, and Veblen to insist that commercialism was not compatible with human freedom. . . .

[T]he tradition which tried to use the origin of inequality as a critical scientific model failed. And when we take in the whole sweep and breadth of the work that went into it, and the stature of the men who contributed to it, we can see that this failure was an historically momentous one. It meant nothing less than the abandonment of Rousseau's vision and the challenge laid down to the science of man.

The crash of the empirical-theoretical edifice that set out to prove scientifically the miscarriage of the economic development of society is a crash that still rumbles in the background of modern anthropology. So we must be very clear about exactly what happened and what was at stake. On the surface it may look as though it sufficed to argue back and forth on empirical aspects of the problem of the origin of the state. But this is only on the surface; it obscures what is at stake at a deeper level of the philosophy of social science. At this deeper level, the matter was already clear before the critical anthropological tradition of this century. . . .

By the time we get to the critical anthropology of this century, not only primitive communism but most of the other components of the origins of inequality paradigm are called into question. Did the state originate in war? Well, it was evident to many that on the primitive level there are often very peaceful mergers of clans and families. . . . It has been fairly well settled that the origin of the state out of a uniform primitive communism based on coercive methods simply cannot be proved. And it cannot be proved for two reasons. In the first place, 'the reality is too complex,'. . . [and secondly] what happened in prehistory cannot be historically documented. And so the origins of inequality paradigm, which Marx, Engels, Oppenheimer, and the whole Rousseau tradition tried to convert into a truly scientific problem, simply failed to carry any scientific weight. 'Not convincing' was the expert judgment.

But alas for those who find Rousseau antipathetic. He is not to be disposed of so easily, as the never-ending volumes on him and his work that stuff our library stacks so eloquently attest. As we are learning today from the new and tougher historians of science, a scientific problem has never been historically merely a scientific problem. . . .

There is something deeper at stake in the origins-of-inequality paradigm than merely its failure to marshal sufficient empirical weight. To make a complex matter simple, what is at stake is whether the community of social scientists want a moral-critical theory of their own social system, or whether they want an apologia for that system, which allows them to continue blithely with their narrow, disciplinary empirical work. Stated this baldly, my position may appear perverse, but the quandary is there for all to see. . . . By the time we get to someone like [W. C.] MacLeod and his 1931 book, *The Origin and History of Politics,* it is painfully obvious where the professor stands. The origin of the state can be explained without the intervention of "conquests, magic, or necessary economic organizational influences." How can they better be explained? By the "psychophysical character of the leadership type of animal [a character which is] not acquired, but inherited. Families of leaders tended to produce leaders continuously." MacLeod's basis for rejecting the conflict theory was that it happened too far back in history to be proved; his hypothesis also cannot be proved for the same reason, but, says he, it is rendered inherently probable because of the improbability of the alternate theories!

When we are treated to such grotesque exercises in logic, we know that something deeper is at stake, whether we find these exercises in a 'scientific' textbook or in a political speech on Vietnam as the war to end all guerrilla wars. And the deeper dilemma, as we said above, is whether or not we wish to opt for a scientific theory that is critical of present social arrangements. This is the whole lesson of Rousseau's tradition and of Rousseau himself. If we have a stake in deep-going social change based on a critical model of present social arrangements . . . [if] we want to use social science to help us to understand what is killing us, what is causing us to fail to adapt to the new challenges of our historical period, then we will accept and be willing to work under even a sketchy theory as long as it gives us a suggestive picture of our plight. . . . If we do not want this, then we can consider that the . . . critical-historical matter would then be settled once and for all.

The Rousseau tradition, of course, was partly at fault. It failed to heed Hume's great caution that you cannot read nature (or history) for moral precepts on which automatically to base your conduct. Marx, Engels, Oppenheimer, and their school erred in thinking that it was enough to build a convincing historical argument and that men of good will would thereby be moved to change the existing social structure. But we saw that they were not moved. You cannot read history for support of social ideals in any conclusive way. You can only find clues to what you think is desirable. If we stay on the level of the ideal, we can find cases to support it; if we try to make it a general empirical law, then we always find cases that are exceptions, and the law is thereby discredited. A reading of history, as the symbolic pragmatists have conclusively taught us, is always the gathering of facts under a point of view.

The fallacy of 'originism,' the nineteenth-century search for precise origins of all and any aspects of human development and social life, was not so much that the origins are veiled in prehistory and thus can never be found. The fallacy was that even if they could be found they are only tangential to the main thrust of symbolic-critical history. As we saw . . . if we do not accept a certain moral and critical stance toward present conditions, then no amount of theory or fact on the origin of things can sway us. The whole lesson of the Rousseau tradition is that it was an ideology for the liberation of man from the malfunctional institutions of society, and this ideology is something that you opt for. The moral disquiet that the individual may feel in any particular epoch is not in the 'nature' of the epoch; it is in his own emotions and dispositions, as Hume taught us. For Metternich, war was moral progress. How can you argue scientifically against this? The challenge that Rousseau flung at the science of man was, in sum, the enjoinder to opt for a better world and to accept whatever clues to betterment it could find. But his tradition failed to deal sufficiently with the armor that society provides to cover the sensitivities of lesser men. And the masses as well as the leaders of the twentieth century, in politics as well as, alas, in science, are for the most part such lesser men.

It is only in the light of the failure of this part of Rousseau's tradition and the reasons for that failure that we can get a bearing on our present situation. We have an excellent accumulation of empirical and theoretical materials, but we no longer know what to do with it; we have no basis of organization. . . . Generally speaking, what is meant these days by 'synthesis' is encyclopedic hodgepodge, conveniently placed between a limited number of covers and inconveniently priced for the scholar. The simple fact has to be repeated again and again, because most social scientists seem to ignore it: a synthesis means an organization of disparate data that is intimately linked together by being fused with a single, organizing principle. What is lacking [currently] is precisely the synthetic principle that would give unity and immediate relevant weight to the historical panorama of human development. As we know so well by now, this principle has to be a moral one, since the science of man itself is in its own origin and nature a moral problem. And the moral organizing principle for the whole tradition of historical synthesis has to be the one set down by Rousseau: we must study historical inequality in the processes of its evolution in order to attack the problem of human freedom in our time. Nothing else will do to organize and make humanly relevant the welter of accumulated facts on man in nature and history.

The contemporary tragedy in the science of man is that there is no longer any community of scientists that would accept a social-critical theoretical model for its science. The moral burden of early anthropology has been forgotten, and the arguments that now rage are only about fact, value-free fact. The new stirring in anthropology ... is attempting to make evolution again respectable . . . by showing it in all its multilinear diversity and complexity. But this historical reconstruction risks becoming the coldest and most detached of tasks, as if we anthropologists who did it were of another species or from another planet. It is as though it were not our story! . . .

[Soviet-Marxist] scientists have properly accused the West of dissipating the original vision and promise of the science of man; but in turn they are guilty of limiting this vision to only one of its aspects. As a result—need it be said?—their social scientists find themselves as much in servitude to the state and to its uncriticized social arrangement as do ours. In order to break through this impasse, we will have to again remind ourselves of the contemporary relevance of the vision of Rousseau and turn to him in order to find the basis for a full examination of the problem of human freedom. As we said in the very beginning of this section of our essay, the problem of freedom has a twofold aspect. We have covered the first one, the origins of inequality, and we have been able to judge its explanatory power, its great historical importance, as well as its inadequacy. Let us now turn to the second aspect.

B. The Primitive Ideal Model as a Critique of the Present Time

The origins of inequality paradigms fail, then, because they are not enough of a critical measure to illuminate the constrictions on human freedom in society today. They only show us what happened, or rather speculate on what happened, in some distant time. And what we need to know in order to have a fully vigorous moral imperative for the present time is what is 'killing us' now. We need a secular moral code that answers to the problem of evil in society, just as the Middle Ages, whose problem we inherited, had their theocentric code. The model that we would use to measure the shortcomings of present social institutions would have to be an ideal image of man. It would have to be an image based solidly on what we know about human nature, on empirical fact; yet it would have to be a constructed model, going beyond man as he is to man as we wish him to be. This would give us something to aim at, something always to be attained; yet because it would be based on known facts about human nature, it would be more persuasive than a mere fantasy. We would hold up to man an image of the most developed person, the highest individuality, and at the same time the other image that keeps the tension of the paradox: an image of the most communal, equalitarian society. Thus it would serve both as a critique of the present and as a utopian figure to draw our best efforts.

This is the composite vision that Rousseau had in mind when he spoke of the *ideal of the primitive*. The use to which he wanted it put was the utopian, social-critical use. There has been much dispute about what Rousseau meant in these state-of-nature speculations, as we noted earlier. But, as we said, the matter is quite clear. He used the ideal type in the same way that Plato had done in *The Republic*. The confusion is not Rousseau's but belongs to those who lost the Enlightenment vision of what was generally known as *ideal-real science*. This in itself is a great and neglected chapter in the history of ideas, this loss of the ideal-real dialectic in social science in the twentieth century. Its meaning was very clear. . . . For [Max] Weber, the ideal model was a fictional accentuation of empirical reality, created for the purpose of being able to gain some kind of conceptual grip on that reality. It was a way of including many disparate kinds of data into one sharp imaginative mold—whether or not this imaginative construction was exactly true. For the ideal-real science of Enlightenment, on the other hand, the ideal model served a moral-critical purpose as well as a scientific-conceptual one. It not only united disparate data, but also served to answer such pressing moral dilemmas as: *What is the highest developed individuality? The 'good life'?*

For example, in the days when political science still partook of the Enlightenment quest, it was an ideal-real science that sought to answer one basic and central question, the question posed right at the beginning of modern political science by Aristotle: *'What are the forces, as far as we know them now, that maintain or destroy states?'* The 'real' aspect of this question is the empirical data gathered on the actual forces that are destroying a given state. But these data cannot be given meaning unless they are played off against an 'ideal' aspect, namely, what social forms would be necessary in order to make a new and intelligent adaptation to present historical conditions?

The important point that I wish to make is that without the 'ideal' or critical aspect of social science, the 'real' aspect is dissipated into an endless search for data, an infinite multiplication of special, technical problems; there is nothing to bring them into focus. J. L. Myres, who early in this century reminded us of Aristotle's question as the basis for political science, went on to bemoan the complexity of the problem: "But if a young student of political science were to set himself to this life work, where could he turn for his facts? What proportion of the knowable things about human societies . . . could he possibly bring into his survey, without a lifetime of personal research in every quarter of our planet?"

The only answer to this is that he must look for the facts that reveal most directly the possible failure of his own political system to meet present world conditions. He must, as we said earlier, try to find those facts that explain why he is in danger of 'being killed.' Political science would then answer the question of the destruction of states anew in each historical epoch, so that citizens might take preventive action. This is why political science, if it is truly functional and dynamic, is inseparable from critical sociology. It is no surprise that modern political science, having forsaken the Enlightenment tradition, is no longer able to answer Aristotle's question in a truly scientific way. In order to answer it, political science would have to abandon its posture as a narrowly empirical discipline, 'realistically' studying political behavior, and instead join with a critical sociology that offers an ideal-real conception of the total social system. It is an interesting speculation, and I think an accurate one, to say that the best contemporary political science has tried to keep its vitality in a way that exempts it from coming to grips with its Enlightenment mandate by 'including' the Enlightenment quest within a more 'sophisticated' and superordinate vision.

I am thinking here of political theorists like Hans Morgenthau and his 'realistic' political science, derived from Reinhold Niebuhr's vision of man. And Niebuhr, as we well know, aimed particularly to show in his life work the failure of the Enlightenment in modern thought. Thus, what these people are saying in effect is that states will be states because man will be man, and power is power, and corruption is eternal in the realm of finitude. In order to be realistic, the political theorist must align himself with certain of the power thrusts of his national state, since this is the only way to 'realistically' promote its more basic humanistic values against the totalitarianism and the untempered power of other states. The Nazi epoch is held to be the paradigm for this mature consciousness. Today, we can in our turn judge this new Greek-Christian 'realism'; its bankruptcy is nowhere more apparent than in Morgenthau's support of the Diem regime in South Vietnam. It is a bankruptcy that Niebuhr himself now seems to realize in his latest writing; but if he was a 'prophetic voice in our time' in the 1930s, as Tillich and others claimed, it is very clear that his time is past and he is no longer speaking intelligibly to the present world crisis.

This failure results, as we had every right to expect, specifically from the overdose of 'realism' that slighted the necessary ideal-critical stance of the Enlightenment. These gentlemen spoke as though ideals had no prominent place in political science. The fitting comeuppance was given to Morgenthau by McGeorge Bundy on the televised national teach-in over Vietnam in the spring of 1965. What right, said Bundy, had Morgenthau to imagine himself any better expert on Vietnam than anyone else, since he had already made the erroneous prediction on backing the Diem regime. Morgenthau was nonplussed; he was a realist being realistically judged. In other words, by allying himself with the government's 'realistic' policy, Morgenthau had forfeited the only vantage point that the social scientist might have: the ideal-critical stance, the higher moral judgment.

From all this it should again be very clear that the social scientist's primary attitude is one of social self-criticism. If he abandons it in time of national danger, he must be very sure about the present reality and the precise character of that danger. But if people of the stature of Niebuhr and Morgenthau go astray, perhaps there is no worthwhile caution that can be laid down, except to the young, that they not repeat the mistakes of their elders. Each historical period has its own mandate, and the task of youth is to find out exactly what it is, on its own terms. C. Wright Mills's work is a perfect ideal-real blend of political science and sociology. It gave a coherent picture of the functioning of the American social system with a view to forestalling the destruction of that system in World War III. Alas, the best testimonial to the failure of ideal-real science in the twentieth century is the fact that the social scientists turned their backs on Mills, and now the laboratory of international political events is relentlessly grinding out empirical support for Mills's ideal-real vision.

When we realize that it is precisely the loss of the ideal-real dialectic that characterizes contemporary social science, we can also get an insight into many of our disputes. For example, the continuing problem of the 'primitive' that we noted earlier. Is the matter merely relative, and the primitive no different from modern man? Is modern man just as irrational, or even more so? Is primitive society more or less desirable than modern society? This is a debate that has quietly smoldered since the eighteenth century, as we noted earlier—from the Baron de Lahontan, through Rousseau and the philosophes, Fourier and the nineteenth century, up to modern anthropology today.

It is clear that it is a sterile debate in its usual form. It is obvious, as it was to many in the eighteenth century, that primitive society and primitive man are in some ways superior to modern society and modern man, and in some ways distinctly inferior. The whole matter could be dismissed as relative, which it usually is. But then, look what we miss, what we throw out, namely, the whole collection of data on primitive societies since scientific anthropology began. We have gathered it for a purpose, a moral-critical purpose, as we know so well by now. What we must do in order to make this debate meaningful is to frame it in the terms Rousseau set up, that is, by integrating our knowledge of the primitive into an ideal-critical model of man. In this way, we have a basis for ideal-real science.

Whatever we find in primitive society that stands in judgment of our present conditions becomes a part of our model; whatever we see in communal society that serves as a clue to our deteriorated social arrangements goes into the construction of our model. Since we know that in many ways we have made definite and momentous gains over primitive and traditional society, we cannot limit ourselves to this one model. We need to construct an ideal-real image of man out of all the social-historical materials available to us. In this way, the whole panorama of evolution would make its weight felt. What does it tell us about what is wrong in our present conditions?

The task of social science in all the disciplines today is to proceed to the construction of such an ideal-real science. We must realize that none of our data makes full sense unless it is focused on present problems of human value, and if it is so focused, then even conjectural data become of vital importance. . . . We must have an ideal-real science, then, and a full-field theory of alienation that rests on both aspects of the problem of freedom, as designed by Rousseau. We need the historical reconstruction, as well as the full-blown critique of present social structures. What would such a theory of alienation look like? It would largely be a *historical-social psychology,* a picture of why man has failed to make the freest possible adaptations to new conditions in each historical period. It would take for granted that man could make such adaptations, that there is nothing in his nature that hinders his potential freedom. It would find the evil in social arrangements and in man's failure to act upon his social structure in a liberating way in any particular period. . . .

At the end of this sketch, let us hope that we have been able to argue effectively about one thing at least, that the science of man took root in the vision and moral dilemma of the eighteenth century, and that it was that century, largely in the person of Rousseau, which laid down the lines for the development of a valid Science of Man. I hope that I have also been able to show that this science has as its main task the maximization of both personal freedom and social community, the paradoxical and ambiguous challenge conceptualized by Kant. And, finally, I hope that it is plain that freedom as a scientific problem can only be conceptualized in its twofold aspect.

If we accept all this, we must now add that there is still another sense in which we must get back to the eighteenth century, and once we get back to it in this new spirit we shall discover still a third dimension of the problem of freedom. It is this aspect of the eighteenth century and this third dimension of the problem of freedom that show, perhaps best of all, how pitifully we have narrowed down and dissipated the grand promise of a science of man in society. Let us merely touch upon it now in closing this essay. It will help us draw together our critique of disciplinary fragmentation and specialization, and at the same time help us to see the real ground of our science in the realm of ethics. If we have inherited the problem of the decline of medieval society, then we must make clear that a science of man grounded in a new secular ethics is itself narrow and limited unless it can offer a total vision of reality. In other words, a full-field theory of alienation cannot have its fullest meaning if it is only two-dimensional. It must be not only historical and social but ontological.

Historians of science are now beginning to bring back into prominence something that has long been obscured: while we knew very well that the triumph of Newtonianism in all the sciences was what made the eighteenth century great, what was obscured by this triumph was precisely the countercurrent of a deep and anguished anti-Newtonianism. It is only today that we can again see what was truly at stake in this struggle, simply because we are paying the full price of the sweeping victory of the one-sided Newtonian world view.

Several voices can be heard on this problem—voices in theology, like Reinhold Niebuhr's and Paul Tillich's, voices in the science of man, like Eric Voegelin's, Alfred Weber's, and Albert Salomon's. What they are calling for is a third dimension to the problem of freedom and human action, the dimension that has been slighted and almost forgotten in the great surge of objective, empirical science. It is the dimension of ontology that would once again give central prominence to the only questions capable of guiding life and science: *What is the meaning of life? What is worth striving for? What may man hope for?* Without these questions, as Voegelin has argued with such brilliance and massive scholarship, science itself is sickly and puerile at best. At worst, it is idiotic and actively antihuman.

We should not be surprised that one of the best minds and most colorful of men of the eighteenth century had already given the matter ample voice in his six volumes of *Antient Metaphysics*. Lord Monboddo's whole life was a protest against Newton and the new breed of 'manual philosophers,' what today we would call the new fetishists of science, the foreground manipulators, who lost the depth and background of nature. Monboddo uttered a warning cry not to abandon the Greeks, not to lose the perspective of ontology in philosophy and science. He warned that we need to deepen the merely material approach to man and nature with the spiritual approach; and that we have as our central task the explaining of—and not simply describing—man's condition on earth.

Monboddo saw that beginning with Descartes and Newton, a new type of man and attitude were becoming ascendant, and he was one of the few in the eighteenth century to realize that this new type of man was not necessarily for the good. He launched a massive attack on the new materialist causality that these men were championing, the secondary causality that took the burden of explanation. We now have to be content, warned Monboddo, with part explanation, with part philosophy, what [George] Santayana later called in his criticism of Dewey, *philosophy of the foreground;* manipulative, scientific, existential, experimental philosophy, which slights the background of nature, the *realm of essence* or substance. We need to keep in view, said Monboddo, the Aristotelian problem of final cause, and not merely material cause. We need to try and understand what life is all about, where it is heading. Otherwise, we ourselves will be headless, undirected, trivial men.

Alas for us, the protest represented by Monboddo lost out, and Newtonianism went on to a long victory substantiated by Darwin. It was he who fully legitimated the focus on material cause even in the life science, biology. But today, a century later, there is the new stirring that we noted above, which promises eventually to usher in an entirely new vision of science. Voegelin predicts that perhaps the most important single fact about the first half of this century will be the complete reappraisal of the character of the science of man. . . . This means that we will have a model for the fullest liberation of man by making a complete accusation of social restraints on his freedom. It means that we will have a vision of a new community that would finally provide the fullest context for civilized living. But it means more as well. By reintroducing the dimension of ontology as the ultimate ground of human freedom, our model of man and community will not be a finished model, as the critics of a manipulative science so rightly fear. It will be only a beginning for the creation of a new man out of the still unknown and untapped energies of the life force itself.

In order for this to happen, the science of man, while working toward the new community, would be partly grounded in a creative new myth of the meaning of life . . . a science of man with a vision of community, working in a community that itself creates the new symbols of a new social order. In other words, we would be scientists working within a living myth of the significance of our own science and of our own lives, scientists working with artists—in a sense subordinate to art because partaking of a creative mythology. . . . Perhaps one day we will have the ultimate courage, the courage to affirm a dream that mankind has collectively been spinning and mellowing for over 2,500 years. We would look in vain for more than a few men who have this kind of courage in the corridors of scientific power and prestige in our universities today. Yet, under the pressure of our world social crisis, the numbers are growing: man seems to reach for the conceptions needed to help him survive. The pressure of our present evolutionary crisis is directly upon man's brain. We can more confidently pass on the vision of the Enlightenment to our young today than perhaps at any other time since it was fashioned. The hope of the authentic spirit of ideal-real science, like that of the life that it was meant to serve, lies in the new birth that defies oblivion.

PART THREE

DENIAL OF DEATH AS INTERPRETIVE ORGANIZING PRINCIPLE (1971–1975)

The chapters in this section present selections written during the last years of Becker's life. In terms of his academic career, this was the best time of Becker's life; the reward, we might say, for the previous years when he hung on by his fingernails. A newly formed interdisciplinary program at Simon Fraser University in Vancouver specifically invited Becker to join their faculty. Becker's ideas on human behavior were congealing into the simple but fascinating thesis outlined in his last three books, particularly in The Denial of Death *(1973). Through these works, his contribution was finally being recognized.*

What Becker came to realize was that all along, he had been working on a closure on religion from the perspective of social science. Following Otto Rank, whose writings Becker devoured during these years, Becker suggested that finally, a critical social science must lead us 'beyond psychology' into an embrace of the transcendental realm. This is not the easy merger between science and religion touted in some corners of church or seminary; it is the recognition that life-affirming meaning in human affairs can only come as a gift from that which is itself beyond human affairs. Becker suggested that there was a certain parallel between his work and that of the great Protestant theologian, Paul Tillich; Tillich moved toward closure on the social sciences from the perspective of religion, while Becker moved toward closure on religion from the perspective of the social sciences.

Becker's writings in this period no longer contain the enthusiastic and optimistic undertone of the previous years. But neither is the tone one of a facile world-weariness of the type to which some sobered writers are prone. His writing reflects a genuine horror, in the best sense of the word, concerning the human prospect, and he openly wondered if Homo sapiens sapiens *is truly a viable species. Yet he remained animated in his writing by the hope that reason finally would win out over irrationality, or better said, that by exposing human beings to their own irrationality, they might somehow gain the tools required for change. In short, Becker, sharing in Freud's stoicism in the face of death, also shared in Freud's hope, that somehow, in some way in human affairs, Ego would come to replace Id. This is the gift of grace 'beyond psychology,' which the thinker can only embrace in faith.*

Chapter 7

MEANING AND SELF-ESTEEM

Self-Esteem (1971)*

WE HAVE TAKEN OUR STORY OF MAN'S HUMANITY step by step and are now ready to fit the central piece of the puzzle into place. We saw that the weakest part of Freud's theory was that he did not explain the nature of conscience, what people feel guilty about; but rather he gave us a masterful analysis of the mechanism of the implantation of conscience: of how children learn their sense of right and wrong, and how it plagues them throughout life. In a word, Freud failed to explain satisfactorily human *motives*. . . . But if Freud was wrong about motives it was because he was wrong about biological instincts. And if instincts do not drive man, what then does? The main reason that the great Alfred Adler is still contemporary is that he broke with Freud very early on this problem, when he very clearly saw and strongly proclaimed that *the basic law of human life is the urge to self-esteem*. Once you make this break with Freud, stand up for it openly, and build your theories and clinical interpretations around it, a whole new world of understanding opens up to you. After all, you have laid bare man's motive, which is what Freud himself set out to do. . . .

Self-esteem, as the psychoanalysts say, begins for the child with the first infusion of mother's milk, of warm support and nourishment. The child feels that all is right in his world, and radiates a sense of warm satisfaction. As the ego grows in mastery and develops adroit defenses against anxiety, the child can count on a fairly stable environment that responds to his wishes and that grants him a steady state of well-being. After all, he has shaped himself into the very person who can take for granted continued parental approval and support, because he has largely tailored his action and desires to suit their wishes. Once he has done this, the problem of maintaining self-esteem is also solved. Self-esteem becomes the child's feeling of self-warmth that all is right in his action world. It is an inner self-righteousness that arms the individual against anxiety. We must understand it, then, as a *natural systemic*

*Original, full text: *The Birth and Death of Meaning,* Second Edition by Ernest Becker. Copyright © 1962, 1971 by The Free Press. Copyright renewed © 1990, 1999 by Marie H. Becker. All rights reserved. Reprinted by permission of The Free Press, a Division of Simon & Schuster Adult Publishing Group.

continuation of the early ego efforts to handle anxiety; it is the durational extension of an effective anxiety-buffer. We can then see that the seemingly trite words, *self-esteem*, are at the *very core of human adaptation*. They do not represent an extra self-indulgence, or a mere vanity, but a matter of life and death. The qualitative feeling of self-value is the basic predicate for human action, precisely because it epitomizes the whole development of the ego.

This cannot be overemphasized. It permits us to take the final step in under-standing the experience of socialization: the entire early training period of the child is one in which he learns to *switch modes* of maintaining self-esteem. The child learns painfully that he cannot earn parental approval, or self esteem, by continuing to express himself with his body. He finds that he has to conduct himself according to symbolic codes of behavior in order to be accepted and supported. In other words, his vital sentiment of self-value no longer derives from the mother's milk, but from the mother's mouth. *It comes to be derived from symbols.* Self-esteem no longer takes root in the biological, but in the internalized social rules for behavior. The change is momentous because of what is implicit in it: the child's basic sense of self-value has been largely *artificialized*. His feeling of human worth has become large-ly a linguistic contrivance. And it is exactly at this point that we deem that he has been socialized or humanized! He has become the only animal in nature who vital-ly depends on a symbolic constitution of his worth.

Once this has been achieved the rest of the person's entire life becomes ani-mated by the artificial symbolism of self-worth; almost all his time is devoted to the protection, maintenance, and aggrandizement of the symbolic edifice of his self-esteem. At first he nourishes it in the appraisal of his playmates, and usually at this time it depends entirely on his physical and athletic prowess—overt qualities that other children easily recognize and admire, especially fearlessness. Later it may depend on earning good grades in school, on dressing well, on dancing expertly at the school prom, and so on. Finally, in the twenties one comes to earn his self-esteem by performing in the roles that society provides: doctor, lawyer, corporation man, teacher, engineer, and so on. Then we get our vital sense of inner worth by repeat-ing, *"I am a good doctor, lawyer, engineer. Look at the operation I performed, the business deal I pulled off, the way that beautiful girl looks at me. . ."* and so on. Almost all of one's inner life, when he is not absorbed in some active task, is a traf-fic in images of self-worth.

The Inner-Newsreel

If our first reaction is to shrug at this as an exaggeration, let us try to be hon-est and admit to ourselves what we do most of the time. We run what I like to call an 'inner-newsreel' that passes in constant review the symbols that give self-esteem, make us feel important and good. We are constantly testing and rehearsing whether we really are somebody, in a scenario where the most minor events are recorded, and the most subtle gradations assume an immense importance. After all, the self-esteem is symbolic, and the main characteristic of symbols is that they cut reality very fine. . . .

Everyone runs the inner-newsreel, even if it does not record the same symbolic events. Always it passes in review the peculiar symbols of one's choice that give him a warm feeling about himself: the girl he seduced, the money he made, the picture he directed, the book he published, the shrewd putdown at the cocktail party, the smooth ordering from the menu in the chic restaurant, the beautifully executed piano suite, and so on and on. All day long we pass these images in review, and most of us even in our sleep. The difference is that while we are awake we have some control over the scenario. When the newsreel records a negative image—the slip-of-the-tongue, the loss of money, the bungled seduction, the bad car purchase, the lousy book—we immediately counter the negative image with a positive one, to try to get our self-esteem in balance and onto the favorable side. But while we are asleep the ego is not working, it has no conscious control over the messages we send to ourselves about our sense of worth. Our deeper experience may have on record that we really feel worthless, helpless, dependent, mediocre, inadequate, finite: this is our unconscious speaking, and when the ego cannot oppose any positive images to counteract these negative ones, we have the nightmare, the terrible revelation of our basic uselessness. . . .

When we think about the terror of the nightmare, or the simple disgust of a bad dream, with its confused and degrading images of ourselves, we can see that something really important is at stake here. The scenario of self-value is not an idle film hobby. The basic question the person wants to ask and answer is "Who am I? What is the meaning of my life? What value does it have?" And we can only get answers to these questions by reviewing our relationships to others, what we do to others and for others, and what kind of response we get from them. Self-esteem depends on our social role, and our inner-newsreel is always packed with faces—it is rarely a nature documentary. Even holy men, who withdraw for years of spiritual development, come back into the fold of society to earn recognition for their powers. [Friedrich] Nietzsche said of [Arthur] Schopenhauer that he was a model for all men because he could work in isolation and care nothing for the plaudits of the human marketplace. The implication is that he had his sense of value securely embedded in himself and his own idea of what his work was worth. Yet this same Schopenhauer spent his lonely life scanning the footnotes of learned journals to see whether there was ever going to be recognition of his work. . . . The anthropologist Robert Lowie once said that primitive man was a natural peacock, so open was he in self-display and self-glorification. But we play the same game, only not as openly. Our entire life is a harangue to others to establish ourselves as peacocks, if only on furtive and private inner-newsreel images. Again the brilliant writer teaches us the scientific truth, as did James Thurber in *The Secret Life of Walter Mitty*.

The Psychoanalytic Characterology

If the reader gets a feeling of pathos in all this, it is only logical: after all, the humanization process is one in which we exchange a natural, animal sense of our basic worth, for a contrived, symbolic one. Then we are constantly forced to harangue others to establish who we are, because we no longer belong to ourselves. Our character has become social. Alfred Adler saw with beautiful clarity that the basic process in the formation of character was the child's need to be somebody in the symbolic world, since physically, nature had put him into an impossible position. He is faced with the anxieties of his own life and experience, as well as the need to accommodate to the superior powers of his trainers; and from all this somehow to salvage a sense of superiority and confidence. And how can he do this, except by choosing a symbolic-action system in which to earn his feeling of basic worth? Some people work out their urge to superiority by plying their physical and sexual attractiveness—what the psychoanalysts call the 'Don Juan' character. Others work it out by the superiority of their minds; others by being generous and helpful; others by making superior things, or money, or playing beautiful music, or being an unusual mimic and joke teller; some work it out by being devoted slaves: 'I am a locus of real value because I serve the great man.' Others serve the corporation to get the same feeling, and some serve the war-machines. And so on and on. The great variation in character is one of the fascinations and plagues of life: it makes our world infinitely rich, and yet we rarely understand what the person next to us really wants, what kind of message he is addressing to us, what kind of confirmation we can give him of his self-worth. This is the problem of our most intimate lives—our friendships and our marriages: we are thrown against people who have very unique ways of deriving their self-esteem, and we never quite understand what they really want, what's bothering them; we don't even know what special inner-newsreel they are running. On the rare occasion that we make a breakthrough and communicate about these things, we are usually shocked by how finely they have sliced their perceptions of reality: 'Is *that* what is bothering you?'

The reason scenarios of self-esteem are so opaque even in our closest relationships is embarrassingly simple: we ourselves are largely ignorant of our own lifestyle, our way of seeking and earning self-esteem. Each of us has a more-or-less unique life-style, formed during our early training. And this formation is largely a process of conditioning that begins even before we learn symbols, it is pre-symbolic. As a result, we have no way of getting on top of this process of conditioning, no way to grasp it, because we did not as children know what was happening to us. The child continually loses battles he does not understand. The psychoanalytic characterology is the study of the efforts that the child makes to salvage an intact self-esteem from this confusion. These efforts become his 'mode of being in the world.'

Now, if this mode of being were simply a matter of finding out what symbol-system one had unwittingly chosen in order to get on top of all the burdens of his early situation, we could all fairly easily get self-knowledge. But the sense of right and wrong, our way of perceiving the world, our feelings for it and for who we are, are not a 'mental' matter—they are largely a total organismic matter, as Dewey saw long ago, and as Frederick Perls has recently reminded us. We earn our early self-esteem not actively but in large part passively, by having our action blocked and reoriented to the parents' pleasure. This is what triggers the process of introjection and appersonization, . . . we take large parts of our parents' images and commands into our own self, without, as Perls so well insisted, 'digesting' them, making them an integral part of ourselves that responds to our honest control. As a result, the self is largely a confusion of insides, outsides, boundaries, alien objects, and it is de-centered and split off from the body in some measure. Also, . . . some children are allowed to be more active, others are made to be largely passive: this passivity results in aggravating the self-body dualism in some people. What we call our character, then, is a peculiar configuration of self-other and self-body relationships. The thing that makes the study of character so fascinating and so difficult is that it is largely a matter of sorting out bizarre collages. These are so confused and so personal in the weight of their meanings and symbolisms that it is impossible to do a complete decoding. Only the person himself can really know what experience means to him, only he can feel the quality of his perceptions; and even he cannot know, because these matters are in large part presymbolic, unconscious. That is why analysis, and self-analysis if one wants to work at it, is a task for more than one lifetime—it can really never be finished. What makes the psychoanalytic corpus so compelling from a scientific point of view is that it has mastered the general problem of character by finding recurrent types, gross groupings into which everyone more-or-less fits: oral-aggressive, oral-passive, anal-sadistic, phallic-narcissistic, and so on. In fact, these groupings are universal because there is a limited spectrum of variation in self-worlds, a limited spectrum of self-body differentiation and confusion, and a limited number of ways we can get satisfaction from others. We can rarely know exactly the unique character a given person has, but his mode of earning self-esteem as a way of keeping action moving out of the confusion of the early training period, is more or less identifiable in terms of the basic psychoanalytic characterology.

If we merge it with the characterology developed by [Wilhelm] Dilthey's followers, the modern existentialists, and the data of anthropology, we have a fairly complete cosmography of the inner worlds of men. This is an immense scientific achievement; I daresay that it has a sophistication equal to that of subatomic theory in physics, and perhaps an even greater difficulty. The Nobel people have never rewarded the great innovators in the study of human character, and perhaps rightly so: so far there is no proof that this has anything to do with the progress of man on this planet; and if most people knew these things about themselves it would probably throw whole nations into chaos. Witness the treatment that the brilliant modern student of character, Erich Fromm, receives at the hands of *Time* magazine which dismisses him with the epithet 'marxist-culture quack.' Better to let the matter rest on the fringes of 'respectable' science.

Culture and Personality (1971)*

IF THERE WERE ANY DOUBT THAT SELF-ESTEEM is the dominant motive of man, there would be one sure way to dispel it; and that would be by showing that when people do not have self-esteem they cannot act, they break down. And this is exactly what we learn from clinical data, from the theory of the psychoses, as well as from anthropology. When the inner-newsreel begins to run consistently negative images of one's worth, the person gives up. We see this clearly in depressive withdrawals and schizophrenic breakdowns. I remember one psychiatric patient who had passed his life in review and concluded that he had been 'kidding himself' all along, that he really was nobody. The psychiatric resident did not take this symbolic balance-sheet seriously enough, and considered it merely self-indulgent, pessimistic ruminations—until the patient acted on his self-appraisal and leaped from a sixth-story window. We can never really know when the *metteur-en-scene* will give the whole thing up for a bad job, or when he is merely reviewing and rearranging, so some skepticism is justified. But of one thing we are sure: to lose self-esteem is to lose the nourishment for a whole, pulsating, organismic life. Anthropologists have long known that when a tribe of people lose the feeling that their way of life is worthwhile, they may stop reproducing, or in large numbers simply lie down and die beside streams full of fish: food is not the primary nourishment of man, strange as that may sound to some ethological faddists. So seriously do we take the self-esteem since Adler, that for over a generation we have been working toward theories of disease based on self-esteem.

In a word, we must understand that the self-esteem is vital. When we do, we can take one further step from our discussion in the last chapter, a thrilling step, really, because it gets at the very essence of what man everywhere is truly trying to do. It is wrong to say that man is a peacock, if we mean thereby to belittle his urge to self-glorification, and make it seem a mere matter of vanity and self-display. The constant harangue that we address to one another: 'notice me,' 'love me,' 'esteem me,' 'value me,' would seem debasing and ignoble. But when we tally the sum of these efforts, the excruciating earnestness of them, the eternal grinding-out of the inner-newsreel, we can see that something really big is going on—really vital, as we said. When the child poses the question 'Who am I? What is the value of my life?' he is really asking something more pointed: *that he be recognized as an object of primary value in the universe.* Nothing less. And this more pointed question has ramifications immediately broad and embracing: He wants to know 'What is my contribution to world-life?' Specifically, 'Where do I rank *as a Hero?*'

This is the uniquely human need, what man everywhere is really all about—each person's need to be an object of primary value, a heroic contributor to world-life—*the heroic contributor* to the destiny of man. This seems to be the logical and inevitable

*Original, full text: *The Birth and Death of Meaning,* Second Edition by Ernest Becker. Copyright © 1962, 1971 by The Free Press. Copyright renewed © 1990, 1999 by Marie H. Becker. All rights reserved. Reprinted by permission of The Free Press, a Division of Simon & Schuster Adult Publishing Group.

result of the symbolic constitution of self-worth in an unbelievably complex animal with exquisitely sensitive and effusive emotions. Once you took the general instinct of self-preservation of the lower animals, the basic irritability of protoplasm, the self-identity of the physio-chemistry, the vague pulsation of the warmth of the animal's inner processes, the nameless feeling of power and satisfaction in carrying out his instinctive behaviors—once you took all this and gave it a directive self-control via the ego, and a precise, symbolic designation in a world of symbols, then you resulted in nothing less than the need for heroic self-identity. Self-preservation, physio-chemical identity, pulsating body warmth, a sense of power and satisfaction in activity—all these tally up in symbolic man to the emergence of the heroic urge. Freud saw the psychic nature of these facts, and he tallied them up under the label of narcissism; it was a truly brilliant formulation, and Fromm recently stressed that this is one of his lasting contributions: the exposure of man's utter self-centeredness and self-preoccupation, each person's feeling that he is *the one* in creation, that his life represents all life, and apotheosizes it. Freud saw the universality of narcissism, and revealed the invertedness and the clinical liabilities of it. Adler too studied the neurotic overemphasis on the 'Will to Power,' and made the idea a central part of his formulations. But it was Nietzsche, earlier, who saw the healthy expression of the 'Will to Power' and glory, the inevitable drive to cosmic heroism by the animal who had become man.

We still thrill to Nietzsche, as we do to [Ralph Waldo] Emerson, because they saw that heroism was necessary and good, and that nothing less than the urge to heroism would do to typify the place of man in the animal kingdom. If you are a psychiatrist or social worker, and want to understand directly what is driving your patient, ask yourself simply how he thinks of himself as a hero, what constitutes the framework of reference for his heroic strivings—or better, for the clinical case, why he does not feel heroic in his life. If you are a student of society, and want to understand why youth opts out of the system, find out why it fails to offer them the possibility of real heroism. If you are a child psychologist you already understand the deeper meaning of what we casually and often scornfully term 'sibling rivalry.' This rivalry is not mere competitiveness, or selfishness; it is too bitterly dedicated and all-absorbing to be anything but vital. The child needs to be an object of primary value, and by definition only one person can be primary; and one can only establish primacy in relation to those around him. The parents are out of the contest since they already enjoy supreme power; their task is to dispense it, and in dispensing it they also serve as judges. So one concentrates on his peers before the tribunal. Hence the daily and often excruciating drama lest the child feel devalued, second-best, left-out: 'You put a band-aid on his cut, but you didn't do anything to the cut I got yesterday!' 'Well, you put a smaller band-aid on it.' 'You let her turn two knobs on the stereo, but I could turn only one!' If the parent, understanding what is at stake, indulgently says that his knob was bigger, he will immediately ask to see and minutely compare. And so on and on. The heroic, as we said, is derived only by being primary, and the self-esteem is constituted symbolically, which means that only the finest gradations of meaning can serve as evidence. When we understand sibling rivalry for the critical problem it reflects, we can understand the naturalness of ambition, and the basic benignancy of competitiveness. Children are not vicious animals struggling to dominate rivals, but culture-heroes in the making, desperately trying to stand out.

Culture and Personality

Culture-heroes have to have available to them some kind of heroic action system in which to realize their ambitions, and this symbolic system is what we call 'culture.' Culture is a structure of rules, customs, and ideas, which serve as a vehicle for heroism. It is a logical extension of the early ego development, and the need for self-esteem. The task for the ego is to navigate in its world without anxiety, and it does this by learning to choose actions that are satisfying and bring praise instead of blame. Only in this way can it earn the vital self-esteem that is a buffer against anxiety. Culture provides just those rules and customs, goals of conduct, that place right actions automatically at the individual's disposal. Therefore, if the function of self-esteem is to give the ego a steady buffer against anxiety, wherever and whenever it might be imagined, one crucial function of culture is to make continued self-esteem possible. Its task, in other words, is to provide the individual with the conviction that he is *an object of primary value in a world of meaningful action.*

If we had to detail the way culture constitutes this action, it would look something like this: As the child learns *mine, me,* and *I* from his parents around the age of two, he is already enmeshed in a world that is conventional and no longer natural. Once the child learns that he is an 'I' in relation to others, he has quickly to bolster this discovery by finding out: 'What does this world mean to me, and how do I act in it?' A self-objectifying animal thus has to bring something to his world in order to act in it. An animal whose behavior is governed by purely instinctual patterns of response needs only to act. But once an animal becomes self-conscious, straightforward action is no longer possible. The prescription for conduct free of anxiety is to choose the 'right' thing to do. And, as soon as one course of action becomes 'right' and another 'wrong,' life becomes moral and meaningful. Morality is merely a prescription for choice; and 'meaning' is born as the choice is carried into action.

The child, given a name, learns the names of others. And, his relationship to the other higher primates in his environment comes to differ markedly from that of his subhuman cousins. His relationship to people of the same or of different sex, in different stages of maturity, carries obligations and rights: pure power and energy differences no longer govern conduct. The child discovers that he is a 'boy' and that boys may have certain rights over 'girls'; he may find that he is the 'first-born' boy and that this serial fixation in time carries obligations from which others may be free. The body that he discovers self-reflexively is compared to others, and he learns that genital appendages, while they may not yet be used, are an insignia of a certain status. He learns that this kind of body is to be carried in a certain way, the legs to be held in a certain position while sitting, the skin entitled to certain kinds of decorations or scarifications and not to others.

The self-reflexive animal discovers his body as something which enables him to transact with the world in a certain way. Society uses that body as the source of the most direct cues for action in the cultural plot. As soon as the child is born, a rudimentary genital appendage can already be the reason for great joy or deception on the part of the parents. A good measure of their part in the plot depends on the symbolic value of that appendage. Many cultures have not hesitated to dispose of newborn females—they had no symbolic value onstage. What the psychoanalysts call 'penis envy' is not the chagrin of a female that she was not born a 'superior' male member of the species and thus suffers a 'natural' inferiority. It is, rather, the result of some body comparison to see what an appendage entitles one to be: it is direct evidence about the possibility of primary heroism in an artificial cultural system. Man has chosen to use his physiology for his most direct cues to action, and the cultural drama is a succession of performances based principally on age and sex differences. Societies arrange their members in categories of infant, boy, girl, adult male, adult female, old male, old female. Old English recognized the adolescent whom we have chosen to ignore, with the designations 'lass' and 'lad.' The designation 'old man' in one culture may entitle the actor to enjoy finally the power over others that he has waited a lifetime for—as the aged males of the Australian Tiwi tribe apportioned the young women among themselves. The same designation in another culture may entitle the holder to being left out in the bush for the hyenas to carry off.

I think it is worth adding, in passing, that the child doesn't see things so symbolically straightforward, and so there is a sense in which 'penis envy' may be a real experience for a little girl, though not in the tragic sense that the patriarch Freud thought. I mean that the child lives in a very concrete physical world where he judges differences very primitively according to size and power. He is often told that he will have greater rights and privileges when he 'gets bigger.' The little girl, then, measuring herself carefully for sheer volume against her brother, might really feel 'cheated' of an added fleshy appendage that visibly increases her size, and might want reassurance that this does not prejudice her status: it might be a real anxiety about having been born 'short' in a competition for size and quick growing up that gives special rights. But aside from these natural perplexities, it is obvious that the parents' views and the role that society cuts out for her will far outweigh whatever childhood feelings she might have about being cheated of mere physical size due to added protuberances.

The world of action is structured in terms of: 'What is the person's position, and what behavior can I expect from him as a result of it?' 'What is my position in relation to him, and what behavior does this position entitle or oblige me to?'

These are questions about status and role, the basic prescriptions for action in the human environment. The anthropologist Ralph Linton's detailing of the place of status and role in a culture, and the place of the personality in this scheme, was a milestone in sociocultural analysis. Status and role are basic to an understanding of human behavior because they tell the individual what he should do in a particular social situation, and how he should feel about himself as he does it. The culture, in other words, cannot provide its members with a feeling of primary value in a world of meaning unless it provides a prescription for meaningful action on the part of all. Status and role serve further to make behavior predictable, so that the meaning in everyday life becomes dependable; the individual can count on others to behave according to his expectations. Role and status are a shared frame of reference that makes joint action possible; they are society's scenario for the theatrical staging of the cultural action plot.

And, as in a high school play, everyone scrambles for the lead parts. Identity is inseparable from the role one is assigned. The self-reflexive animal asks continually: 'Who am I? How am I supposed to feel about myself in this situation? How are others supposed to feel about me?' The answer to the last question, particularly, is the most convincing way of finding out who one is. The child derives his identity from a social environment. The social environment remains to his death the only source for validating that identity.

One of the great and lasting insights into the nature of society is that it is precisely a drama, a play, a staging. . . . The child who learns the *I* and begins to refer his action to those around him *is trained primarily as a performer.* His entire life is a training, preparation, and practice for a succession of parts in the plot—parts he can show himself worthy of filling, simply by handling them. Individuals are given parts to play in the status-role system, based on their specialized occupations, their family membership, and the particular associations that they form. Seeing his identity reflected in each of these designations the individual carries with him a sense of value proper to that designation. The designation is a claim for a part to play in the cultural plot. When others recognize that claim, as the culture provides that they do, meaningful motivation and value become an inseparable part of daily action.

The word *status* is not to be confused with status used in the everyday sense, as a position which a few may enjoy but which is denied to most. In sociological terms, everyone has a status, a formalized cue that makes it possible to predict how he will act in a certain situation. It is easy to understand that the culture as a whole has the most to gain from this predictability; life can go on with a minimum of confusion, as the actors navigate on the basis of status cues. Sometimes these cues can be intricately complex. For example, the culture may provide variations in grammatical form to be used in addressing people of various statuses, like the *you* and *thou* of Old English. But the Balinese have seventeen gradations of status language! The only way we might, perhaps, capture the flavor of this is to imagine ourselves talking only in Old English to social superiors, and in Brooklynese to social inferiors. In traditional Japan, two interlocutors remained tongue-tied until a rapid exchange of calling cards gave to each the other's positional cue in the status hierarchy; then, the appropriate language form could be used.

Why does man unnecessarily complicate his life? Because in this very complexity there is a challenge to ego mastery, and a denial of meaninglessness. How else would heroism be possible? The Australian aborigine structured his interpersonal world in the most intricate terms of kinship avoidance, mating taboos, and so on. The individual undoubtedly derives the greatest stimulus from this conceptual ordering, like those in our culture who remember baseball scores from many years back. The more intricate the staging, the more all-absorbing the play. Furthermore, if everything is split down to the finest possible point, there is less chance of chaos. Everyone uses the toilet, some have keys to toilets, and some have keys to 'executive' toilets.

Culture, then, provides man with a highly involuted and meaningful schema of action, which makes fine shades of self-esteem possible. But that is its function on a symbolic level; there is also the physical aspect of man's existence: culture has to provide man with safety as well as self-esteem. This is its other crucial function. Action has to be dependable and predictable. And the area of least dependability in social life is, naturally, people. After all, each person is working out the peculiar scenario of his self-esteem needs, and we never really know what he is about. As [Jean-Paul] Sartre so bitingly puts it: "Hell is other people." The child quickly finds that his environment contains two kinds of objects—thing-objects and person-objects. Thing-objects are dependable, controllable. A schizophrenic child may develop a deep attachment to, say, a radiator, in preference to his mother. Both function, but the radiator more warmly and more predictably. Person-objects, on the one hand, are powerful and capricious. They can be galvanized into hostile mobility seemingly without cause. Suddenly, they are capable of flaring up into a violent, overpowering rage. Thing-objects don't shout back; they have no idling emotional motor. The ego thrives on control, but person-objects, theoretically, are always beyond control. One can never be sure about them—his most dependable inferences about someone can suddenly be violently or humiliatingly baffled. A person-object is a locus of causality, capable of introducing undreamed of events into one's life. The person-object with whom one has lived for years with mathematical dependability may one day calmly slaughter a brood of children.

The problem of 'What will the next person be like' is at the core of human adaptation, because self-preservation may depend on it. 'How are they going to act next?' allows one to frame an adequate response based on a reasonable inference. Animals do it all the time without, of course, linguistically formulating the question. [Otto] Fenichel calls this *the rational component of social fear:* in a hundred ways every individual's existence depends on his taking other people's reactions into account. But when one is dealing with massively unpredictable human objects, dependable cues for inference are not easy to come by. Therefore, man is given to stereotyping in the interests of his own security. People are forever trying to put each other into neat little boxes, and file them away in the cabinet, said Joyce Cary in *The Horse's Mouth*. Any cue is a port in a storm, and as the self-reflexive animal uses his own physiology for social purposes, he uses also the qualities of animals. To say that someone is as 'smart as a fox' is a sort of plebeian character analysis. We want to know what an individual's plan is, and how he is going to go about implementing it.

So it is easy to understand that status cues and role prescriptions for behavior take care not only of self-esteem, but of the vital matter of our safety as well. When we know the other person's role, we can proceed to the familiar 'role-taking.' That is, we place ourselves in his shoes, knowing what his behavior is going to be, and thereby permit ourselves to formulate an appropriate response in advance. Most of our interpersonal fantasy life is merely role-taking in advance of projected action. We carry on imaginary dialogues of: "Then he will say . . . And I'll answer . . . To which he will probably respond . . ." and so on. We do not let our ordering of the world rest for a moment. Probably, if most of us had our way, we would try to maximize the predictability of everyone else, while leaving ourselves free to inject novelty into our relationships. Only this kind of power would give us complete safety and control. But it would also be dull.

The Paradox of Hero-Systems

The most impressive thing about the study of culture and personality is how very neatly the two elements dovetail into one coherent picture. When anthropologists and sociologists had succeeded in formulating this picture, they were struck by the genius of man's ordering of his world. Did the child need self-esteem as his most vital need? Did symbols provide for this need, as well as for safety and control of the environment? Was the outgrowth of this need for self-esteem the urge to be a primary hero? Then let us raise children within a codified hero-system that will permit us to survive and thrive according to our peculiar needs. The whole thing tended to be beautifully standardized. Anthropologists found that there were any number of different patterns in which individuals could act, and in each pattern they possessed a sense of primary value in a world of meaning.

But as early as the beginning of culture and personality studies, anthropologists of the stature of Franz Boas and Ruth Benedict saw the underside of these genial arrangements—the cost in human freedom that they represented. Benedict even spoke of the 'megalomaniac' and 'paranoid' styles of whole cultures, and we will look at the serious implications of this kind of judgment later on. When psychoanalysts of the caliber of Geza Roheim, Abram Kardiner, Erik Erikson, and Erich Fromm dissected culture and personality systems, they saw in detail how fatal the early child training everywhere was.

The child is shaped to follow automatically certain rules in a world which automatically executes those rules. Socialization, in this sense, is a kind of 'instinctivization' of the human animal—a paradoxically symbolic instinctivization, but one that represents the same hardening of behavior as that found among lower animals. As Fromm so well put it, children are trained to want to do as the society says they have to do. They have to earn their prestige in definitely fixed ways. The result is that people willingly propagate whole cultural systems that hold them in bondage, and since everyone plays in the same hero-game, no one can see through the farce. This is the momentous scientific problem posed by culture and personality studies, and we will want to dwell on it in the concluding chapters of this book. Here, we can again draw an already familiar conclusion: for every genial invention of man in evolution, for every simplified ordering of his world, and most of all for the expression of his unique humanness, there is a tragic paradox.

Social Encounters (1971)*

USUALLY WE THINK OF MAN'S LIFE IN SOCIETY as a rather routine thing, people going about their business so that the work can be done, saying what they have to say on the job or at the union hall. Even if we know about roles and statuses, how they structure social life, we tend to consider the whole thing as matter-of-fact; there shouldn't be much at stake in social encounters, since everything is fairly well pre-coded and automatic. So many of us may think, and we would be wrong. Ever since the early sociologists discovered that man was dependent on society for the fashioning of his self, his identity, we began to turn our attention to what was really going on. We began to understand that the individual's view of himself depended hopelessly on the general reflection he received back from society. . . . [M]an makes a pact with society in the preservation and creation of himself. The fundamental task that every society on earth must face is truly monumental. Society must protect its person-objects at their sorest point, the fragile self-esteem of each and every member. In the social encounter each member exposes for public scrutiny, and possible intolerable undermining, the one thing he needs most, the positive self-valuation he has so laboriously fashioned. With stakes of this magnitude, there can be nothing routine about social life. Each social encounter is a hallowed event.

The crucial problem of protecting one's self-esteem in hazardous social encounters is handled by society in the form of an intricate series of conventions. [Erving] Goffman has coined the perfect word for these conventions—he calls them *face ritual*. In the social encounter, the individual entrusts his face to others, and has the right to expect that they will handle it gently. Face rituals are codes for interaction, and they serve this function of gentle handling.

Now, we cannot understand how crucial this process of face protection is unless we shed our old habits of understanding face as a kind of vanity, or as a curious preoccupation of a decrepit Chinese culture. We have to reorient our understanding of the word *face*, as we did for the word *self-esteem*. They are both grounded, in short, in the basic anxiety-buffering function of the self-system, and reflect crucial aspects of human adaptation.

Face is the positive feeling of self-warmth turned to the world for others' scrutiny and potential sabotage. Face is society's window to the core of the self. We can only fully appreciate the importance of face when we realize that nothing goes deeper than the exposure of the self-esteem to possible intolerable undermining in the social encounter.

This is the delicate charge that face rituals must protect. There are two claims that have to be met. On the one hand, society has a right to engage the self, to lay a social claim on it and include it in intercourse with similar selves. This is the major claim which permits social action. On the other hand, each individual has the right to keep others at a distance, and insist on his body privacy, his separateness, the simple fact that he is a person. The self must submit to being socially engaged, if this engagement is done with proper deference to the self-esteem. . . . There is a delicate tension to be maintained in social life, between avoiding and approaching others, a recognition and respect for the self, and a tacit claim on it. The individual helps maintain this delicate balance by a necessary degree of self-containment; there are times when one must be silent, a silence infused with separateness, yet with a willingness to be approached. . . .

The problem of deference is an extremely touchy one precisely because self-esteem is at stake. We must exercise a social claim on each other, and yet not seem to manipulate. The simple act of engaging someone by offering him a seat is fraught with possibilities of bungling. Rituals of farewell are delicately sensitive because here the self is being released from a social situation. The release must be gentle, and not an ejection into isolation. . . . As Goffman has so elegantly put it, society is tasked to show the self proper deference; the individual must maintain a certain demeanor. The double-sided process of social ceremony and self-governance is the theatrical drama for which the child has been laboriously trained. Let us not forget that the process of socialization is the fashioning of a skillful performer. The child is trained in all the subtle qualities necessary to maintain a proper tension between approaching others and avoiding them. We are familiar with training in deportment, dress, and bearing. The child is taught to be perceptive, to have dignity, considerateness, and poise: his self, in other words, is fashioned in his own awareness; he is taught to have feelings attached to himself. This attitude of self-regard makes itself felt in the social context. . . .

We are used to considering qualities like honor and pride basic to man's nature. And so they are. Without them, social performance could not go on. If we are properly proud, we have learned not to submerge others with what may be uncomfortable private data. We may tell our boss that we are ill, but we will not tell him the shape and color of our stool. To have learned honor is to know when to refrain from encompassing others with one's inappropriate designs. It is this overflow that we call *privatizing* the social context. A fellow commuter must be spared the gleefully imparted confidence that one is going to get by without paying a fare. In order for society to function, we must be trained to handle each other lightly and well. Man must make provision for the utmost sensitivity in social intercourse. . . . That marvelous performer Goethe, who even in his old age radiated an aura of indomitable selfhood, said that there was a "courtesy of the heart which is akin to love." The courtesy is the delicate handling of other selves. The love is the control of oneself so that social life can go on. . . .

The Self as a Locus of Linguistic Causality

The psychiatrist Harry Stack Sullivan liked to use the term 'self-system' instead of the Freudian divisions of the psyche, because he saw that you cannot arbitrarily chop up the child's total ongoing action and experience. For Sullivan, this self-system was largely a linguistic device fashioned by the child to conciliate his world. Words are basic to the formation of his self, and words are the only way he can control his environment. This is a powerful formulation, because it permits us to understand that what we term *personality* is largely a locus of word possibilities. When we expose our self-esteem to possible undermining by others in a social situation, we are exposing a linguistic identity to other *loci* of linguistic causality. We have no idea what words are going to spout forth from another's self-system. The self-system, in this sense, is an ideational, linguistic device, in a continual state of modification and creation. We sit comfortably in our armchairs, pouring forth conventional symbolic abstractions. In this shadowy monotone, we exercise and modify our fragile selves, while our pet cat sits purringly by, convinced probably that we are only purring too.

After the child has fashioned a transactable self, his work has hardly begun. He must then learn to use the ritual rules for social interaction. Children are notoriously termed *cruel*, the only way we find of expressing the idea that they have not yet learned to use the face-preserving social conventions. . . . We can only consider the socialization process complete when the child has learned to interact outside the family. The early peer group contacts are crucial in learning to transact with others, to protect their selves and to maintain one's own. *"If you keep calling my doll ugly, I won't come play over at your house tomorrow."* This is not a threat, but a plea for gentle handling, an enjoinder to exercise mutuality.

Sociologists insist on the importance of early training in role-playing. The child plays at various adult roles and learns the proper lines for each part—husband, wife, policeman, robber. By the time he grows up, he is already skilled at assuming the identity of some of the major figures in the cultural plot. But there is a more subtle side to early role-playing. The child learns to put forth and sustain a self and learns to modify the demands of that self, as well as to evaluate the performance of his peers. He learns that there are certain reactions to his cues that he can discount. . . .

If the self is primarily a linguistic device, and the identity of the self primarily the experience of control over one's powers, one fundamental conclusion is inescapable. To present an infallible self is to present one which has unshakable control over words. . . . This simple and crucial fact for understanding human behavior stares us so disarmingly in the face that we pass on to more involved and less important things. The proper word or phrase, properly delivered, is the highest attainment of human interpersonal power. The easy handling of the verbal context of action gives the only possibility of direct exercise of control over others.

We already saw that this fact is central to the development of the ego, how magically the child gets his gratification if he learns the right words. The word, a mere sound, miraculously obliges the adult to do one's bidding; it brings food and warmth, and closeness. The word which pleases the angry adult transforms him before one's eyes into a smiling, appreciative protector. So it is no wonder that in our adult life we carry over some of this early enchantment with the magical efficacy of words, this conviction that everything in the universe can hang delicately on the proper sound. . . . The efficacy of words, then, has from the beginning been at the very basis of our adaptation to anxiety, and respect for this talent is what the adult retains. . . . We are uncomfortable in strange groups and subcultures largely because we cannot frame the appropriate verbal context for sustaining the action or the ceremonial. We do not hear cues familiar to us, nor can we easily give those that make for smooth transitions in conversation. . . .

By using word ceremonial properly the individual can navigate without fear in a threatening social world. He can even ignore the true attitudes of others, as long as he can get by them with the proper ritual formulas of salutation, sustaining conversation, farewells, and so on. The actor has only to be sure of the face-saving ritual rules for interaction. Everyone is permitted the stolid self-assurance that comes with minute observation of unchallengeable rules — we can all become social bureaucrats.

However, there is a more subtle aspect to this mutual protection of fragile self-esteem. . . . [N]ot only do words enable us to protect ourselves by confidently manipulating the interpersonal situation; also, by verbally setting the tone for action by the proper ritual formula, we permit complementary action by our interlocutor. That is, the ability to use formulas with facility actually implies the power to manipulate others indirectly, by providing the symbolic context for their action. We know this only too well, at least subconsciously. We need only reflect on the inordinate amount of time we spend in anguished self-recrimination over having failed merely to say the right thing at a given point in a conversation. . . . Even the slave enjoys power by skillfully using the obsequious formulas of deference appropriate to his status. These ingratiating and respectful expressions for engaging others in anxiety-free fashion are his only tools for manipulating the interpersonal situation. They are proved methods of control. What is more, by doing his part in permitting the action to continue, he actually calls the tune for his superior, even from his inferior position. . . .

[T]he fundamental task of culture is to constitute the individual as an object of primary value in a world of meaning. Without this, he cannot act. Now, the proper exercise of ritual formulas provides just this. The actor can feel himself an object of primary value, motivated to act in a mutually meaningful situation. *"Private Johnson reporting, sir!"* affirms the self, the proper motivation, and the life meaning which forever is. And when we permit our interlocutor as well as our self to act in a fabric of shared meaning, we provide him with the possibility of self-validation. As we act meaningfully in pursuit of agreed goals, we exercise our self-powers as only they can be exercised. This is vitally important. It is easy to see the reverse side of this same coin: namely, that if we bungle the verbal context for action, if we deliver the wrong lines at the wrong time, we frustrate the possibility of meaningful action and unquestioned motivation. . . . Directness is self-convincing. For any animal, meaning dies when action bogs down; for man, it suffices that verbal action bog down in order for meaning to die. And so, unflinching mastery of the lines actually serves to create meaning by providing an unequivocal context for action. . . . Thus, the word not only sustains us by outlining a context of action in which we can be meaningfully motivated. It also 'creates' us, in a sense, by infusing our action with meaning. That is, as we act meaningfully, we exercise our powers and create our identity.

And so we see that not only is motivation reinforced by the flawless performance, but agreement in values is also cemented by the mutuality of performance. The actors are quickened in their commitment: man lives the cultural fiction. The linguistic self-system is an ideational device in continued movement—scanning, questioning, assimilating. It needs reinforcement and something to feed on. As the individual exercises his creative powers in the social encounter, and basks in the radiation of fabricated meaning, his identity is revealed to himself. He forms himself into a meaningful ideational whole, receiving affirmations, banishing contradictions. . . . And so we can understand that there is another side to the social credo. *Let us all protect each other so that we can carry on the business of living.* Man is a social creator as well as a social creature. By the social exercise of linguistic power, man creates his own identity and reinforces that of others. In this sense, identity is simply the measure of power and participation of the individual in the joint cultural staging of self-enhancing ceremony. Only by proper performance in a social context does the individual fashion and renew himself by purposeful action in a world of shared meaning. Loneliness is not only a suspension in action and stimulation; it is a moratorium on self-acquaintance. It is a suspension in the very fashioning of identity; cut off from one's fellows, one cannot add his power to the enhancing of cultural meaning or derive one's just share of it. Social ceremonial is a joint theatrical staging whose purpose it is to sustain and create meaning for all its members.

Subtler Aspects of the Social Creation of Meaning

If social encounters are largely a theatrical staging, part of the basic training of the players will be an inordinate sensitivity to cues. We want to know that everyone is playing correctly. . . . Status, remember, is a social technique for facilitating action. It divides our social environment into a behavioral map, and by living according to the positional cues, our actions take on the only meaning they can have. Our alertness to the performance of others, therefore, is an expression of our concern over sustaining the underlying meaning of the plot. . . . [W]e must feel that the performer deserves his status, and if he didn't deserve it he wouldn't be able to play it convincingly.

Goffman observes that skilled mimics who admit that their intentions are not serious may provide one way to work through our anxieties in this delicate area. We want to know that the performance represents the real thing when it is supposed to. . . . Illegitimacy implies above all that legitimacy exists.

In every culture, man is alert to the discovery of fraud, because it implies the basic legitimacy of the plot he is playing in. That is why we devour the cues in every performance, searching for conviction, for unshakable veridicality. The performance takes on such a life-and-death flavor precisely because life-meaning is being created. This is why it is important for each actor to bring to the social scene his own special dramatic talent, whereby the quality of the performance is enriched. It would be impossible to over-insist on the importance of this talent for social life. It is probably the most subtle and most important area of social creativity, a creativity in which everyone takes part, and in which there are the widest differences in skill. Part of our talent in this creativeness is our inordinate sensitivity to cues, both verbal and nonverbal, kinesic and unconscious. The inferences upon which our lines are based must be gathered from as many cues as possible, if we are to judge accurately and perform creatively in a given part.

Anselm Strauss points out that each person has to assess three things about another. He must be alert to a myriad of cues to determine:

1. The other's general intent in the situation.
2. The other's response toward himself.
3. The other's response or feelings toward me, the recipient or observer of his action.

This interweaving, observes Strauss, of signs of intent, of self-feeling, and of feeling toward the other, must be exceedingly complex in any situation. Why is the assessment of these three things so important? Simply because this trilogy allows one to fulfill his 'social human nature' — it allows him to exercise those unique capacities into which he has been schooled. The adept performer should be able to:

1. Save his own face (protect his fragile self-esteem) against unwarranted attack or privatization.
2. Prepare the appropriate lines that may be necessary to protect the other's self-esteem, if the other inadvertently makes a gaffe. Part of one's social obligation is to protect the other person, as well as oneself, against undermining in the social context.
3. Frame creative and convincing lines that carry the interaction along in the most meaningful, life-enhancing fashion. Or, wanting that, try to get out of the interaction gracefully, and at the other's expense. (Goffman is the acknowledged modern master at detailing the subtleties of these maneuvers.)

A person's response toward himself, his self-alert, critical eye, is a transaction with what Sullivan so beautifully called his *fantastic auditor*. Other psychoanalysts call it the *observing ego*. We direct our performance to this imaginary judge, who sets the standards for it and keeps us in line, saying just the right things. Now and again, we slip out of the alert censorship of our fantastic auditor, as when we explode into a mess of uncontrolled nonsense. When we watch another perform, we think that we can see how he feels about himself. Actually, we don't see this at all; we can have little idea how he feels about himself. What we do see is how smoothly the individual is staging himself, controlling his performance.

We do not like to see another who is too absorbed in his own staging at the expense of convincing delivery of the lines. This kind of stage ineptitude is like performance in a high school play, where self-conscious actors deliver stilted, halting, unconvincing lines, or overly fluent ones. When we talk about someone who is 'phony,' we mean that his staging of himself is overly obvious. He is unconvincing because he allows us to see his efforts at delivering the right lines. . . .

Of course, the masking of inappropriate elements is never sure, precisely because the social encounter is not (in our culture, anyway) completely rigid and structured. One wants to come out of it somewhat aggrandized in his own image, and so he has to overextend himself. Part of the delicate subtlety of the encounter is its potential for increasing the value of the self in one's own eyes. This is what the social psychologists call *status-forcing*. But one needs to be a most skillful performer to come out of an interaction better than he came in. He needs to have an acute sensitivity to the manifold cues, deliver the proper lines necessary to sustain his image and that of the others; he must enhance the cultural meaning as well as the personal meaning of all the selves concerned.

We see a clear example of inept performance, and of constant attempt to force status, in the phenomenon called *riding*. Riding is simply clumsy acting, a grotesque attempt to heighten one's self-esteem by denigrating another. It is a continuous preoccupation of close in-groups temporarily thrown together in distasteful occupations, like waiters and counter-girls. Riding makes a mockery of the delicate skill of cue-sensitive performance. We would expect this where people are thrown together without rigid ceremonial rules for protecting against privatization. A similar phenomenon occurs when a line is used: to employ a line usually means trying to get something out of an interaction that is grossly at the other person's expense. In traditional society there is less of this because cues are more dependable, and the situation tightly structured. There is very little line that one can employ on a date that is chaperoned, for instance. Line is a probing for advantage in the absence of standardized prescriptions for behavior, an attempt to emerge from the fluid interaction much better than one came in. Of course, every interaction has this creative element, the possibility of emerging from it somewhat enhanced in one's feeling of warmth about oneself. . . .

One of the impetuses to the fragmentation of society into subgroups is that they provide some respite from the continual strain on creative alertness of the self-system. In the subgroup, conversation is familiar, automatic, untaxing for the most part. In some primitive societies 'joking relationships' are established between certain individuals. These people, when they meet, engage in an unashamed mockery, teasing, and joking that is denied to others. Joking relationships seem to be established at points of tension in the social system—among in-laws, for example—and relieve the individuals of the strain of meeting these encounters, and the necessity of facilitating them creatively. . . .

One thing we can conclude at this point—and it should be very sobering, even unsettling, and that is that man's meaning hangs by a ludicrously fragile thread, such as a proper amount of silence. Most of us never realize the artifacts that make symbolic life believable, the flimsy stuff out of which man draws conviction and self-aggrandizement. . . . And the main thing that gives conviction to social performance is self-conviction on the part of the actor. Key men in corporation and diplomatic posts are routinely chosen because they have this quality. The self, after all, is largely an attitude of self-regard, inculcated into the child during his socialization. . . . Little wonder that it was Goethe himself who remarked that the influences of the young on each other are the purest. They are not so subtle or indirect as the adults' involved, symbolic cues to action. The world of children is still a world where the convincing self alone carries the brunt of meaning.

The psychoanalysts have added rich evidence to support our earliest sociological insights into these fascinating matters. When we add up the insights from both fields, we have a fairly clear picture of what goes into the phenomenon of 'natural leadership.' A pattern of mothering feeds into the self-system of the child a boundless self-regard. He is taught that he can do no wrong, that he is to be an indomitable locus of causality destined to enrich the world. This gives him an intense self, a militant, *gloating I,* as [Charles Horton] Cooley again so beautifully put it. When he grows up, he convinces by his conviction, and we do not doubt for a moment that life is rich with meaning. Furthermore, he may use us to help create it. By putting forth a convincing self, the actor obliges others to a more careful deference. The strong self forces others to make an effort at performance that may often be beyond their means. Thus, the aura of his infallibility is enforced as their performance stumbles or becomes painfully effortful. This painful effort then generates a further conviction of meaningfulness in which all those around the leader can share. No wonder the leader radiates such power: not only does he embody it in himself, in his aura of self-reliant strength, but he also creates it in his interpersonal performance. We succumb to the leader because we want to share in this power and will accept any that is doled out to us. Again we can judge very clearly where man has departed from his subhuman cousins. We share the same awe and fear of power as the baboons, or any animal that is transcended by nature and by the strength of others. But in order for this power to truly captivate us, it has to be generated in the creation of meaning and in social performance, and not simply in brute animal strength. We may fear the bully, and may admire physical strength; but unless the bully also broods, and unless the strength serves a symbolic design, we will not sit in its shadow.

And so we may conclude that we are *metteurs-en-scene* not only in the fabrication of our inner-newsreels, but also in the action of our social world. We not only edit the images of our films with great skill, but also fashion our spoken lines. Some are more fortunately endowed to set the implicit tone for the performance because they present a model self. The less fortunate are obliged to dance a lifetime to the performance cues of others. Of course, we understand that each culture and even subgroup has its own model for commanding the most meaningful performance in its plot. In South India even a timid child who resembles Hanuman the monkey god is destined to have a favored part in the plot. In Western films the self must above all be silent and self-sufficient, but capable of exploding into brutal murder while maintaining a disarming smile. The Western hero, in fact, provides the best proof that sustaining a convincing self is the basis for enhancing cultural meaning. With nothing but penetrating eyes, charged silence, and an IQ of 80, why does this character thrill audiences to the core? The Western hero conveys little more (but nothing less) than unshakable conviction that underneath it all there is genuine meaning in man's action. The particular conspiracy to be worked on the world is preordained for each cultural plot. But in each case the object of social cynosure can be confident that he will be sustained by all others, if he plays his part well.

But what if he does not? What if the individual presents an unconvincing or even repugnant self? What happens if he does not deliver his lines correctly, if he fails to sustain his own face and that of others, if he digs obtrusively into his nose, or salivates nonchalantly? What happens, in sum, if by his performance he undermines the precariously constituted cultural meaning from which everyone draws the vital sustenance of motivation and value? This is the critical characteristic of those we term abnormal, and presents a major problem in the study of society.

Biological Imperialism (1972)*

AT A TIME WHEN WORLD ARMS SPENDING has reached a total of 204 billion dollars in one year, a book called *The Imperial Animal* [by Lionel Tiger and Robin Fox] already has truth in its title. The problem is how much truth and how vital it is.

Let me stress the serious character of this book: it is in a league all by itself and is not to he confused with the pop-ethology of film writers like Robert Ardrey or the potboilers of Desmond Morris. It happens to have some kinship with these works by virtue of its focus on zoology as a basic explanatory level for all behavior, but this is only coincidental; I can't see the authors laughing all the way to the bank on reading a bad review.

What Tiger and Fox have done is to take the work that has accumulated in zoology and especially in primatology, to merge it with the conclusions that can now comfortably be drawn from almost a half-century of East and South African diggings on early hominid evolution, and to present a picture of man's place in the animal kingdom.

*Original, full text: E. Becker, "Biological imperialism." *Transaction: Social Science and Modern Society,* 9: 5 (March) 40-43 (1972). Reprinted with permission from Transaction Publishers.

Experts will, of course, find things to disagree with in some of their interpretation of linkages between humans and subhumans. But they have presented an outstanding critical synthesis of a vast range of empirical data; what they have actually tried to do is to bring the whole Darwinian picture of man in evolution up-to-date with all the new research data.

The basis for their argument is that man is behaviorally embedded in the vertebrate phylum, and so carries its heredity, predispositions, and limitations—especially those of the primate order and most particularly those of the hunting primate that developed over a million years of human evolution. The nexus of the argument is the now-accepted one that man was a hunter *while* his large brain was being developed. Hunting behavior, then, is a sort of basic appetitive predisposition of the whole human organism. The authors borrow Earl Count's term *biogram* and talk about the basic primate hunting biogram that is built into the human animal. They see this as a *wiring* or a programming, a *biogrammar* that represents man's nature. It orients him in the direction of the search for power and self-perpetuation within a hierarchy of dominance and subordination characterized by competitiveness, the real hunger for triumph and the celebration of triumph.

Man is a heroic hunter sprung out of the vertebrate phylum and has all the needs that derive from this heritage—these are fundamental and durable truths that I don't see can reasonably be argued against. The authors' presentation of the basic needs of a hunting primate is also first rate, and we should get general agreement on some such image of man as soon as possible.

Then the book takes off on an exploration of man's various behaviors in order to show how faithfully they reflect the basic evolutionary wiring—politics, mating, male associations, economics, medicine and religion, education. Even those readers who already have a fairly good idea of the upshot of the recent work in primatology and early man finds will be regaled by this excursion from biology into culture. Frankly, this reviewer was not prepared to be treated to a spectacle of such penetration and scope developed so brilliantly with complete command of facts, without fanaticism and, what is more, interwoven with real style, wit, and even an occasional spurt of poetic beauty reminiscent of a Loren Eisley.

What I liked particularly was the discussion of the hunting biogram as again reflected in the organization of small businesses, the executive level of corporations, the outlaw band, the Mafia, the labor union and, of course, the military. I see no other way to explain the rapt fascination that is still shown over the panoply of emblems and insignias the Nazis designed: men are oriented to self-celebrating triumph and want to have finely and colorfully measured the gradations of their bravery and exclusivity. *Viola tout.*

Another thing that I did not expect and was moved by was the authors' use of their perspective throughout in a frankly critical way: they came out against the wasting of sons in wars for the pleasures of the old baboon males. They come out for the naturalness of welfare sharing, against the inhumanity of unemployment, the cowardice and inhumanity of bussing, the futility of specialist medicine that does not treat the whole person in a community of persons, the failure of an educative system that is not a total, mobile experience of learning-while-doing in a living, human world, and many other things as well.

None of these criticisms are new, but what is new is the way they have developed them against the hunting biogram. This leads them to a nonRousseauian prehistorical romaticism, and if it were realistic, they would want a world frankly based on the hunting level of social organization. From this point of view, they are moved to call the agricultural level "the great leap backward" and to lament, as Marx did, the grotesque creatures who emerged in history and filled the roles of peasant, worker, bureaucrat—untriumphant slaves of the plot of ground, the time clock, the pile of paper. On all this they very aptly call themselves *biological Fabians* and want to see a better world built on human (hunting) principles.

So the book is written on several levels—empirical, critical, and also prophetic. The authors take their realism seriously, and frankly want to call the world away from its erroneous ways. The message is clear: "again and yet again, man is an animal." The authors declare their preference for the old medieval view of evil as fatally locked in the human breast, and they have scorn for Rousseau's uncritical view of man as a blank slate. The work is thus frankly directed against all dreamy utopians who turn away from the data on man—the idealists in science as well as the Marxist revolutionaries, who imagine that a new society will bring with it a totally new human nature.

In this the authors again show how abreast they are of the Zeitgeist, the new move to creature-consciousness that extends over the spectrum all the way from the work of Paul Tillich to that of Norman O. Brown, John Arthur Passmore, and Philip Rieff. Only in this way can the real viciousness of man be explained—the fact that, no matter what the idealists proclaim, man is a trembling and limited creature.

Cultural anthropologists like Ashley Montagu can continue to lamely echo the notion that violence is learned, but it is no good. It is estimated that between 1820 and 1945, human violence caused 59 million deaths. Tiger and Fox are not saying that man is a killer by instinct; they go beyond this with an excellent discussion of violence as following logically from the hunter biogram; and so it is not a lust or an instinct, but flows from a style of heroism, of dedication to one's group, to survival.

The hunting biogram, as we know, caused very little ravage on primitive levels of life; but with civilization and the rise of the state it began to be worked on abstract symbolic levels, and piles of bodies began to be fed into purely symbolic calculators. There is very little to argue with in this tableau of the hunters' fall from evolutionary Eden. On this the authors join hands with Jean-Jacques Rousseau, Adam Ferguson, Adam Smith, and countless others.

All in all, this is a book of great scope and ambition, the offering of a single synthetic perspective on human nature and human ills. And it is on this self-conscious task that the authors ask to be judged. They claim explicitly that they are offering a more comprehensive and economical grammar for understanding man than that offered by cultural anthropology, behaviorist psychology, or instinct theory. And it is, here that my enthusiasm for the book suddenly dips grievously. One of the ironies of the creative process is that it partly cripples itself in order to function. I mean that, usually, in order to turn out a piece of work, the author has to exaggerate the emphasis of it, to oppose in a forcefully competitive way other versions of truth; and he gets carried away by his own exaggeration since his whole distinctive image is built on it. If man is a competitive, imperial animal, there is no reason to expect that Tiger and Fox will be exempt from the biogram—and indeed they are not; this is an imperialistic work, and it brings up forcibly some minor and major disagreements.

For one thing, if you stretch a *grammar* as broadly as they have done, you are bound to do your own violence and lapse into your own struttings and posings. There are occasional pages that seem little more than sophisticated and updated Clarence Day *(This Simian World)*; there are lapses into facile reductionism on the theory of the incest taboo and elsewhere; there are irresponsible statements on the nature of mental illness as useful which are never clarified; at a few points the reductionism becomes truly ridiculous, as in a nine-line theory of delusions, mania, and depression or a seven-line theory of sexual perversion. Brilliance and style both work to the authors' advantage to disguise these shortcomings, but they are real.

These are perhaps trivial matters in such an ambitious work. But there are larger matters. For one thing, their grammar has better competitors than the authors seem to know. After all, the present dissatisfaction with idealism in social science did not jump full-blown out of their heads. It goes back at least to Kenneth Burke and Hugh Duncan and was very forcefully stated by Dennis Wrong. Tiger and Fox colorfully denounce the "Christian Scientists of sociology" and ask why, if men are not violent creatures, they seem inevitably to create situations that lead to violence. They answer this question very well and without instinct or learning theory, it is true, but so did Duncan, [Lewis] Mumford, and many others. In fact, in some ways they answered it much more fully and deeply than do Tiger and Fox, who do not talk about a major dynamic of human evil—the expiation of guilt through victimage and sacrifice.

This may seem like grudging criticism of a book that succeeds so well in developing and defending its main thesis and in presenting between two covers a consistent and integrated theory. But it helps us see beyond Tiger and Fox to the really competing grammars of sophisticated social scientists, psychoanalysts, and existential phenomenologists—and these are not mentioned. In fact, Freud's monumental *Group Psychology and the Analysis of the Ego* is not even touched on, yet it explains so richly many of the dynamics of dominance-subordination and the problem of followership. I would argue emphatically that Norman O. Brown's distillation of psychoanalysis *(Life Against Death)* and his perspective on history and evolution explain human evil just as economically and even more profoundly than Tiger and Fox's book.

Or even more emphatically, I would point to Otto Rank's unparalleled historical synthesis of a general theory of evil based on the animal motives of fear and self-perpetuation. Now too we have Mumford's brilliant historical thesis which also takes the picture of man from animal origins to the present. And in a more specialized vein, who has developed richer and more comprehensive explanations of the perversions than the existential psychoanalysts?

Admittedly, this introduces a dimension of "uneconomy" into the problem of explaining human nature that the authors might not be comfortable with. They have followed only part of [A. N.] Whitehead's enjoinder: to seek simplicity and to mistrust it. No one grammar on human nature is going to win the field of hunting competition and bring back the prize to the victor celebration in one's academic office. There are too many serious and responsible scholars working, with too many rich data and sound theories developed over decades. Somehow all this will have to be integrated into a general theory.

If nothing has advanced in the use of the hunting biogram in sixty years, what good is it? Tiger and Fox say that their conclusions are neither conservative nor radical, but real. They feel that we can build a new society, ever radically new, but it will have to be on the ground; and the ground is the knowledge accumulated in the century since Darwin on man's basic hunting nature. William James wanted a "moral equivalent of war" that would enable men to be heroic, to fulfill their hunting natures, yet with real benefit to mankind instead of destruction. Tiger and Fox want the same thing, now that they have powerfully filled in more of the details; and they believe that this possibility is the one hopeful outcome of their realistic orientation—just as James did.

Then the final sad observation that we have to make on this book is not a judgment on the authors, but a sharing of sadness with them. The book is beyond ideology—not in the smug sense that this thought was put forward in the fabulous fifties—but in the sense that responsible science is always beyond ideology: ideologies are easy for men to achieve; scientific social reconstruction is evidently beyond them. The planning for communities based on man's animal nature is itself utopian! We are no nearer to it today than when James wrote—in fact, we are further away. The lesson we have learned is that the future is no longer up to scientists alone. We know what men are; it is up to the people and their politicians to begin to focus on evil that triumphant hunters can overcome with benefit to all.

Toward the Merger of Animal and Human Studies (1974)*

ONE OF THE GREAT OBSTACLES TO THE DEVELOPMENT of a theory of human nature that would command scientific respect has been the bitter dispute between the biological and cultural scientists themselves. This argument has been going on since the nineteenth century and instead of being bridged, the gap between the two camps is ever widening. To judge by the intransigence and bitterness of the

Original, full text: E. Becker, "Toward the merger of animal and human studies." *Philosophy of the Social Sciences,* 4: 235-254 (1974). Copyright © 1974 by E. Becker. Reprinted by permission of Sage Publications, Inc.

dispute, it has all the earmarks of a battle about basic dogma, holy truth, and who is entitled to utter it. The recruitment of new experts in biology and the multiplication of subspecialties make everyone more jealous to protect the boundaries of his field, while at the same time wanting to arrogate to himself unshakable authority within these boundaries. This would be all right if these experts did not, at the same time, call down the holy writ of the nineteenth century, which said that all things can be reduced to the most minute and elemental levels. This means that they want eventually to pull every study about man into their own boundaries because that is where the essence of pure truth will be distilled by breaking down all levels to the ones they are working on.

This problem is familiar enough; we know how even [Sigmund] Freud—the student of the mind, culture, society, and even history—believed the holy writ of pan-reductionism. There have also been many very biting and accurate things said about the facts and politics of this belief. Like all dogmatic disputes, the facts are less important than the need to believe, and the confrontation could go on forever with hardly anyone being converted. What I would like to do in a sketchy way is to show that the two camps could easily be reconciled if they so desired, that there is obviously secure truth in both, and that these truths do not negate each other but instead are complementary and mutually reinforcing. My hope would be that instead of continually arguing at conference levels all the way up to the recent Fourteenth Nobel Symposium, and printing one tract after another against unbelievers, the two sides would get together and make mutual capital out of their profound insights into the human condition. This hope is probably naive, dealing as it does with a dispute about sacred academic prerogatives, but the facts are clear enough.

Probably the best way to proceed is to take the central figure in biology, around whom the conflict has mostly raged, and to try to make sense and gain out of his work. This means taking Konrad Lorenz's immensely popular book *On Aggression* and trying to see what is left after the assault of the critics. And what an assault it has been! There is hardly any point in repeating any of it here; let us just note that an array of men of unquestionable scientific stature have attacked just about everything theoretical that Lorenz has said. He has been attacked for false facts, false generalizations, superficial analogies, wrong inferences, for reporting fanciful things that no other observer had ever seen, for tautological reasoning, ridiculous speculations on social evolution and, of course, for blatant reductionism—quite a catalogue of scientific sins. . . . [The criticism] is very clear: Lorenz wants to show the *precise equivalency* of men and geese—nothing less; his argument is that there are hereditary instincts in man just like other animals, and his main thesis is that this holds true especially for the instinct of aggression. But as we said, the judgment of the experts on all this, including the idea of an hereditary instinct of aggression in man, has been adamant. No less a student of animals than Sir Solly Zuckerman summed it up: ". . . hardly a serious work of science."

The only thing the experts seem to agree on is the charm and persuasiveness of

Lorenz's personal observations on animals and men. In this sense he would be a successor to La Fontaine and his *Fables* or to George Orwell of *Animal Farm* fame: a raconteur who uses imaginative metaphor to give mankind moral instruction through bitingly satiric self-exposure. After such an authoritative dismissal we are entitled to wonder what can be left of Lorenz except charm and style? Well, a few very important things, I believe: the serious purpose for which the book was written; the real meaning of its popularity and persuasiveness even among serious scientists who are not part of the mindless mass readership seeking satiric titillation; and probably most important of all, the keen observations of a dedicated and seasoned student of the world of organismic events. If Lorenz's observations are correct, they raise a final question, then: what is the larger current of scientific thought into which he fits?

As for his purpose in writing, Lorenz makes no attempt to disguise it—on the contrary. One of the chapters is titled 'On the Virtue of Humility,' and he makes it plain that he means the humility of the scientist in the face of fact. The book is sprinkled with criticisms of men for being 'arrogant' and 'pride-inspired' because they refuse to see that they are a part of nature. Instead, man should be 'modest,' a 'humble seeker of biological truth'; it is time 'to preach humility.' All that Lorenz has written, by his own admission, "should be a warning to the spiritual pride of many people." It is this that is one of the great obstacles to human self-knowledge, and it is summed up historically in the heritage of idealistic philosophy. What is the teaching of this heritage that obstructs self-knowledge? That man is not a part of nature and has not originated by natural evolution, but that he has been made in the image of God. This, says Lorenz, "is certainly the most arrogant and dangerous of all untenable doctrines." Instead of this we must have the humility to 'consider that our ancestors, at a time fairly recent in relation to the earth's history, were perfectly ordinary apes . . . .' The enemy of human enlightenment, then, is the "resistance to the discoveries of Charles Darwin." Here Lorenz allies himself also with Freud, in his realization that we are still driven by the same instincts as our prehuman ancestors. In fact, he really wants to repeat and affirm Freud's achievement: that the moral law within man is not the spiritual entity that awed the great Kant, but instead there is a natural explanation for morality: it grew up in evolution. There is only one way, finally, to get rid of the spiritual fantasies of the idealists, and that is to promote Darwin and Freud, the really sound opinions about mankind. Only expert teaching of biological fact can do this: "It is plain biology . . . that ought to be considered the 'big science.'"

The cumulative effect of the book's onslaught by the phalanx of Imperial Biology and its Divine King Darwin and consuls Freud and Lorenz is overwhelming. Lorenz —like a brooding, finger-pointing Biblical prophet—is out to shock us with the reality of our condition. The tone of the whole book is in many places unmistakably Lutheran; it admonishes us to "look what you really are, not what you pretend or hope to be!" And all through these Biblical accusations, Lorenz is also unmistakably delighting in anticipation of his own revelations, relishing his role as a truth-teller, no matter how bitter a pill it makes—or rather especially because it is bitter. We are reminded again of Freud's famous reflection about how surprised the Americans are going to be when they hear what he has in store for their tender ears. Here is Lorenz's equivalent of a Freudian shocker, "the paradigmatic illustration," as he himself says, of his whole argument. He is describing the phenomenon called 'militant enthusiasm,' and we have only to admire his descriptive skills, his fineness of observation of men, and we can consent to be chilled into submission by it just as we would by Freud: "A shiver runs down the back and, as more exact observation shows, along the outside of both arms. . . . The tone of the entire striated musculature is raised, the carriage is stiffened, the arms raised from the sides and slightly rotated inward so that the elbows point outward. The head is proudly raised the chin stuck out and the facial muscles mime the 'hero face,' familiar from the films. On the back and along the outer surface of the arms the hair stands on end. This is the objectively observed aspect of the shiver!"

The triumphant emphasis on objective observation is meant to lead us further, to the true origin of it: "Anybody who has ever seen the corresponding behavior of the male chimpanzee defending his band or family with self-sacrificing courage will doubt the purely spiritual character of human enthusiasm. The chimp, too, sticks out his chin, stiffens his body, and raises his elbows; his hair stands on end, producing a terrifying magnification of his body contours as seen from the front. The inward rotation of his arms obviously has the purpose of turning the longest-haired side outward to enhance the effect."

And now that we see the precise equivalence of human and chimpanzee enthusiasm, Lorenz draws his obvious and sobering lesson: "Our shiver, which in German poetry is called a *heiliger Schauer,* a 'holy' shiver, turns out to be the vestige of a prehuman vegetative response of making a fur bristle which we no longer have."

There we have it. Lorenz has brought up to date with a vengeance Darwin's famous *Expression of the Emotions in Man and Animals.* It remains only to take the next logical and necessary step: to link the observations of fact into a theoretical structure, to make ultimate closure between the most precise modern investigation and Darwinian philosophy: "Militant enthusiasm is a specialized form of communal aggression. . . . Like the triumph ceremony of the Greylag goose, militant enthusiasm in man is a true autonomous instinct: it has its own appetitive behavior, its own releasing mechanisms, and like the sexual urge or any other strong instinct, it engenders a specific feeling of intense satisfaction. . . . To the humble seeker of biological truth there cannot be the slightest doubt that human militant enthusiasm evolved out of a communal defense response of our prehuman ancestors."

Why is it important to stress humbly these fatal links between animals and men? To show something that the idealists and rationalists could never explain: the inevitability of human drivenness, the precariousness of reason. "One soars elated, above all the ties of everyday life, one is ready to abandon all for the call of what, in the moment of this specific emotion, seems to be a sacred duty. All obstacles in its path become unimportant. . . . Rational considerations, criticism, and all reasonable arguments against the behavior dictated by militant enthusiasm are silenced by an amazing reversal of all values, making them appear not only untenable but base and dishonorable. . . . Conceptual thought and moral responsibility are at their lowest ebb."

From all this we can immediately see that the power of Lorenz's argument springs from the absolute seriousness of the problem that he has staked out; he is not engaging in simple roguish self-titillation, destroying and disrobing illusions just out of sadistic pleasure. Far from it: if his book is full of Biblical propheticism it also witnesses to the dedicated humanist and rationalist; if he assumes the Biblical mantle, it is only the better to lead to really sound reason, to a true humaneness, even to a better humanity than we have ever yet seen. He wants man to take himself less seriously, be less pompous; he deflates us in order to defuse our megalomania; he even calls for humor as an antidote to the hard-bitten seriousness that is making such a wreck out of our world. And so, it is all very correct and beautiful, this Biblical realist telling the world the painful truth so that it may abandon pride and ignorance, and doing it with a really humble enjoinder to Erasmian humor. We are almost ready to forgive him his biological imperialism because it is dedicated to so noble an end, by so obviously a warm humanitarian.

The interesting question historically is why he had to be moved to write such a powerful Biblical statement from within biology. Was not Darwinism securely established in all fields; is he not whipping a dead horse by attacking nineteenth-century idealism? Well, the answer is no. The fact is, as the noted student of society Morris Ginsburg pointed out, that ethology is an historical reaction. It represents the swing of the pendulum from the 1920s and 30s when instinct theory was wiped out in social science. It was then that a picture of man as a wholly malleable creature took over; we saw man as totally shaped by his environment, amenable to education, to guidance by reason. But alas, none of this happened; education failed and so did the best reason and tradition. Instead, we came into an epoch of the direst evil and were bereft of any scientific means to explain it. Lorenz represents historically the renewed search for those means along cumulative lines from Darwin through Freud. His main task is to explain the conflict between the rational and the irrational that always swamps man. And there seems to be no scientific way to do this without instinct theory, without specifically calling into the picture the animal backgrounds of human behavior. Lorenz sets out to show that man is defeated by the unreason that takes over when his animal instincts are triggered; that unreason thus has its roots in evolution and is a powerful physical force that defeats man—whatever the rosy idealists say; that the most dangerous form this force takes is the aggressive behavior of militantly enthusiastic groups just as modern history has so bitterly shown us.

No wonder there has been such a favorable reaction to Lorenz among both scientists and the general public, despite the expert misgivings that we noted earlier. He is fulfilling an historical purpose within the science of man itself by correcting the facile Rousseauian liberal view of human nature; and he is fulfilling a public purpose by giving to modern men the scientific means to understand those forces that were pulling them apart as they tried vainly to make a saner world.

The Truth of Lorenz

But now there is one big question that arises after we admit all this, and that is, how can a man who has been criticized for so much falsehood be said to be speaking an historical and human truth? The answer is that he can do this if he has been speaking the truth 'falsely' in some sense—which is exactly where the scientific judgment on Lorenz must come to rest, in my opinion. Let us linger on this important denouement because it leads us exactly to the merger of animal and human studies that we started out to explore. What does it mean to say that ethology 'speaks the truth falsely'? Let me illustrate, using his own paradigm example, 'militant enthusiasm.'

Who cannot be thrilled by his use of the idea of a 'holy shiver' in man, and his description of its acute resemblance to behavior of animals? Even more, who can argue with his description of the situations that elicit this holy shiver? He lists four things that bring it out in man: "Militant enthusiasm can be elicited with the predictability of a reflex when the following [environmental] situations arise. First of all, a social unit with which the subject identifies himself must appear to be threatened by some danger from outside. . . . A second key stimulus which contributes enormously to the releasing of intense militant enthusiasm is the presence of a hated enemy from whom the threat . . . emanates . . . . A third factor contributing to the . . . response is an inspiring leader figure. . . . A fourth, and perhaps the most important, prerequisite for the full eliciting of militant enthusiasm is the presence of many other individuals, all agitated by the same emotion."

We would not want to argue with this description, because it composes the *very things* that we have been able to identify in the terrifying destructiveness of human groups all though history: the narcissistic identification with one's own group, which is a primary life-symbol to all its members; an outside enemy that serves as a scapegoat for the death-anxiety of the group; a leader who is the focal life-symbol and from whom the members of the group get both the power and the permission to rid themselves of guilt, anxiety, and conflict; and fourth, the presence of many other individuals all intent on the same heroic victory over evil (anti-life), gives to each member the unmistakable support to enjoy his righteous self-expansion. No wonder that Lorenz draws exactly the same moral from his observations as a zoologist, as we do from psychoanalysis and social psychology: Men may enjoy the feeling of absolute righteousness even while they commit atrocities. . . . As a Ukranian proverb says: "When the banner is unfurled, all reason is in the trumpet."

But now our paths diverge. It is obvious that he is drawing the same conclusions but on quite different premises; he is saying that reason evaporates in man because he still carries within him a phylogenetic instinct that is triggered when conditions are exactly right. Lorenz is claiming to explain from within the single field of zoology the paradox of the irrational that has perplexed observers of man, the 'rational' animal, since the beginning of history. This is very neat but as we can already judge, too neat; this is just where the cultural anthropological criticisms of Lorenz come to rest. If man carries an instinct of aggression triggered when the conditions are right, then how, ask the anthropologists, do we explain the fact that there are groups which know no warfare or even milder strife? This would seem to mean that man does not infallibly have an instinct that makes him militantly aggressive. Many sociologists have argued the same way; as [Stanislav] Andreski recently put it, "If human beings were in fact endowed with an innate proclivity for war, it would not be necessary to indoctrinate them with warlike virtues; and the mere fact that in so many societies, past and present, so much time has been devoted to such an indoctrination proves that there is no instinct for war." Lorenz might answer that in these groups the instinct has been 'inhibited' (which is a favorite argument of his school), but it is just such makeshift reasoning that undermines the scientific validity of some ethologists' claims. It reinforces a theoretical claim with an additional theoretical possibility, much as psychoanalysis turned away serious students when it claimed that the lack of sexual attraction in a given case could only mean that it was 'repressed,' etc.

Let me quickly assure the reader that I do not intend to dwell on the dispute between Lorenz and the social scientists, or to enter into the labyrinth of theory construction in science; I only want to show that the direct strength of Lorenz's description is not upheld by an equal impregnability of theory. Having shown this, we can also indicate the most direct way out of the problem which accomplishes what we wanted: to get at the truth of Lorenz after all the exaggerations and false claims have been laid aside. There is one way to include both Lorenz's theoretical argument and the cases that do not fit it (the ones from anthropology). And that is not by introducing further precise theoretical postulates from ethology, but to proceed to a more general level of theoretical explanation that includes them both. Why are there groups which are not aggressive and warlike? Why is it that soldiers have to be trained to hate and kill, and are often so reluctant to go to war or to remain in it, even after the most sustained training, after the strongest indoctrination? The answer can only be that the militant enthusiasm of war is itself a special case of a more general human urge. And here I must refer the reader to a literature that we do not have room to expand on here (and with which, in any case, he is surely familiar): I mean the explanation of human motives that has come out of the best distillation of psychoanalytic theory, specifically in the work of Otto Rank, Norman O. Brown, and Robert J. Lifton. What this work shows is that the things that drive men are their urges to self-perpetuation and heroic victory over evil. The sense of powerful transcendence in which man revels can be gained in many different ways—not only by killing (although historically killing has been a form that is both widespread and capable of giving men real pleasure). From the writings of Rank, Brown, and Lifton we are now justified to include these various games under a general category: immortality games. They all refer to ways in which men seek their continued self-perpetuation in the face of death. In modern times especially, there is a wide latitude of hero-games, and war is only one of them—and a lesser one for many people. Which explains why so many soldiers yearn for home (the family, the career, political agitation, the playboy life, etc.). That is where the primary hero-games may be played.

In other words, when we consider man as the culturally modifiable creature that he is, even given his fundamental appetites and predispositions, we still get the scientific and moral lesson that Lorenz wants, but we get it not on the basis of exact homology between animals and men. (We will see at the conclusion of this essay why it is important to get this same factual result but from different theoretical assumptions.) We know that the individual is carried on a wave of heroic transcendence by the very things that Lorenz observes; and so we can agree with him that no matter to what cause man dedicates his holy shiver, we have to "doubt the purely spiritual character of human enthusiasm." And we have to doubt it for the very reason that Lorenz keeps pointing his prophetic finger toward: that man is an animal. We agree with Lorenz that Darwinism is still haunting modern man with its essential message, the same one that threatened and rocked the nineteenth century, and the one that mankind everywhere is struggling to deny with all its anal might and symbolic ingenuity: that man is not the righteous, spiritual creator that he imagines himself, but a finite animal creature.

And so, despite the fallibility of his instinct theory, Lorenz takes his historical place just as he sees it, in the radical Darwinian recognition of the fundamental role of animality in human affairs. In other words, he stands side by side not only with Darwin and Freud, but with Rank and Brown. Irrationality is a fundamental part of man and we explain it in terms of animal fears. Militant enthusiasm and the conditions that trigger it are part of the drama of a vulnerable animal trying to overcome fundamental animal problems; they are part of the organismic creature's attempt to control mystery, power, and finitude.

With such a fundamental message at stake we are ready to overlook Lorenz's biological imperialism. Plain biology *is* the big science, since man is basically a creature, whatever else he might try to be. From this point of view there is large truth in saying that the mass enthusiasm of man is the same as the flocking behavior of Greylag geese. We could even leave out the symbolic aspects of man's attempt to triumph over evil, and call it the 'communal defense response' now programmed in the direction of symbolic meaning. After all, what essential difference would it make? In each case we are talking about an animal who enjoys organismic self-expansion, the feeling of the plenitude of his powers, and the banishing of the anxiety of death to which he is subject. Overstating one's case does not abolish the basic truth of it. All the while that the Freudians were talking about sexuality, they were really talking about the problems of the human condition, the timeless existential dilemmas. Similarly, all the while that the ethologists were talking about the fatality of precise animal instincts, they were talking about the general determinism of organismic limitations. Freud overstated his case because he was a medical doctor trained in the nineteenth century; Lorenz overstates his case because he is a zoologist researching animal instincts. How can we expect people to abandon the position of expert training which alone gives their insight its authority?

Still, the world never takes us on our own terms, and the ethologists have to accept their victory on the conditions of the scientific community, and not on their own. This means that, however uncomfortable it may be, they are really phenomenological ontologists talking about the general problem of organismic expansion and transcendence. By viewing the matter on a more general level, we get at both the basic animality and the larger ontological and phenomenological problems that are missed by a simple instinctual reductionism—just as Freud himself missed them. The monsters that are unleashed from the id are not primal drives from the dim recesses of racial memory. They are forces of hate and destruction that struggle against the insignificance of the creature, and that will take their toll to overcome that insignificance. Freud was right, we now see, to steadfastly maintain the link to phylogeny; there is something in the animal creature that overshadows all his social and human training, and that is animal anxiety. The fear of death and abandonment is grounded in the physiology of the animal; it is part of the general instinct of self-preservation. But as a general instinct it derives from a general organismic seating in the world, and so can be satisfied in any number of general ways. The enthusiastic victory over creatureliness is a phenomenological problem in sum, and in this way we have an intimate reconciliation of Lorenz and his critics in cultural anthropology and sociology. They were all talking about the same thing—transcendence of creature limitations.

The Authentic Closure on Darwin

If this kind of reconciliation has been hard to make with Lorenz, it becomes much easier and clearer when we look at a different approach to the tradition of Darwin. I am referring to the recent brilliant major work *[The Imperial Animal]* of Lionel Tiger and Robin Fox. It, too, is part of the Lorenzian onslaught on human illusion, and it is animated by the same prophetic spirit; it contains the same pleading for humble realism about man's basic animality; it voices the same warning about falsely optimistic expectations, about the difficulty of realizing grandiose human hopes on the evolutionary foundations of animal fallibility. The writers very self-consciously oppose their 'realistic' perspective to what they colorfully denounce as the 'Christian Scientists of sociology', the descendants of the naive Rousseau, that is, to all dreamers, idealists, cultural anthropologists, Marxists and other utopians who imagine that they can wish any kind of world into being without reckoning with basic human nature. Their basic prophetic message is identical to that of Lorenz and can be summed up in the single admonition: ". . . again and yet again, man is an animal." But here the identity ends, for the range of facts used to get this message, and the conclusions drawn from these facts, put the whole matter on a quite different level. They attempt nothing less than a summing-up and synthesis of the accumulated studies on early man and the subhuman primates, of the last several decades. This is a large body of data based both on the East and South Africa diggings of the early man-apes which has been going on since 1924, and also on the new studies of primates in their natural habitat. It gives the following unmistakable picture of man.

The most striking thing revealed by the data from pre-human evolution is that the human brain evolved over a couple of million years while man was already a hunter. This means that hunting behavior is built into the human organism. We now understand man as a primate hunter embedded in the whole vertebrate phylum, sharing all the distinctions and appetites that flow from this: he has been selected for competitiveness, the ability to fit into hierarchies of dominance and subordination, to use power ruthlessly in the service of self-perpetuation and especially group survival, to band together with other males in the exercise of mutual skill and power, to close in on prey, kill it, share it with his group, and to celebrate the sharing in a triumphant self-exalting way. To put it as briefly as possible, all organisms like to fill themselves by trapping and ingesting others; man is a particularly agile and developed searcher and trapper, one who enjoys the thrills and dangers of it, and who likes to celebrate his gifts once the triumph is consummated.

The crucial thing about this picture of man as embedded in a distinctive evolutionary history or 'biogram' is this: it gives us a quite different understanding of human viciousness than that put forth by Lorenz and the instinctivists. We can understand that one does not have to be an instinctive killer in order to use and enjoy killing. Men use violence as heroic hunters giving play to their whole evolutionary heritage, the skills and dedications it orients them toward; *man is a dedicated victory seeker.* This means, further, that although he has no specific 'lust to kill', still, killing is a kind of logical outcome of a disposition or appetite for victorious consummation of his distinctive powers in the service of his group. This gives us quite a different theory of evil than that we get from Lorenz. Let me quote a few crucial passages: "The catalogue of blood letting, cruelty, sadism, and cavalier disregard for the suffering of others is so extensive as to suggest that these crudities may result not from something as private as 'instinctive cruelty' or the fact that man is 'evil', but as a direct consequence of a process of male bonding which is deeply related to the social nature of human beings and which is linked both to political structure and the hunting method of ecological exploitation."

This is already quite different from the mass enthusiasm of 'flocking' behavior, and the precise instinct it is triggered by. Evil and the irrational are products of a general kind of organismic disposition. Tiger continues: "I am suggesting, then, that the phenomena of human cruelty, blood-craving, sacrifice, and pseudo-specific killing and abuse are directly related to the sense of personal manly validation individual men feel in terms of their male groups, and that perhaps the chief effect of intercultural difference in this matter is to specify object, instrument, and mode for the validation of individual maleness and group power in different cultures."

This takes us even further from holy shivers that can be turned on and off. We are in a different atmosphere entirely, an atmosphere of a sense of maleness, or organismic importance; a sense that varies with cultural learning. And finally: "In the same way, we can look at the behavior of frustrated Nazis in the early days of Hitler's movement, in the disciplined aggressive cadres of the Black Muslims, or the cells of the Ku Klux Klan, and we may see an attempt by men feeling relatively deprived to establish themselves as full and effective men in significant and dramatic groups. Not only political unrest, and not just anomie, and not only class conflict or racial hauteur is here, but also the expression of a need to be a man among men. This yields privileges and duties and goals and the experience of a sense of strength and personal moment. . . . "

Do we wonder about the rapt fascination that is still shown over the panoply of emblems and insignias the Nazis designed? Men are oriented to self-celebrating triumph, and want to have finely and colorfully measured the gradations of their bravery and exclusivity; *voila tout.*

The curious thing about this picture of man is that it puts us back to the Harvard of the turn of the century, to Josiah Royce's *Philosophy of Loyalty* and to William James, a time when both philosophers of religion and experimental psychologists realized that the thing that men want most is heroic belonging to a victorious cause. James had already put the almost identical case of modern ethology: "The earlier men were hunting men, and to hunt a neighboring tribe, kill the males, loot the village and possess the females, was the most profitable, as well as the most exciting, way of living. Thus were the more martial tribes selected. . . . Modern . . . man inherits all the innate pugnacity and all the love of glory of his ancestors. Showing wars irrationality and horror has no effect upon him. The horrors make the fascination. War is the strong life; it is life *in extremis;* war-taxes are the only ones men never hesitate to pay, as the budgets of all nations show us."

Tiger and Fox have merely repeated this same thing, only now in a brilliant synthesis of a much broader and more detailed factual base. Their work represents the cumulative updating of the Darwin–James tradition, and must be seen in that light to be appreciated for its importance, for its utterly non-idiosyncratic nature.

When we put the matter in this historical perspective we can see the more-or-less exact significance of modern ethology. It brings man into the animal kingdom but it does not lock him fatally into it in a programmed, reflexive way. Tiger and Fox talk about the firm building-in of the basic vertebrate biogram and there is no doubt that a disposition and physical equipment that evolved through millions of years of evolution has to be there somewhere in the orientation of our sense of organismic closure, of proper power and delight. The question that has to be cleared up is how tightly our evolutionary history orients us and in what fixed ways. Tiger and Fox make an argument for a rather heavy determinism of the hunting biogram, and they use the terms 'wiring' and 'programming' to pin that determinism down into the organism. Yet at the same time they talk about man in a more general way, as subject to the dispositions and appetites of a vertebrate hunter, and not as an animal who reacts to a fixed trigger mechanism. They see man as in danger of negating himself in the contradictions between his natural needs and dispositions and the self-defeating and alienated ways of life that civilization maps out for him. But it is not at all clear how much the hunting biogram determines the particular ways of life or the social forms in which men have to live and act while they search out and celebrate their victories. Is human society as close an echo of the primal horde as Tiger and Fox want to make out? I doubt it, but I agree with them that it will be important to know the degree of the resemblance for really intelligent social planning.

But the more important and immediate conclusion is right on the surface: there is nothing in our evolution which seems at all to determine the *nature* of the evil that we must hunt down. Men could enjoy chasing and cornering almost anything they define as evil, from moon viruses to industrial pollutants. This is where [William] James rested his case for a 'moral equivalent of war', right after he talked about the hunter's natural thirst for glory (a thirst that can be quenched by almost anything). This leads us to our most important conclusion about the zoological picture of man that has taken shape since Darwin. It features the very same central motives that we get from a mature psychoanalysis, existential phenomenology, and even a general organismic ontology: the motives of fear, power, hierarchy, self-perpetuation, expansiveness, group loyalty, victory over evil and limitation. We see that the real step to large-scale evil in the evolution of man was when he switched from a merely physical self-perpetuation to a symbolic self-perpetuation based on the absolutes of his cultural world view. Man was the first animal who could aggrandize himself infinitely in his fantasy, and this is what began to take such a toll of pulsating life. With all this we see that the modern Darwinian picture merges its full explanatory power with these other rich theoretical perspectives without seriously compromising their generality and large relativity. I think it is significant that the noted student of primitive war, [Harry H.] Turney-High, could conclude his study, despite the record of bloodshed, without being able to say that man is naturally a bloodthirsty or violent creature: the Omaha were peaceful and hated war, as other tribes learned war. The reason, we now know, is that all motives that lead to bloodshed are subsumed under the flexible one of self-expansion in a direction to transcend evil. This is what still gives James's case for a moral equivalent of war its force, despite the wealth of linkages between men and animals that have been revealed since he wrote.

As far as I can make out, not only ethology, but also traditional behaviorism has its place in the delayed historical closure on Darwinism. This is what the fight has been about ever since J. B. Watson right through to B. F. Skinner in our time: the primary reality of our physical, organismic condition. Skinner's latest book *Beyond Freedom and Dignity* follows the same lines as the ethologists: the same inflammatory title and Biblical message that man is not what he imagines; his main problem is his arrogance, his pretension to freedom, dignity, spiritual autonomy. It is just this pretension that is written in blood. But, unlike ethologists such as Lorenz, Skinner throws the whole weight of his scientific authority against the idea of instincts. And in contradistinction to Tiger and Fox, he even denies the storage of evolutionary histories in the organism; as he forcefully puts it, Man is not a naked ape.

On the face of it this scientific disagreement among noted authorities seems to confuse the matter beyond the possibilities of achieving an agreed nexus of theory. But actually it helps us boil down the essence of the whole historical dispute. No matter who may eventually be right or wrong about instincts or biograms, there is one thing they all agree on now. When one clears away all the matters of dispute, the thing that is left starkly and simply is man's basic animality—the fact that he is conditioned by his environment, that he does not act freely, altogether rationally or in full self-knowledge. James, Freud, [William] McDougall, Lorenz, Tiger and Fox, and Skinner all agree on this but in different ways.

We are entitled then, to call this the agreed scientific nexus of the whole movement of modern psychology in all its schools: the attempt to rehabilitate man by freeing him of his self-delusion, by showing him the correlates of his determinism. We can thus see that, historically, the problem of Darwinism has been how to include it in social science in a truly sophisticated and empirically correct way. What began as a crude social Darwinism (evolution continuing to work out the survival of the fittest in the social arena) has now been refined down to a question of how the human animal contrives to deny its own animality, and the price it pays for this blind denial.

The further problem, of course, is that each school has its own particular option on how man's rehabilitation through self-exposure should be accomplished, and this is where the bed-fellows fall out. Lorenz, for all of his reduction of men to animals, is far more attractive to me than Skinner: he gives more prominence to man's will, to his inner development and self-control; Skinner leans far too much toward total environmentalism, toward making man an object of external programming. Skinner's program, even while denying instincts belittles man much more than does Lorenz's. These repercussions of the various approaches are scientifically crucial and have to be carefully argued out.

The Drawbacks of the Zoological Approach to Man

Now that we have reviewed the historical importance of the Darwinian reminder about the human condition, it is important for us to draw the balance and show some of the real drawbacks of this approach. The first obvious thing that jumps to our eyes is that no serious student of man would want to exchange the richness of our understanding of man gained from fields like psychoanalysis and social psychology for the one we get from zoology (even broadly considered). Admittedly, it is basic, graphic, sometimes even humorous, warm, and poetic, but it is thin. A whole book on flocking behavior does not give us the depth and complexity of a single page on group dynamics; a whole shelf on the viciousness of animal aggression, or even on the inhibitors of it does not convey the subtlety of a single page on human scapegoating, on the psychology of buying off one's own death; one page of Erwin Straus on the dynamics of miserliness is worth a volume on primate selfishness. There is no need to labor this after all the literature that has been written, but we do need to be reminded of it after reeling under the Lorenzian juggernaut. We would like humbly to enjoin him to practice some of the scientific humility in the face of facts that he so convincingly preaches.

The same caution applies, although to a lesser degree, to Tiger and Fox. They too fall victim to the temptations of imperialistic claims, and in spite of the regaling suggestiveness of their insights, they cannot match these claims with a uniform richness of explanation. They pretend to offer a more comprehensive and economical theory of human nature than anyone else, and in the process, they give us a feast of insights into many areas of human motivation. Yet one can only marvel at their bravado in throwing off a theory of incest in a few lines, or taking nine lines for a theory of delusions, mania, and depression, and seven lines for a theory of sexual perversion. I am not saying that economical theories are false, but that they are competitive and can be empirically evaluated on the basis of how adequately they reflect the phenomenon. One has only to compare facile reductionist theories of mental illness with the richness of psychoanalytic and existential-phenomenological ones. At least Tiger and Fox have proved that they are no exceptions to the urges of imperial animals.

But behind all this is a more critical problem than mere imperialism or even thinness of explanation, and it is on that I want to dwell a bit. We can approach the complexities of human behavior in two ways: in terms of their spread over a total phenomenal field, or in more economical terms like vertebrate biograms or instinctual structures. In either case, we see man tugging at his limitations, trying to pull away from his animal substratum. If we use a total phenomenal field approach, we see this tugging compromised by man's animal nature in a general way; but if we use an ecological or instinctive approach we see something quite different—man is compromised by specific adaptive mechanisms that grew up in evolution. This may seem to be merely a fussy matter of how one prefers to understand animal determinism, but it is more than that: it is very crucial and represents the principal drawback of the ethnological approach to human problems.

Let me elaborate a bit, using Lorenz's own language. Here is one key statement that I must quote at length: ". . . even the simple and seemingly innocuous mechanisms of anonymous flocking can turn into something not only inhuman but *truly terrible*. In human society, these mechanisms remain more or less hidden . . . but there is one contingency in which they erupt with the *uncontrollable power of a volcano and gain complete mastery over man,* causing behavior that can no longer be called human. This *horrible recrudescence of the ancient mechanisms* of flocking behavior occurs in mass panic. I was once an unwilling witness of the sudden emergence and rapidly snowballing effect of this process of dehumanization, and if I was not drawn into its vortex it was only because, thanks to my knowledge of flocking behavior, I had seen the *approaching danger* sooner than others and had had time to guard against my own reactions. To me there is small pride in the memory; on the contrary, no one can put much trust in his own self-mastery who has ever seen men more courageous than himself, men fundamentally disciplined and self-controlled, rushing blindly along, closely huddled, all in the same direction, with eyes protruding, chests heaving, and trampling underfoot everything that comes in their way, exactly like stampeding ungulates, and no more accessible to reason than they."

Here, again, is the master of description using adjectives that project the atmosphere of a science-horror story that engulfs us. In another place he talks about the "essential spontaneity of instinctive drives," and says that trying to eliminate or diminish them would be "about as judicious as trying to counteract the increasing pressure in a continuously heated boiler by screwing down the safety valve more tightly."

Note the atmosphere that Lorenz projects in the words I have italicized. They paint the unmistakable picture of a kind of fatal danger that man carries within himself, mysterious inner forces just waiting to take the ascendancy over us in an unguarded moment. And this is not Lorenz's own preference but is part of an ethnological picture of man, since Tiger too warns us not to tamper with an ancient and central pattern of human behavior. It is truly as though man were sitting on top of a volcano, but now a volcano of instinctual structures or at least biogram 'wirings'. The image is not unfamiliar to us because we already recognize it from Freud: that man may be swamped from within by the monsters of the id. Or, in Lorenz's language, man's "animal properties bring with them . . . danger."

In other words, Lorenz repeats the scientific contradiction that had so long hamstrung psychoanalysis. On the one hand, Freud finally delivered to the science of psychology what it had always wanted: to take the inner life of man and make it an object for scientific investigation, *which means making it free of irrationality and mystery.* On the other hand, he gave psychology this ultimate gift but took it away at the same time, by placing irrationality at a deeper level than the psychological inner fife of man: at the level of built-in neuro-chemical instinctual processes. And so, instead of giving to the irrational the complete and open structure that his work had promised, he again hid it and kept it mysterious. It is one thing to say that man is an animal swamped from within by evolutionary adaptations which can break out in the midst of his highest aspirations. This is scientifically bad because, as we said, it leaves the irrational unstructured and mysterious. It is another thing to say that man is an animal who aspires to transcend his organism, but who causes the greatest evil in doing this because he does not realize what he is doing. This is scientifically good because it gives to the irrational a complete openness and structure. We know that the irrational in man's inner life is his unconscious horror of insignificance and death: this is an open and unmysterious problem. Even if we reduce it to its most elemental level as the general instinct of self-preservation, it is a clear object of study: it is a reasonable motive. Or, put another way, it is unreasonable to give way to flocking behavior in a crisis situation, but it is very reasonable not to want to die. The terror of death is not only an 'ancient mechanism' but it is an existential problem: we know we do not want to vanish forever, even if we admit that we fear it.

Ethology not only hamstrings our scientific quest but also our moral one, and this is equally critical. Lorenz's whole book is a plea for self-knowledge, and hence self-control and rational behavior—once we find out what is really jerking us about.

The problem is to find out what our precise instincts are and to know the situations that release them. Then we could go on to try to envisage ideals and social forms of aggression that are creative and altruistic, instead of violent and destructive. Again, here is the Freudian program of trying to replace id with ego, to gain control of one-self by knowing the truth, and to try to sublimate in the direction of creative work and love. There is nothing to be said against this; it is a restatement of James's plea for a 'moral equivalent for war'. But scientifically the question still is: what is gained or lost in this moral venture by remaining on the level of the analysis of specific instincts? And the answer has to be that anything that distracts us from the real problem makes our task of self-knowledge so much harder than Lorenz suspects. And the real problem of the human condition is terror of death and the need for heroic transcendence.

Scientifically, we are distracted by shuffling off to the side of the problem, to flocking instincts and bonding biograms. I am reminded here of the eminent William Ernest Hocking's criticism of psychoanalysis and its focus on sexual problems: he said that these only served to distract us from the real problem of the meaning of the world and of one's life. Similarly, the ethologists distract us. What we want is the central scientific problem at all times; only this can give us any hope of the rational victory that Lorenz, as a scientist, wants.

Man's fate ,then, has to be an open mystery instead of a closed one. This is where, I think, the criticisms of the cultural anthropologist and even some zoologists come to rest. I am not saying that this makes the task any the less monumentally difficult than Lorenz claims it is. If we say that man is a creature with human motives which deny that creatureliness, we are not making it any easier to admit the creatureliness or to relieve the evils of the struggle against it. This is where ethology joins Freud and Hobbes in their merger with Rousseau and Marx. Even if we omit all the excess scientific baggage of 'phylogenetic mechanisms,' we still see exposed the animal underside to the human quest for glory, the fated limitations of man's condition. Today, anyone is scientifically relevant to the enterprise of social science who stands with one foot in somberness and realistic accusation of the self-deceptions of man, of the undersides of human ambition. This is what makes Lorenz, Tiger and Fox and even Skinner, exciting and sobering reading, just as it still keeps the dark Freud contemporary. This, after all is said and done, is the locus of the merger of biology and social science. The Enlightenment mandate of obtaining a realistic picture of human motives has in fact never been closer to being fulfilled.

Chapter 8

DEATH AND DENIAL

The Terror of Death (1973)*

T HE FIRST THING WE HAVE TO DO WITH HEROISM is to lay bare its underside, show what gives human heroics its specific nature and impetus. Here we introduce directly one of the great rediscoveries of modern thought: that of all things that move man, one of the principal ones is his terror of death. After Darwin the problem of death as an evolutionary one came to the fore, and many thinkers immediately saw that it was a major psychological problem for man. They also very quickly saw what real heroism was about . . . heroism is first and foremost a reflex of the terror of death. We admire most the courage to face death; we give such valor our highest and most constant adoration; it moves us deeply in our hearts because we have doubts about how brave we ourselves would be. When we see a man bravely facing his own extinction, we rehearse the greatest victory we can imagine. And so the hero has been the center of human honor and acclaim since probably the beginning of specifically human evolution. But even before that, our primate ancestors deferred to others who were extrapowerful and courageous and ignored those who were cowardly. Man has elevated animal courage into a cult. Anthropological and historical research also began, in the nineteenth century, to put together a picture of the heroic since primitive and ancient times. The hero was the man who could go into the spirit world, the world of the dead, and return alive. . . .

We already have volumes of work and thought on the subject, from religion and philosophy and—since Darwin—from science itself. The problem is how to make sense out of it; the accumulation of research and opinion on the fear of death is already too large to be dealt with and summarized in any simple way. The revival of interest in death, in the last few decades, has alone already piled up a formidable literature, and this literature does not point in any single direction.

There are 'healthy-minded' persons who maintain that fear of death is not a natural thing for man, that we are not born with it. An increasing number of careful studies on how the actual fear of death develops in the child agree fairly well that the child has no knowledge of death until about the age of three to five. . . . Only gradually does he recognize that there is a thing called death that takes some people away forever; very reluctantly he comes to admit that it sooner or later takes everyone away, but this gradual realization of the inevitability of death can take up until the ninth or tenth year.

If the child has no knowledge of an abstract idea like absolute negation, he does have his own anxieties. He is absolutely dependent on the mother, experiences loneliness when she is absent, frustration when he is deprived of gratification, irritation at hunger and discomfort, and so on. If he were abandoned to himself, his world would drop away, and his organism must sense this at some level; we call this the anxiety of object-loss. Isn't this anxiety, then, a natural, organismic fear of annihilation? . . .

The 'healthy-minded' argument just discussed is one side of the picture of the accumulated research and opinion on the problem of the fear of death, but there is another side. A large body of people would agree with these observations on early experience and would admit that experiences may heighten natural anxieties and later fears, but these people would also claim very strongly that nevertheless the fear of death is natural and is present in everyone, that it is the basic fear that influences all others, a fear from which no one is immune, no matter how disguised it may be. William James spoke very early for this school, and with his usual colorful realism he called death 'the worm at the core' of man's pretensions to happiness. No less a student of human nature than Max Scheler thought that all men must have some kind of certain intuition of this 'worm at the core,' whether they admitted it or not. Countless other authorities . . . belong to this school: students of the stature of Freud, many of his close circle, and serious researchers who are not psychoanalysts. What are we to make of a dispute in which there are two distinct camps, both studded with distinguished authorities? Jacques Choron goes so far as to say that it is questionable whether it will ever be possible to decide whether the fear of death is or is not the basic anxiety. In matters like this, then, the most that one can do is to take sides, to give an opinion based on the authorities that seem to him most compelling, and to present some of the compelling arguments.

I frankly side with this second school—in fact, this whole book is a network of arguments based on the universality of the fear of death, or *terror*, as I prefer to call it, in order to convey how all-consuming it is when we look it full in the face. . . . In other words, the fear of death must be present behind all our normal functioning, in order for the organism to be armed toward self-preservation. But the fear of death cannot be present constantly in one's mental functioning, else the organism could not function. . . . And so we can understand what seems like an impossible paradox: the ever-present fear of death in the normal biological functioning of our instinct of self-preservation, as well as our utter obliviousness to this fear in our conscious life. . . . The argument from biology and evolution is basic and has to be taken seriously; I don't see how it can be left out of any discussion. Animals in order to survive have had to be protected by fear responses, in relation not only to other animals but to nature itself. They had to see the real relationship of their limited powers to the dangerous world in which they were immersed. Reality and fear go together naturally. As the human infant is in an even more exposed and helpless situation, it is foolish to assume that the fear response of animals would have disappeared in such a weak and highly sensitive species. It is more reasonable to think that it was instead heightened, as some of the early Darwinians thought: early men who were most afraid were those who were most realistic about their situation in nature, and they passed on to their offspring a realism that had a high survival value. The result was the emergence of man as we know him: a hyper-anxious animal who constantly invents reasons for anxiety even where there are none.

The argument from psychoanalysis is less speculative and has to be taken even more seriously. It showed us something about the child's inner world that we had never realized: namely, that it was more filled with terror, the more the child was different from other animals. We could say that fear is programmed into the lower animals by ready-made instincts; but an animal who has no instincts has no programmed fears. Man's fears are fashioned out of the ways in which he perceives the world. Now, what is unique about the child's perception of the world? For one thing, the extreme confusion of cause-and-effect relationships; for another, extreme unreality about the limits of his own powers. The child lives in a situation of utter dependence; and when his needs are met it must seem to him that he has magical powers, real omnipotence. If he experiences pain, hunger, or discomfort, all he has to do is to scream and he is relieved and lulled by gentle, loving sounds. He is a magician and a telepath who has only to mumble and to imagine and the world turns to his desires.

But now the penalty for such perceptions. In a magical world where things cause other things to happen just by a mere thought or a look of displeasure, anything can happen to anyone. When the child experiences inevitable and real frustrations from his parents, he directs hate and destructive feelings toward them; and he has no way of knowing that malevolent feelings cannot be fulfilled by the same magic as were his other wishes. Psychoanalysts believe that this confusion is a main cause of guilt and helplessness in the child. . . . The child is too weak to take responsibility for all this destructive feeling, and he can't control the magical execution of his desires. This is what we mean by an immature ego: the child doesn't have the sure ability to organize his perceptions and his relationship to the world; he can't control his own activity; and he doesn't have sure command over the acts of others. He thus has no real control over the magical cause-and-effect that he senses, either inside himself or outside in nature and in others: his destructive wishes could explode, his parents' wishes likewise. The forces of nature are confused, externally and internally; and for a weak ego this fact makes for quantities of exaggerated potential power and added terror. The result is that the child—at least some of the time—lives with an inner sense of chaos that other animals are immune to.

Ironically, even when the child makes out real cause-and-effect relationships, they become a burden to him because he overgeneralizes them. One such generalization is what the psychoanalysts call the 'talion principle.' The child crushes insects, sees the cat eat a mouse and make it vanish, joins with the family to make a pet rabbit disappear into their interiors, and so on. He comes to know something about the power relations of the world but can't give them relative value: the parents could eat him and make him vanish, and he could likewise eat them; when the father gets a fierce glow in his eyes as he clubs a rat, the watching child might also expect to be clubbed— especially if he has been thinking bad magical thoughts.

I don't want to seem to make an exact picture of processes that are still unclear to us or to make out that all children live in the same world and have the same problems; also, I wouldn't want to make the child's world seem more lurid than it really is most of the time; but I think it is important to show the painful contradictions that must be present in it at least some of the time and to show how fantastic a world it surely is for the first few years of the child's life. Perhaps then we could understand better why [Gregory] Zilboorg said that the fear of death "undergoes most complex elaborations and manifests itself in many indirect ways." Or, as [C. W.] Wahl so perfectly put it, *death is a complex symbol* and not any particular, sharply defined thing to the child.

We could understand, too, why children have their recurrent nightmares, their universal phobias of insects and mean dogs. In their tortured interiors radiate complex symbols of many inadmissible realities—terror of the world, the horror of one's own wishes, the fear of vengeance by the parents, the disappearance of things, one's lack of control over anything, really. It is too much for any animal to take, but the child has to take it, and so he wakes up screaming with almost punctual regularity during the period when his weak ego is in the process of consolidating things.

Yet, the nightmares become more and more widely spaced, and some children have more than others: we are back again to the beginning of our discussion, to those who do not believe that the fear of death is normal; who think that it is a neurotic exaggeration that draws on bad early experiences. Otherwise, they say, how explain that so many people—the vast majority—seem to survive the flurry of childhood nightmares and go on to live a healthy, more-or-less optimistic life, untroubled by death? . . . . Repression takes care of the complex symbol of death for most people. But its disappearance doesn't mean that the fear was never there. The argument of those who believe in the universality of the innate terror of death rests its case mostly on what we know about how effective repression is. The argument can probably never be cleanly decided: if you claim that a concept is not present because it is repressed, you can't lose; it is not a fair game, intellectually, because you always hold the trump card. This type of argument makes psychoanalysis seem unscientific to many people, the fact that its proponents can claim that someone denies one of their concepts because he represses his consciousness of its truth.

But repression is not a magical word for winning arguments; it is a real phenomenon, and we have been able to study many of its workings. This study gives it legitimacy as a scientific concept and makes it a more-or-less dependable ally in our argument. For one thing, there is a growing body of research trying to get at the consciousness of death denied by repression that uses psychological tests such as measuring galvanic skin responses; it strongly suggests that underneath the most bland exterior lurks the universal anxiety, the 'worm at the core.'

For another thing, there is nothing like shocks in the real world to jar loose repressions. . . . But even more important is how repression works: it is not simply a negative force opposing life energies; it lives on life energies and uses them creatively. I mean that fears are naturally absorbed by expansive organismic striving. Nature seems to have built into organisms an innate healthy-mindedness; it expresses itself in self-delight, in the pleasure of unfolding one's capacities into the world, in the incorporation of things in that world, and in feeding on its limitless experiences. This is a lot of very positive experience, and when a powerful organism moves with it, it gives contentment. As [George] Santayana once put it: a lion must feel more secure that God is on his side than a gazelle. On the most elemental level the organism works actively against its own fragility by seeking to expand and perpetuate itself in living experience; instead of shrinking, it moves toward more life. Also, it does one thing at a time, avoiding needless distractions from all-absorbing activity; in this way, it would seem, fear of death can be carefully ignored or actually absorbed in the life-expanding processes . . . everyone enjoys a working amount of basic narcissism, even though it is not a lion's. The child who is well nourished and loved develops, as we said, a sense of magical omnipotence, a sense of his own indestructibility, a feeling of proven power and secure support. He can imagine himself, deep down, to be eternal. We might say that his repression of the idea of his own death is made easy for him because he is fortified against it in his very narcissistic vitality. This type of character probably helped Freud to say that the unconscious does not know death. Anyway, we know that basic narcissism is increased when one's childhood experiences have been securely life-supporting and warmly enhancing to the sense of self, to the feeling of being really special, truly Number One in creation. The result is that some people have more of what the psychoanalyst Leon J. Saul has aptly called *Inner Sustainment*. It is a sense of bodily confidence in the face of experience that sees the person more easily through severe life crises and even sharp personality changes; it almost seems to take the place of the directive instincts of lower animals. One can't help thinking of Freud again, who had more inner sustainment than most men, thanks to his mother and favorable early environment; he knew the confidence and courage that it gave to a man, and he himself faced up to life and to a fatal cancer with a Stoic heroism. Again we have evidence that the complex symbol of fear of death would be very variable in its intensity; it would be, as Wahl concluded, "profoundly dependent upon the nature and the vicissitudes of the developmental process."

But I want to be careful not to make too much of natural vitality and inner sustainment . . . even the unusually favored Freud suffered his whole life from phobias and from death-anxiety; and he came to fully perceive the world under the aspect of natural terror. I don't believe that the complex symbol of death is ever absent, no matter how much vitality and inner sustainment a person has. Even more, if we say that these powers make repression easy and natural, we are only saying the half of it. Actually, they get their very power from repression. Psychiatrists argue that the fear of death varies in intensity depending on the developmental process, and I think that one important reason for this variability is that the fear is transmuted in that process. If the child has had a very favorable upbringing, it only serves all the better to hide the fear of death. After all, repression is made possible by the natural identification of the child with the powers of his parents. If he has been well cared for, identification comes easily and solidly, and his parents' powerful triumph over death automatically becomes his. What is more natural to banish one's fears than to live on delegated powers? And what does the whole growing-up period signify, if not the giving over of one's life-project? I am going to be talking about these things all the way through this book and do not want to develop them in this introductory discussion. What we will see is that man cuts out for himself a manageable world: he throws himself into action uncritically, unthinkingly. He accepts the cultural programming that turns his nose where he is supposed to look; he doesn't bite the world off in one piece as a giant would, but in small manageable pieces, as a beaver does. He uses all kinds of techniques, which we call the character defenses: he learns not to expose himself, not to stand out; he learns to embed himself in other-power, both of concrete persons and of things and cultural commands; the result is that he comes to exist in the imagined infallibility of the world around him. He doesn't have to have fears when his feet are solidly mired and his life mapped out in a ready-made maze. All he has to do is to plunge ahead in a compulsive style of drivenness in the *ways of the world* that the child learns and in which he lives later as a kind of grim equanimity. . . . This is why people have psychotic breaks when repression no longer works, when the forward momentum of activity is no longer possible. . . .

I think we have reconciled our two divergent positions on the fear of death. The 'environmental' and the 'innate' positions are both part of the same picture; they merge naturally into one another; it all depends from which angle you approach the picture: from the side of the disguises and transmutations of the fear of death or from the side of its apparent absence. I admit with a sense of scientific uneasiness that whatever angle you use, you don't get at the actual fear of death; and so I reluctantly agree with [Jacques] Choron that the argument can probably never be cleanly 'won.' Nevertheless, something very important emerges: there are different images of man that he can draw and choose from.

On the one hand, we see a human animal who is partly dead to the world, who is most 'dignified' when he shows a certain obliviousness to his fate, when he allows himself to be driven through life; who is most 'free' when he lives in secure dependency on powers around him, when he is least in possession of himself. On the other hand, we get an image of a human animal who is overly sensitive to the world, who cannot shut it out, who is thrown back on his own meager powers, and who seems least free to move and act, least in possession of himself, and most undignified.

Human Character as a Vital Lie (1973)*

IF THE BASIC QUALITY OF HEROISM IS GENUINE COURAGE, why are so few people truly courageous? Why is it so rare to see a man who can stand on his own feet? Even the great Carlyle, who frightened many people, proclaimed that he stood on his father as on a stone pillar buried in the ground under him. The unspoken implication is that if he stood on his own feet alone, the ground would cave in under him. This question goes right to the heart of the human condition, and we shall be attacking it from many sides all through this book. I once wrote that I thought the reason man was so naturally cowardly was that he felt he had no authority; and the reason he had no authority was in the very nature of the way the human animal is shaped: all our meanings are built into us from the outside, from our dealings with others. This is what gives us a 'self' and a superego. Our whole world of right and wrong, good and bad, our name, precisely who we are, is grafted into us; and we never feel we have authority to offer things on our own. How could we?—I argued—since we feel ourselves in many ways guilty and beholden to others, a lesser creation of theirs, indebted to them for our very birth.

But this is only part of the story—the most superficial and obvious part. There are deeper reasons for our lack of courage, and if we are going to understand man we have to dig for them. . . . It all boils down to a simple lack of strength to bear the superlative, to open oneself to the totality of experience—an idea that was well appreciated by William James and more recently was developed in phenomenological terms in the classic work of Rudolf Otto. Otto talked about the terror of the world, the feeling of overwhelming awe, wonder, and fear in the face of creation—the miracle of it, the *mysterium tremendum et fascinosum* of each single thing, of the fact that there are things at all. What Otto did was to get descriptively at man's natural feeling of inferiority in the face of the massive transcendence of creation; his real creature feeling before the crushing and negating miracle of Being. We now understand how a phenomenology of religious experience ties into psychology: right at the point of the problem of courage. . . .

But nature has protected the lower animals by endowing them with instincts. An instinct is a programmed perception that calls into play a programmed reaction. It is very simple. Animals are not moved by what they cannot react to. They live in a tiny world, a sliver of reality, one neuro-chemical program that keeps them walking behind their nose and shuts out everything else. *But look at man, the impossible creature!* Here nature seems to have thrown caution to the winds along with the programmed instincts. She created an animal who has no defense against full perception of the external world, an animal completely open to experience. Not only in front of his nose, in his *umwelt*, but in many other *umwelten*. He can relate not only to animals in his own species, but in some ways to all other species. He can contemplate not only what is edible for him, but everything that grows. He not only lives in this moment, but expands his inner self to yesterday, his curiosity to centuries ago, his fears to five billion years from now when the sun will cool, his hopes to an eternity from now. He lives not only on a tiny territory, nor even on an entire planet, but in a galaxy, in a universe, and in dimensions beyond visible universes. It is appalling, the burden that man bears, the *experiential* burden. . . .

[M]an can't even take his own body for granted as can other animals. . . . Man's body is a problem to him that has to be explained. Not only his body is strange, but also its inner landscape, the memories and dreams. Man's very insides—his *self*—are foreign to him. He doesn't know who he is, why he was born, what he is doing on the planet, what he is supposed to do, what he can expect. His own existence is incomprehensible to him, a miracle just like the rest of creation, closer to him, right near his pounding heart, but for that reason all the more strange. Each thing is a problem, and man can shut out nothing. . . .

The historic value of Freud's work is that it came to grips with the peculiar animal that man was, the animal that was not programmed by instincts to close off perception and assure automatic equanimity and forceful action. Man had to invent and create out of himself the limitations of perception and the equanimity to live on this planet. And so the core of psychodynamics, the formation of the human character, is a study in human self-limitation and in the terrifying costs of that limitation. The hostility to psychoanalysis in the past, today, and in the future, will always be a hostility against admitting that man lives by lying to himself about himself and about his world, and that character . . . is a vital lie. . . .

This formulation indicates a great broadening of perspective. Add to it a generation or two of psychoanalytic clinical work, and we have achieved a remarkably faithful understanding of what really bothers the child, how life is really too much for him, how he has to avoid too much thought, too much perception, too much *life*. And at the same time, how he has to avoid the death that rumbles behind and underneath every carefree activity, that looks over his shoulder as he plays. The result is that we now know that the human animal is characterized by two great fears that other animals are protected from: *the fear of life and the fear of death*. In the science of man it was Otto Rank, above all, who brought these fears into prominence, based his whole system of thought on them, and showed how central they were to an understanding of man. At about the same time that Rank wrote, [Martin] Heidegger brought these fears to the center of existential philosophy. He argued that the basic anxiety of man is anxiety *about* being-in-the-world, as well as anxiety *of* being-in-the-world. That is, both fear of death and fear of life, of experience and individuation. Man is reluctant to move out into the overwhelmingness of his world, the real dangers of it; he shrinks back from losing himself in the all-consuming appetites of others, from spinning out of control in the clutchings and clawings of men, beasts and machines. As an animal organism, man senses the kind of planet he has been put down on, the nightmarish, demonic frenzy in which nature has unleashed billions of individual organismic appetites of all kinds—not to mention earthquakes, meteors, and hurricanes, which seem to have their own hellish appetites. Each thing, in order to deliciously expand, is forever gobbling up others. Appetites may be innocent because they are naturally given, but any organism caught in the myriad cross-purposes of this planet is a potential victim of this very innocence—and it shrinks away from life lest it lose its own. Life can suck one up, sap his energies, submerge him, take away his self-control, give so much new experience so quickly that he will burst; make him stick out among others, emerge onto dangerous ground, load him up with new responsibilities which need great strength to bear, expose him to new contingencies, new chances. Above all there is the danger of a slip-up, an accident, a chance disease, and of course of death, the final sucking up, the total submergence and negation. . . .

We called one's life style [character] a vital lie, and now we can understand better why we said it was vital: it is a necessary and basic dishonesty about oneself and one's whole situation. This revelation is what the Freudian revolution in thought really ends up in and is the basic reason that we still strain against Freud. We don't want to admit that we are fundamentally dishonest about reality, that we do not really control our own lives. We don't want to admit that we do not stand alone, that we always rely on something that transcends us, some system of ideas and powers in which we are embedded and which support us. This power is not always obvious. It need not be overtly a god or openly a stronger person, but it can be the power of an all-absorbing activity, a passion, a dedication to a game, a way of life, that like a comfortable web keeps a person buoyed up and ignorant of himself, of the fact that he does not rest on his own center. All of us are driven to be supported in a self-forgetful way, ignorant of what energies we really draw on, of the kind of lie we have fashioned in order to live securely and serenely. Augustine was a master analyst of this, as were Kierkegaard, Scheler, and Tillich in our day. They saw that man could strut and boast all he wanted, but that he really drew his *courage to be* from a god, a string of sexual conquests, a Big Brother, a flag, the proletariat, and the fetish of money and the size of a bank balance.

The defenses that form a person's character support a grand illusion, and when we grasp this we can understand the full drivenness of man. He is driven away from himself, from self-knowledge, self-reflection. He is driven toward things that support the lie of his character, his automatic equanimity. But he is also drawn precisely toward those things that make him anxious, as a way of skirting them masterfully, testing himself against them, controlling them by defying them. As Kierkegaard taught us, anxiety lures us on, becomes the spur to much of our energetic activity: we flirt with our own growth, but also dishonestly. This explains much of the friction in our lives. We enter symbiotic relationships in order to get the security we need, in order to get relief from our anxieties, our aloneness and helplessness; but these relationships also bind us, they enslave us even further because they support the lie we have fashioned. So we strain against them in order to be more free. The irony is that we do this straining uncritically, in a struggle within our own armor, as it were; and so we increase our drivenness, the second-hand quality of our struggle for freedom. Even in our flirtations with anxiety we are unconscious of our motives. We seek stress, we push our own limits, but we do it with our screen against despair and not with despair itself. We do it with the stock market, with sports cars, with atomic missiles, with the success ladder in the corporation or the competition in the university. We do it in the prison of a dialogue with our own little family, by marrying against their wishes or choosing a way of life because they frown on it, and so on. Hence the complicated and second-hand quality of our entire drivenness. Even in our passions we are nursery children playing with toys that represent the real world. Even when these toys crash and cost us our lives or our sanity, we are cheated of the consolation that we were in the real world instead of the playpen of our fantasies. We still did not meet our doom on our own manly terms, in contest with objective reality. It is fateful and ironic how the lie we need in order to live dooms us to a life that is never really ours. . . .

The irony of man's condition is that the deepest need is to be free of the anxiety of death and annihilation; but it is life itself which awakens it, and so we must shrink from being fully alive. . . . What exactly would it mean on this earth to be wholly unrepressed, to live in full bodily and psychic expansiveness? It can only mean to be reborn into madness. [Norman O.] Brown warns us of the full radicalness of his reading of Freud by stressing that he resolutely follows [Sandor] Ferenczi's insight that "Character-traits are, so to speak, secret psychoses." This is shaking scientific truth. . . . But the chilling reality behind this truth is even more upsetting, and there doesn't seem to be much that we can do with it or will ever be able to do with it. I mean that without character-traits there has to be full and open psychosis. At the very end of this book I want to sum up the basic contradictions of Brown's argument for new men without character defenses, his hope for a rebirth of mankind into a 'second innocence.' For now, it is enough to invoke [poet] Marcia Lee Anderson's complete scientific formula: "Stripped of subtle complications [i.e., of all the character defenses — repression, denial, misperception of reality], who could regard the sun except with fear?"

The Nature of Social Evil (1975–posthumous)*

WE HAVE SEEN WITH RANK THAT THE DRIVING FORCE behind evil in human affairs stems from man's paradoxical nature: in the flesh and doomed with it, out of the flesh in the world of symbols and trying to continue on a heavenly flight. The thing that makes man the most devastating animal that ever stuck his neck up into the sky is that he wants a stature and a destiny that is impossible for an animal; he wants an earth that is not an earth but a heaven, and the price for this kind of fantastic ambition is to make the earth an even more eager graveyard than it naturally is. . . .

Our great wistfulness about the world of primitive man is that he managed willy-nilly to blunt the terrible potential destructiveness of the drama of heroism and expiation. He didn't have the size, the technological means, or the world view for running amok heroically. Heroism was small scale and more easily controlled: each person, as a contributor to the generative ritual, could be a true cosmic hero who added to the powers of creation. Allied to this cosmic heroism was a kind of warfare that has always made military men chuckle. Among the Plains Indians it was a kind of athletic contest in which one scored points by touching the enemy; often it was a kind of disorganized, childish, almost hysterical game in which one went into rapture if he brought back a trophy or a single enemy for torture. . . . Today we are agreed that the picture looks something like this: that once mankind got the means for large-scale manipulation of the world, the lust for power began to take devastating tolls. This can be seen strikingly at the rise of the great civilizations based on divine kingship. These new states were structures of domination which absorbed the tribal life around them and built up empires. Masses of men were forged into obedient tools for really large-scale power operations directed by a powerful, exploitative class. It was at this time that slaves were firmly compartmentalized into various special skills, which they plied monotonously; they became automaton objects of the tyrannical rulers. We still see this degradation of tribal peoples today, when they hire themselves out for money to work monotonously in the mines. Primitive man could be transformed, in one small step, from a rich creator of meaning in a society of equals to a mechanical thing.

Something was accomplished by this new organization of labor that primitive man never dreamed of, a tremendous increase in the size of human operations: huge walled cities, colossal monuments, pyramids, irrigation projects, unprecedented wars of booty and plunder. . . .

From the point of view of a Marxist level of analysis, this perspective on history attacks social evil at its most obvious point. From the very beginning, the ravages of large-scale warfare were partly a function of the new structure of domination called the state; the state was an instrument of oppression that had come into being 'artificially' through conquest, and with it began mankind's real woes. The new class society of conquerors and slaves right away had its own internal frictions; what better way to siphon them off than by directing the energies of the masses outward toward an 'alien' enemy? The state had its own built-in wisdom; it 'solved' its ponderous internal problems of social justice by making justice a matter of triumph over an external enemy. This was the start of the large-scale scapegoating that has consumed such mountains of lives down through history and continues to do so today . . . what better way to forge a nation into a unity, to take everyone's eyes off the frightening state of domestic affairs, than by focusing on a heroic foreign cause? . . .

Why has mankind remained locked into such a demonism of power all through history? It is not simply because the slaves have not had the power to throw off their chains; or, as the early Marxists argued, simply because men have forgotten how it was 'in the beginning' before the state stepped on their necks. . . . [This] thesis is still too Marxian and unpsychological; and this has to be remedied . . . only by being completely clear about sacrifice can we get a truly subtle picture of historical demonism.

The Mystery of Sacrifice

[Freud] revealed to us that *the irrational had structure* and so we could begin to understand it. . . . [S]acrifice has been adequately explained on its many levels of meaning, so fortunately we need not go into them all here. Let us just say a few things about sacrifice on its most basic level, where it reveals its essential meaning. At this level sacrifice is . . . an admission of the pitiful finitude and powerlessness of man in the face of the *mysterium tremendum* of the universe, the immensity of what transcends him and negates his significance. At this level, sacrifice affirms *reality*, bows to it, and attempts to conciliate it. Sacrifice, then, is not an irrational aberration, but a basic human reflex of truth, a correct expiation of natural guilt. One basic motive of society, as Brown said, is the symbolic expiation of guilt, which we saw as a very complex phenomenon grounded in the truth of the human condition. Guilt is one of the serious motives of man . . . people bear tyranny because of its rewards not only to their stomachs, but also to their souls. They support tyranny by willingly marching off to war not only because that reduces the frustration they feel at home toward authority, not only because it enables them to project their hatreds on the enemy, but also because it expiates *their guilt*. How else explain the parents that we read about during each war who, when told about the tragic death of their son, have expressed regret that they had not more to give? This is the age-old essence of primitive gift giving; it chills us only by the nature of the sacrifice that they make so willingly and by the secondhand god to whom it is offered—the nation-state. But it is not cynical or callous: in guilt one gives with a melting heart and with choking tears because one is guilty, one is transcended by the unspeakable majesty and superlativeness of the natural and cultural world, against which one feels realistically humbled; by giving one draws oneself into that power and merges one's existence with it.

Furthermore (and this takes us deeper into the problems), sacrifice and scapegoating are not technical tricks to overcome anxiety. [Lewis] Mumford says that the spilling of blood, because it is a life substance, may be a magical effort to make crops grow. Of course. In one of its forms, scapegoating is also magical in origin: a ritual is performed over a goat, by which all the tribe's uncleanliness (sin) is transferred to the animal; it is then driven off or killed, leaving the village clean. But we know by now that all these technical efforts are inseparably sacred ones, which means that they represent not only an arrangement of life but a real spiritual purge that qualifies one to triumph over death. . . . Men spill blood because it makes their hearts glad and fills out their organisms with a sense of vital power; ceremoniously killing captives is a way of affirming power over life, and therefore over death. . . . It relates not only to guilt but fundamentally to power. The sacrifice is a gift, a gift to the gods which is directed to the flow of power, to keeping the life force moving there where it has been blocked by sin. With the sacrifice, man feeds the gods to give them more power so that he may have more. . . . The sacrifice was a means for establishing a communion with the invisible world, making a circle on the flow of power, a bridge over which it could pass. . . . [T]his idea of the flux and flow of power is hard for us to understand today—or rather would be hard if we had not had some experience with it: I mean of course the psychology of the Nazi experience, which served as a grim refresher course on the metaphysics of mass slaughter. . . . Nazis were animated by what [Leo Alexander] calls a 'heathen concept': they had a whole philosophy of blood and soil which contained the belief that death nourishes life. This was 'heathen' indeed: we recognize it as the familiar archaic idea that the sacrifice of life makes life flow more plentifully. Alexander calls the Nazi delight in death a 'thanatolatry,' but I would prefer to talk about a 'death potlatch,' by means of which death is thought to mystically replenish life. . . .

If we understand sacrifice in both its dimensions—as guilt and as the unblocking of power—we can see how logically and unmysteriously warfare had to increase in viciousness: men staged whatever size death potlatch they were technically capable of, from Genghis Khan to Auschwitz. The general opinion is that at the most primitive level of religious organization—that of shamanism—sacrifice of war captives was a rarity; captives could be taken in small number for a variety of reasons, but usually simple sadistic ones like gloating over torture or personal ones like avenging the loss of members of one's own family. . . . [I]n simpler societies expiation for guilt was easier to achieve and required no massive expenditure of life. But as societies increased in scale and complexity, incorporating high gods, a priesthood, and a king, the motive for sacrifice became frankly one of pleasing the gods and building power, and then mountains of war captives began to be sacrificed. When much booty and many slaves were brought back from raiding expeditions, it may have seemed that the purpose was secular and economic, but it was basically religious: it was a matter of arming one's power over life and death; and the lure of economic gain was always outweighed by the magical power of war, no matter how this was disguised. . . . The affirmation of the king's power was much more important than mere possession: power is the ability to dispense life and death for the whole tribe and in relation to all of nature. Allied to this dynamic is another one which we have trouble understanding today: the one who makes the sacrifice dispenses not only power but fate; if you kill your enemy, your life is affirmed because it proves that the gods favor you. . . . [War] was a test of the will of the gods; to see if they favored you; it forced a revelation of destiny and so it was a holy cause and a sacred duty, a kind of divination. Whatever the outcome was, it was a decision of holy validity—the highest kind of judgment man can get—and it was in his hands to be able to force it: all he had to do was to stage a war. . . . As Winston Churchill discovered in one of his first military experiences: "Nothing in life is so exhilarating as to be shot at without result." And as Hitler concluded—after miraculously surviving the bomb blast that was meant to take his life but instead took several others, "Providence has kept me alive to complete my great work." . . . [T]he larger and more frequent the heaps of dead which attest to one's special favor, the more one needs this confirmation. It becomes a kind of addiction to proving an ever-growing sense of invulnerability, to tasting the continually repeated pleasure of survival. . . .

Man is an animal organism who must naturally aggress on his world in order to incorporate the energy-power he needs from it. On the most elemental level this power resides in food, which is why primitives have always acknowledged food power as the basic one in the sacrificial meal. From the beginning, man, as a meat-eating hunter, incorporated the power of other animals. But he himself was a peculiarly weak animal, and so he had to develop a special sensitivity to sources of power, and a wide latitude of sources of power for his own incorporation. This is one way to understand the greater aggressiveness of man than of other animals: he was the only animal conscious of death and decay, and so he engaged in a heightened search for powers of self-perpetuation. Any study of the early evolution of warfare and the natural viciousness of it has to take this into account. Very early in human evolution men aggressed in order to incorporate two kinds of power, physical and symbolic. This meant that trophy taking in itself was a principal motive for war raiding. . . . [T]he piece of the terrible and brave animal and the scalp of the feared enemy often contained power in themselves: they were magical amulets, 'powerful medicine,' which contained the spiritual powers of the object they belonged to. And so trophies were a major source of protective power: they shielded one from harm, and . . . the visible proof of survivorship in the contest and thus a demonstration of the favor of the gods. What greater badge of distinction than that? No wonder trophy hunting was a driving obsession among primitives: it gave to men what they needed most—extra power over life and death. We see this most directly, of course, in the actual incorporation of parts of the enemy; in cannibalism, after victory the symbolic animal makes closure on both ends of his problematic dualism—he gets physical and spiritual energy. An *Associated Press* dispatch . . . quotes a Sgt. Danh Hun on what he did to his North Vietnamese foes: "I try to cut them open while they're still dying or soon after they are dead. That way the livers give me the strength of my enemy."

The Logic of Scapegoating

From the beginning, men have served the appetites of one another in the most varying ways, but these were always reducible to a single theme: the need for fuel for one's own aggrandizement and immunity. Men use one another to assure their personal victory over death. Nothing could be further from the 'irrationality' that Mumford complained about. In one of the most logical formulas on the human condition, [Otto] Rank observed, "The death fear of the ego is lessened by the killing, the sacrifice, of the other; through the death of the other, one buys oneself free from the penalty of dying, of being killed." No wonder men are addicted to war. . . .

Modern man lives in illusion, said Freud, because he denies or suppresses his wish for the other's death and for his own immortality; and it is precisely because of this illusion that mankind cannot get control over social evils like war. This is what makes war irrational: each person has the same hidden problem, and as antagonists obsessively work their cross purposes, the result is truly demonic. . . . Not only enemies but even friends and loved ones are fair fuel for our own perpetuation, said Freud. . . . This is the price of our natural animal narcissism; very few of us, if pressured, would be unwilling to sacrifice someone else in our place. The exception to this is of course the hero. We admire him precisely because he is willing to give his life for others instead of taking theirs for his. Heroism is an unusual reversal of routine values, and it is another thing that makes war so uplifting, as mankind has long known: war is a ritual for the emergence of heroes, and so for the transmutation of common, selfish values. In war, men live their own ennoblement. But what we are reluctant to admit is that the admiration of the hero is a vicarious catharsis of our own fears, fears that are deeply hidden; and this is what plunges us into uncritical hero worship: what the hero does seems so superlative to us. Thus from another point of view we see how right Freud was on enslavement by our own illusions based on our repressions.

The logic of scapegoating, then, is based on animal narcissism and hidden fear. If luck, as Aristotle said, is when the arrow hits the fellow next to you, then scapegoating is pushing the fellow into its path—with special alacrity if he is a stranger to you. . . . If anyone still thinks that this is merely clever phrasing in the minds of alienated intellectuals trying to make private sense out of the evil of their world, let him consult the daily papers. Almost every year there is a recorded sacrifice of human life in remote areas of Chile to appease the earthquake gods. There have been fifteen recent officially reported cases of human sacrifice in India—one being that of a four-year-old boy sacrificed to appease a Hindu goddess, and another involving a West Indian immigrant couple in England who sacrificed their year-old son, following prayer and meditation, to ward off the death of the mother. Freud was right; in the narcissism of earthly bodies, where each is imprisoned fatally in his own finite integument, everyone is alien to oneself and subject to the status of scapegoat for one's own life. . . .

It seems that the Nazis really began to dedicate themselves to their large-scale sacrifices of life after 1941, *when they were beginning to lose* and suspected at some dim level of awareness that they might. They hastened the infamous 'final solution' of the Jews toward the closing days of their power, and executed their own political prisoners—like Dietrich Bonhoeffer—literally moments before the end. Retreating Germans in Russia and Italy were especially apt to kill with no apparent motive, just to leave a heap of bodies. It is obvious they were offering last-minute hostages to death, stubbornly affirming in a blind, organismic way, "I will not die, you will—see?" It seems that they wanted some kind of victory over evil, and when it couldn't be the Russians, then it would be the Jews and even other Germans; any substitute scapegoat would have to do. . . . I don't know how much of a burden of explanation we would want to put on the pool of life-stuff in modern, secular society. For one thing, we no longer believe in the balance of nature; for another, we don't often grant to others the same life quality that we have. But whether or not we believe in a steady pool of life-stuff, numbers are important to man: if we 'buy off' our own death with that of others, we want to buy it off at a good price. . . . This explains the obsessive nature of 'body counting' of the enemy as well as the universal tendency to exaggerate his losses and minimize those of one's own side. People can only lie so blatantly and eagerly when their own lives are at stake; these exaggerations always seem silly to outsiders to the conflict precisely because their lives are not involved. . . . We couldn't understand the obsessive development of nationalism in our time—the fantastic bitterness between nations, the unquestioned loyalty to one's own, the consuming wars fought in the name of the fatherland or the motherland—unless we saw it in this light. 'Our nation' and its 'allies' represent those who qualify for eternal survival; we are the 'chosen people.' . . .

Cultures as Styles of Heroic Death Denial

It is fairly easy to draw the moral from all this, even though it will be shocking to some of the older styles of doing social theory. . . . The important thing about the analyses of Rank, [Kenneth] Burke, [Hugh] Duncan, and [Robert Jay] Lifton is that they reveal precisely those secular forms which the traditional religious dramas of redemption now take. It would be easy to argue that we now have a fairly good working catalogue of the general range of social expressions of basic human motives, and that this represents the completion of the work of the great Max Weber, who had already shown the social dramas of several historical societies, both eastern and western, in the round.

But with our greater and even more tragic historical experience, which includes Hitler and Stalin, we can give the Weberian tradition even more life and critical force: we can extend it from primitive man right up to the modern revolutionary monoliths, all the while basing it on a few universal principles of human motivation. Since there is no secular way to resolve the primal mystery of life and death, all secular societies are lies. And since there is no sure human answer to such a mystery, all religious integrations are mystifications. This is the sober conclusion to which we seem to be led. *Each society is a hero system which promises victory over evil and death.* But no mortal, nor even a group of as many as 700 million clean revolutionary mortals, can keep such a promise: no matter how loudly or how artfully he protests or they protest, it is not within man's means to triumph over evil and death. For secular societies the thing is ridiculous: what can 'victory' mean secularly? And for religious societies victory is part of a blind and trusting belief in another dimension of reality. Each historical society, then, is a hopeful mystification or a determined lie.

Many religionists have lamented the great toll that the Hitlers and the Stalins have taken in order to give their followers the equivalent of religious expiation and immortality; it seemed that when man lost the frank religious dimension of experience, he became even more desperate and wild; when he tried to make the earth alone a pure paradise, he had to become even more demonic and devilish. But when one looks at the toll of scapegoats that religious integrations have taken, one can agree with Duncan that religious mystifications have so far been as dangerous as any other. No world view has a claim on secure truth, much less on greater purity—at least as it has been practiced historically in the social world. [Alan] Harrington, as usual, sums it up very colorfully: "The plotters of earthly and heavenly paradise have fought, slandered and sabotaged one another for hundreds of years. One stands accused of unbridled hubris (risking divine retaliation, jeopardizing everybody's chances); the other of superstition (cringing before mystery); and each finds the other obstructing the road to eternal life." . . .

We don't have to get embroiled in any abstract arguments, because the shape of social theory is clear. If each historical society is in some ways a lie or a mystification, *the study of society becomes the revelation of the lie*. The comparative study of society becomes *the assessment of how high are the costs of this lie*. Or, looked at from another way, cultures are fundamentally and basically styles of heroic death denial. We can then ask empirically, it seems to me, what are the costs of such denials of death, because we know how these denials are structured into styles of life. These costs can be tallied roughly in two ways: in terms of the tyranny practiced within the society, and in terms of the victimage practiced against aliens or 'enemies' outside it. . . .

[Our task is . . .] assessing the cost of scapegoating and by trying to plan for alternative ideals that will absorb basic human fears . . . although death is a natural fear, this fear has always been used and exploited by the established powers in order to secure their domination. Death is a 'culture mechanism' that was utilized by societies from primitive times on as a means of social control and repression, to help an elite enforce its will on a meek and compliant populace. . . . And so we see the fatality and naturalness of human slavishness: man helps secure his own domination by the tribe, the polis, the state, the gods, because of his fears.

When we phrase the problem in these terms, we can see how immense it is and how far it extends beyond our traditional ways of doing science. If you talk about heroics that cost mountains of human life, you have to find out why such heroics are practiced in a given social system: who is scapegoating whom, what social classes are excluded from heroism, what there is in the social structure that drives the society blindly to self-destructive heroics, etc. Not only that, but you have to actually set up some kind of liberating ideal, some kind of life-giving alternative to the thoughtless and destructive heroism; you have to begin to scheme to give to man an opportunity for heroic victory that is not a simple reflex of narcissistic scapegoating. You have to conceive of the possibility of a nondestructive yet victorious social system. It was precisely this problem that was designed by William James over two generations ago, in his famous essay *The Moral Equivalent of War,* but needless to say we have done nothing about it even on a conceptual level, much less on an active social level. Little wonder that things are in a mess.

Chapter 9

BEYOND PSYCHOLOGY

A Conversation with Ernest Becker (1974)*

Ernest Becker: You are catching me *in extremis.* This is a test of everything I've written about death. And I've got a chance to show how one dies. The attitude one takes. Whether one does it in a dignified, manly way; what kinds of thoughts one surrounds it with; how one accepts his death.

Sam Keen: This conversation can be what you want it to be. But I would like to relate your life to your work and I would like to talk about the work you haven't been able to finish.

Becker: That's easy enough. As far as my work is concerned, I think its major thrust is in the direction of *creating a merger of science and the religious perspective.* I want to show that if you get an accurate scientific picture of the human condition, it coincides exactly with the religious understanding of human nature. This is something Paul Tillich was working on but he didn't achieve because he was working from the direction of theology. The problem is to work from the direction of science. . . . I think I have delivered the science of man over to a merger with theology.

Keen: How have you done this?

Becker: By showing that psychology destroys our illusions of autonomy and hence raises the question of the true power source for human life. Freud, Wilhelm Reich, and particularly Otto Rank, demonstrate how we build character and culture in order to shield ourselves from the devastating awareness of our underlying helplessness and the terror of our inevitable death. Each of us constructs a personality, a style of life or, as Reich said, a character armor, in a vain effort to deny the fundamental fact of our animality. We don't want to admit that we stand alone. So we identify with a more

*Original, full text: "The heroics of every day life: A conversation with Ernest Becker by Sam Keen." *Psychology Today,* April (1974), pp. 71-80. Copyright © Sussex Publishers. Reprinted with permission.

powerful person, a cause, a flag, or the size of our bank account. And this picture of the human condition coincides with what theology has traditionally said: man is a creature whose nature is to try to deny his creatureliness.

Keen: And when the half-gods go, the gods arrive? When we abandon our pseudo-control we discover that we are lived by powers over which we have no control? [Friedrich] Schleiermacher, the nineteenth-century theologian, said the human condition was characterized by absolute dependency, or contingency.

Becker: Exactly. I also see my work as an extension of the Frankfurt School of sociology and especially of the work of Max Horkheimer. Horkheimer says man is a willful creature who is abandoned on the planet; he calls for mankind to form itself into communities of the abandoned. That is a beautiful idea and one that I wanted to develop in order to show the implications of the scientific view of creatureliness.

Keen: What are the implications?

Becker: This gets us into the whole problem of evil. One of the things I won't be able to finish, unfortunately, is a book on the nature of evil. I wrote a book called *The Structure of Evil,* but I didn't talk much about evil there. When I got sick, I was working on a book in which I try to show that all humanly caused evil is based on man's attempt to deny his creatureliness, to overcome his insignificance. All the missiles, all the bombs, all human edifices, are attempts to defy eternity by proclaiming that one is not a creature, that one is something special. Searching out a scapegoat comes from the same need to be special. As Arthur Miller said, everybody needs his Jew. We each need . . . someone to kick to give us a feeling of specialness. We want an enemy to degrade; someone we can humiliate, to raise us above the status of creatures. And I think this is an immense datum, the idea of the dynamic of evil as due fundamentally to the denial of creatureliness. Obviously, the idea is that if you accept creatureliness, you no longer have to protest that you are something special.

Keen: But in your writing you stress the need to believe that we are special. You say that we must all be heroes in order to be human.

Becker: That is true. But the important question is, *how we are to be heroes?* Man is an animal that has to do something about his ephemerality. He wants to overcome and be able to say, "You see, I've made a contribution to life. I've advanced life, I've beaten death, I've made the world pure." But this creates an illusion. Otto Rank put it very beautifully when he said that the dynamic of evil is the attempt to make the world other than it is, to make it what it cannot be, a place free from accident, a place free from impurity, a place free from death. The popularity of cults like Nazism stems from the need for a heroic role. People never thrive as well as when they are bringing purity and goodness into the world and overcoming limitation and accident.

Keen: Do you think any of the present political crisis is due to our lack of heroic ideals? Whatever the reality of the Kennedy administration, it did produce a sense of Camelot and a new heroic image. Nixon has given us lackluster and short-haired plumbers.

Becker: Well, America is very much looking for heroes, isn't it? I think one of the tragedies of this country is that it hasn't been able to express heroics. The last heroic war was World War II. There we were fighting evil and death. But Vietnam was clearly not a fight against evil. It is a terrible problem and I don't pretend to solve it. How does one live a heroic life? Society has to contrive some way to allow its citizens to feel heroic. This is one of the great challenges of the 20th century. Sometimes there is a glimpse of constructive heroics—the CCC in the mid-30s, the camaraderie in a just war, the civil rights campaigns. Those people felt that they were bringing a certain amount of purity and justice into the world. But how do you get people to feel that society is set up on a heroic order without grinding up some other society, or finding scapegoats the way the Nazis did?

Keen: In the terms of your understanding of society, it seems to be a Catch 22 problem. If the mass of people are encapsulated in character armor that prevents them from facing the horror of existence, and therefore seeing the necessity for a heroic life, then the mass heroic models must be, by definition, unconscious. Isn't the idea of heroism an elite idea? In The Hero With a Thousand Faces, *Joseph Campbell says the hero's journey is not taken by every man.*

Becker: I am using the idea of heroism in a broader sense. *To be a hero means to leave behind something that heightens life and testifies to the worthwhileness of existence.* Making a beautiful cabinet can be heroic. Or for the average man, I think being a provider is heroic enough. . . . [T]hose are the heroics of the average man. It is not something that one should disparage. . . . But I don't think one can be a hero in any really elevating sense without some transcendental referent like being a hero for God, or for the creative powers of the universe. The most exalted type of heroism involves feeling that one has lived to some purpose that transcends oneself. This is why religion gives the individual the validation that nothing else gives him. . . . In primitive cultures, the tribe was the heroic unit because its members and the ancestral spirits were an audience. The tribe secured and multiplied life and addressed itself to the dead ancestors and said, "You see how good we're doing. We are observing the shrines and we are giving you food." Among some Plains Indians, each person had a guardian spirit, a personal divine referent that helped him to be a hero on earth. I think this accounts for a good deal of the nobility and dignity in some of those

Indian faces we see in photographs. They had a sense that they were contributing to cosmic life.

Keen: It may be much harder for modern man to be a hero. In tribal cultures, heroism had to do with repeating archetypal patterns, following in the footsteps of the original heroes. The hero was not supposed to do anything new. We have thrown away the past and disowned traditional models. So the terror of the modern hero is that he has to do something new, something that has never been done before. We are justified only by novelty. I think this is why modern man (and with women's liberation, modern woman) is anxious and continually dissatisfied. We are always trying to establish our uniqueness.

Becker: Yeah, that's very true. Tillich concluded that for modern man to be heroic, he has to take nonbeing into himself in the form of absurdity and negate it.

Keen: In Buddhism and Eastern philosophy there is an even greater fascination with embracing the Void. The hero is the one who can overcome the desire to exist and embrace nonbeing.

Becker: I have a feeling there is a certain cleverness in Buddhism. Since you can't have what you want in the world, you renounce it altogether; since you can't beat death, you embrace it. They keep talking about getting off the wheel of karma but with tongue in cheek, hoping they will get on again. Buddhism never appealed to me because it lacks an explanation of why we're here. Western man is interested in whys, and causes. Here we are all eggs, placental eggs. We all hatched on this planet and our main life's task becomes to deny that we're eggs. We want to protest that we're here for some higher reason and we've been trying to find out what this reason is. There is no answer, but the reason must be there. And it seems to me Buddhism never tries to answer these questions: Why are we here? Why do eggs hatch on this planet in the form of embryos? This seems to me to be our major question, the one that torments us all.

Keen: You will need to tell me when you are becoming tired because I can come and go as your energy permits.

Becker: Well, I don't know what course my illness is going to take, so I would just as soon get the conversation finished. This fatigue is not going to hurt me terribly. I would like to talk about some of the misgivings I have about my earlier work. One of the big defects with my early work is that I tried to accommodate ideas to the opportunities of the '60s, to be relevant. Recently I have tried to present an empirical picture of man irrespective of what we need or want. Today I hold, with the Frankfurt School, that the only honest praxis is theory. There is nothing honest for the intellectual to do today in the world mess except to elaborate his picture of what it means to be a man. Man is the animal that holds up a mirror to himself. If he does this in an entirely honest way, it is a great achievement. To just run, to be driven without elaborating an image, without showing oneself what one is, this makes a creature very uninteresting.

Keen: Perhaps. But Hegel made just the opposite point: it is in blindness rather than self-knowledge that man serves the purposes of the Absolute Spirit. The cunning of the Spirit is that it uses the partial passions of man to serve the ends of the cosmos. And somehow our self-ignorance is necessary to the whole drama.

Becker: I think Hegel may be right after all. We are here to use ourselves up, to burn ourselves out. But it is still the job of the thinker not to be blindly driven and to try to hold up a mirror for man. It doesn't follow that everyone should be in the business of trying to figure things out. In his study of primitive man, Paul Radin makes the distinction between the thinker and the man of action. The Shaman is a thinker and everybody knows he is an oddball, and not a model for other members of the tribe. But the thinker of today imagines that it is the task of everybody to gain insight and be self-realized. . . .

Keen: Is it accidental that you became fascinated with the question of death and wrote The Denial of Death *and then became ill? Was the fascination a kind of premonition?*

Becker: No. That book was finished a full year before I became sick. I came upon the idea of the denial of death strictly from the logical imperatives of all my other work. I discovered that this was the one idea that tied up the whole thing. It was primarily my discovery of the work of Otto Rank that showed me that the fear of life and the fear of death are the mainsprings of human activity. . . .

Keen: Sometime I want to push you on some critical points. Is your energy high of enough now, or should I wait until this afternoon?

Becker: My energy is good. My mother [Becker points to the intravenous glucose] is working well.

Keen: OK. Here goes. It seems to me you do an excellent job in reviving the lost character realism of the tragic vision of life, but I find a certain distortion in your perspective. Rudolf Otto said that if we look at the holy, at life in the raw, it can be characterized by three ideas. It is a mystery; it is terrifying or awesome; it is fascinating and desirable. You seem to overstress the terror of life and undervalue the appeal. Life, like sexuality, is both dreadful and desirable.

Becker: Well, all right. I think that is very well put, and I have no argument with it except to say that when one is doing a work, one is always in some way trying to counter prevailing trends. My work has a certain iconoclastic bias. If I stress the terror, it is only because I am talking to the cheerful robots. I think the world is full of too many cheerful robots who talk only about joy and the good things. I have considered it my task to talk about the terror. There is evil in the world. After the reports that came out of Nuremberg about the things that were done in the death camps, it is no longer possible to have a naturally optimistic view of the world. One of the reasons we are on the planet is to be slaughtered. And tragedy strikes so suddenly. We must recognize this even as we shield ourselves against the knowledge. All of our character armor is to shield us from the knowledge of the suddenness with which terror can strike. People are really fragile and insecure. This is the truth. . . . I don't know what people would do if they had to live with the knowledge of the suddenness of catastrophe. You just can't worry that any car on the street might strike your child on the way to school. But it might. It is natural for man to be a crazy animal; he must live a crazy life because of his knowledge of death.

Keen: Another critical probe. You say man lives on two levels. He is an animal and a symbol-maker, hence he lives in one world of fact and another of illusion. And our character armor builds the illusory edifices that keep us from the threatening knowledge of the raw facts of life. But it seems to me you fall into the old positivist distinction between fact and interpretation or data and meaning. I doubt that we have anything like a raw world of facts to which we then add a layer of symbolic interpretations. Tillich always insisted: "Never say only a symbol." Symbolic knowledge is the highest form of knowledge we have. How can you justify the position that the factual world elicits only primal terror and certainty of the finality of death? The fact is, we do not know. As Kierkegaard might have said, "Where do you, Ernest Becker, a historical individual, stand in order to give so certain a separation of fact and illusion?"

Becker: Yes, I see. That is a very good point. I don't really know how to answer that. What you are saying is that the symbolic transcendence of death may be just as true as the fact of death.

Keen: Right, but let me elaborate a little. Our modes of thinking about the world are basically dual. We can call them right- and left-brain dominance, or Dionysian and Apollonian, or primary and secondary process thinking. If we take our clues from the rationalistic, or Apollonian, mode of thinking, time is linear and we are all individual atoms that end in death. But in the unconscious there are no straight lines, no time, and no death.

Becker: I see what you mean. I would have to agree that the transcendence of death symbolically, or from the point of view of the whole universe, may be very real. But as a philosopher, I am trying to talk to the consciousness of modern man, who by and large doesn't live in a Dionysian universe and doesn't experience much transcendence of time. I am speaking to the man who doesn't have a canopy of symbols to surround himself with and who is, therefore, quite afraid.

Keen: But our experience of being captives within time and victims of time may be more a sociological than a philosophical datum. It may reflect a judgment we should make about our society rather than about the universe. In most pre-technological cultures, death was not as much of a problem as it is today. In some cultures, death was seen as analogous to the transition from winter to spring and the resurrection of the earth.

Becker: That's right. Certain peoples believed that death was the final ritual promotion, the final rite of passage where the person became individuated to the highest degree. But we don't hold those beliefs anymore.

Keen: But we have to ask ourselves why we don't. . . . Your personal philosophy of life seems to be a stoic form of heroism.

Becker: Yes, though I would add the qualification that I believe in God.

Keen: And to come to that point of trust you must break all illusions?

Becker: Right. The fundamental scientific, critical task is the utter elimination of all consolations that are not empirically based. We need a stark picture of the human condition without false consolations.

Keen: I prefer a more pluralistic approach. On certain days, I operate dominantly as a thinking being; on other days, I am dominantly a compassionate being. And on some few lucky days, I live largely in sensations. From which type of experience should I draw my clues to interpret the world? On hard days, I am a stoic and I know that the courageous thing to do is look straight at the wintry smile on the face of truth. But on those soft days when I am permeable to everything around me, anything seems possible and I know that the courageous way is the one with greater trust and greater openness to what is strange.

Becker: I think that is good and true but it represents a level of achievement. Joy and hope and trust are things one achieves after one has been through the forlornness. They represent the upper reaches of personality development and they must be cultivated. But for people to talk of joy and happiness and to be dancing around completely under the control of their Oedipus complexes, without any self-knowledge, completely reflexive, driven creatures, doesn't seem honest to me. . . . And at that level I don't like to talk about faith and joy. But in the way you express it, I would want to begin talking about a higher human achievement where intellect is left behind and emotional and other types of experience start coming into play. I suppose that in my writing I have been doing an intellectual house-cleaning to make room for the higher virtues.

Keen: In the moment when your mind flips into the space where you can say, 'I am a stoic but I believe in God,' what does the world look like? How do you see yourself?

Becker: Well, I suppose the most immediate thing I feel is relieved of the burden of responsibility for my own life, putting it back where it belongs, giving it back to whoever or whatever hatched me. I feel a great sense of relief and trust that eggs are not hatched in vain. Beyond accident and contingency and terror and death, there is a meaning that redeems, not necessarily in personal immortality or anything like that, but a redemption that makes it good somehow. And that is enough.

Keen: I realize that this morning, I held you at arm's length. My attitude was a perfect illustration of your thesis about the denial of death. I wanted to exile you in a category from which I was excluded—namely, the dying. That is human enough but very silly because it prevents me asking you some questions I would like to ask. As a philosopher, you have thought as hard about death as anybody I know. And now, as it were, you are doing your empirical research.

Becker: It only hurts when I laugh.

Keen: And somehow, I would like to ask you what you can add now that you are closer to experience.

Becker: I see what you mean. . . . What makes dying easier is to be able to transcend the world into some kind of religious dimension. I would say that the most important thing is to know that beyond the absurdity of one's life, beyond the human viewpoint, beyond what is happening to us, there is the fact of the tremendous creative energies of the cosmos that are using us for some purposes we don't know. To be used for divine purposes, however we may be misused, this is the thing that consoles. I think of [John] Calvin when he says, 'Lord, thou bruises me, but since it is You, it is all right.' I think one does, or should try to, just hand over one's life, the meaning of it, the value of it, the end of it. This has been the most important to me. I think it is very hard for secular men to die.

Keen: Has this transcendent dimension become more tangible to you since you became ill or were you always connected through some religious tradition?

Becker: I came out of a Jewish tradition but I was an atheist for many years. I think the birth of my first child, more than anything else, was the miracle that woke me up to the idea of God, seeing something pop in from the void and seeing how magnificent it was, unexpected, and how much beyond our powers and our ken. But I don't feel more religious because I am dying. I would want to insist that my wakening to the divine had to do with the loss of character armor. For the child, the process of growing up involves a masking over of fears and anxieties by the creation of character armor. Since the child feels powerless and very vulnerable, he has to reinforce his power by plugging into another source of power. I look at it in electrical circuit terms. Father, mother, or the cultural ideology becomes his unconscious power source. We all live by delegated powers. We are utterly dependent on other people. In personality breakdown, what is revealed to the person is that he is not his own person. . . . [T]he fundamental deception of social reality is that there are persons, independent, decision-making centers walking around. But the human animal has no strength and this inability to stand on one's own feet is one of the most tragic aspects of life. When you finally break through your character armor and discover your vulnerability, it becomes impossible to live without massive anxiety unless you find a new power source. And this is where the idea of God comes in.

Keen: But that is only one side of the story. When the personality defenses are surrendered, there is more anxiety but there is also automatically more energy, more Eros, available to deal with the world, since less of it is being invested in a holding action. So there is an overflow, a net increase in joy.

Becker: Yes, definitely. There is an increase in creative energies. . . .

Keen: . . . [T]raditionally women satisfied their immortality drive more by creating children than by a fabricating artifacts. Men must create ex nihilo while women have the option of biological reproduction. I think because men's creativity inevitably involves the ephemeral world of symbols, there is greater insatiability among males than females. We make a building or write a book and then we have to do it all over again to keep proving to ourselves that we are creative.

Becker: A book is such a shallow phenomenon compared to a child, isn't it? And it is such transient heroics compared to a baby. I don't know about my work. I think there is an awful lot of femininity in it in terms of the kinds of things I had to feel in order to write. When it comes to the drive toward heroism, I think men are more competitive than women. The whole drama of history is the story of men seeking to affirm their specialness. One war after another has been caused by the efforts of man to make the world into something it can't be. And look at the energy we put into symbolic pursuits. You just can't imagine a feminine Bobby Fischer with that fantastic, energetic devotion to a symbolic game like chess.

Keen: If you were assigned to the job of creating a symbolic portrait of Ernest Becker to accompany this conversation, what would it look like.

Becker: If I had to do a symbolic portrait? Maybe what is significant is that I hesitate every time you ask a personal question. My personality is very much in the background in my work. The only distinctive thing I think I have really achieved as a person is a self-analysis of an unusually deep kind. . . . If I were forced to paint a portrait of myself, the things that come to mind are Rembrandt's successive self-portraits, in which we see him aging and see the effects of his life on his face. First, there would be the young man and every successive portrait would show the face marked by the teachings of life, by the disillusionments. It would show maturity as disillusionment turning into wisdom. But my first choice would be to let my ideas be presented without an accompanying portrait of me. I am very much against the cult of personality. I can't stand actors' faces, or gurus' faces. I object to pushing the image of oneself as the answer to things, as the one who is going to figure things out. . . .

Keen: [Could you talk about your self-analysis?]

Becker: I think that was a big event in my life lasting over a period of years. In my mid-thirties, I suddenly started to experience great anxiety, and I wanted to find out why. So I took a pad and pencil to bed and when I would wake up in the middle of the night with a really striking dream, I would write it down, and write out what feeling I had at certain points in the dream. Gradually my dream messages, my unconscious, told me what was bothering me, that I was living by delegated powers. My power sources were not my own and they were, in effect, defunct. I think if you are talking about analysis, what you are revealing to the person is his lack of independence, his conditioning, his fears and what his power source is. To find my way out of the dilemma, I started exploring other dimensions of reality, theological dimensions and so on.

Keen: How has the theological perspective changed the way you view man?

Becker: Well, for instance, I was once a great admirer of Erich Fromm, but lately I believe he is too facile and too optimistic about the possibilities of freedom and the possibilities of what human life can achieve. I feel there may be an entirely different drama going on in this planet than the one we think we see. For many years, I felt like

Fromm and almost everybody else, that the planet was the stage for the future apotheosis of man. I now feel that something may be happening that is utterly unrelated to our wishes, that may have nothing to do with our apotheosis or our increasing happiness. I strongly suspect that it may not be possible for mankind to achieve very much on this planet. So that throws us back to the idea of mankind as abandoned on the planet and of God as absent. And the only meaningful kind of dialogue is when man asks an absent God, "Why are we here?" I suppose, to use Tillich's terms, I am changing from the horizontal to the vertical dimension: I think a person must address himself to God rather than to the future of mankind. It would be funny, wouldn't it, if Jerusalem did win out over Athens?

Keen: The most passionate statement I heard Tillich make in the years I studied with him was that the genuinely prophetic thinkers in the modern age were those who spend a lifetime combating the Grand Inquisitor. It seems that the visions of apotheoses, of ideal states and of utopias in which there is to be no repression inevitably lead to the five-year plans and the bloodiest political purges.

Becker: The beautiful thing about America is that whatever is wrong with us, we have not gone the road of sacrificing people to a utopian ideal. . . . I think it is the task of the science of man to show us our real condition on this planet. So long as we lie to ourselves and live in false hopes, we can't get anywhere. I don't know where we are going to get, but I think truth is a value, an ultimate value, and false hope is a great snare. . . . It is this passion for truth that has kept me going. . . . It's funny, I have been working for fifteen years with an obsessiveness to develop these ideas, dropping one book after another into the void and carrying on with some kind of confidence that the stuff was good. And just now, these last few years, people are starting to take an interest in my work. Sitting here talking to you like this makes me very wistful that I won't be around to see these things. It is the creature who wants more experience, another ten years, another five, another four, another three. I think, gee, all these things going on and I won't be a part of it. I am not saying I won't see them, that there aren't other dimensions in existence, but at least I will be out of this game and it makes me feel very wistful.

Keen: I hope I will feel that way too. I think the only thing worse would be not to feel wistful. So many people are finished before they die, they desire nothing more, they are empty. . . .

Becker: Well, if you are really an alive person, I don't see how that is possible. You are bound to be more and more interested in experience. There is always more to discover.

The Spectrum of Loneliness (1974)*

WHAT I WANT TO DO IN THIS BRIEF PAPER is to give an overview of the different types of loneliness that emerge in a human life. The first part will be a short introduction to the general problem of loneliness, that is, why people are lonely at all. Then I will talk about the types of loneliness that people are subject to and conclude with the scientific problem that emerges from the study of loneliness: namely, how to incorporate loneliness into an ideal image of man.

The Conditions for the Emergence of Loneliness in Evolution

It is important for us to emphasize, even at the risk of repeating things we already know, how distinctive loneliness is in evolution. Plants have been called poetically and probably truly sleeping animals. They can't move towards one another in any event, They transact with the earth beneath them and the sun, and we can't imagine loneliness to be a part of their experiential being. We can't imagine, either, lower animals such as clams being lonely. If there is loneliness among lower animals, it would be at times of mating when driven by hormonal tonus. Or, for those animals who live with a constant mate, it would be when that mate is absent. Or, finally, for herd animals and primates, it would be when separated from the pack. But these are all instinctive and purely physical reasons. The thing that makes human loneliness unique is that it develops out of a non-physical, non-instinctive sphere.

Man is unique in the animal kingdom because he has the richest interior life. And this is where authentic loneliness emerges. The clam and the rock . . . have little or no interior life. As the cartoon *Broom Hilde* recently put it: Who would want a stupid rock for a friend? It is all exterior, but people are interested in the interiors of objects—which is what makes organisms carry with them more meaning.

What makes this rich interior life? Many things contribute. We know that apes are volatile, highly emotional animals who, because of their large brains, probably already have incipient egos. . . . This means that they already have considerable interiority in the form of images, memories, ability to delay their reactions to the world and keep sensations sorted out. In man, these things are carried to their highest pitch with an inordinately large brain, a long period of mother-child dependence, and the learning of language that results from it. This gives rise to a dual nature with which we are very familiar from the writings of J. M. Baldwin and G. H. Mead: the body and the self come to form distinct areas of experience. The result is that man, alone in the animal kingdom, develops self-objectivity, the ability to look at his body as an object in his field, as something separate from himself, from his insides, where he feels himself authentically to be.

All this is well enough known, but I want to emphasize how implicated it is in

*Original, full text: E. Becker, "The spectrum of loneliness." *Humanitas*, 10: 237-246 (1974). Reprinted by permission.

the problem of loneliness. To an animal who is self-conscious, the body becomes his fate. As [Soren] Kierkegaard already taught us, and as [Otto] Rank, [Erich] Fromm, and others have repeated, this is the meaning of the myth of the Fall. Man is the one animal who does not enjoy oblivious, instinctive living. He is self-conscious, which means that he knows about life and death. The body is the thing that will die, and hence it becomes a major problem to a creature who wants to continue experiencing. The self is the thing that is even more intimate in some ways, but it too has to be explained. Language and thought give one an I that he now has to make sense out of. He must then ask: what does it mean to inhabit a body? to have been created? what am I doing on this planet? Man is placed in the peculiar position of having to make connection with his own inner self. . . .

[T]he main fact of the individual life is that one's existence is a question which must be answered. And the answer can never come from oneself: one cannot explain or justify one's own existence. Self-validation is an impossibility for any creature. A life can only be validated by some kind of beyond which explains it and in which it is immersed. One simply does not know who he is, what his existence means, or even what it can contribute to the life of the universe. These are things one wants to know, that he counts for something, that he makes a difference in the world, that his distinctive face has a meaning, that his insides are there for a reason. And so he must address his existence as a question to the other who is beyond him. First, the other who validates is the parent, then the friend, the lover, the spouse, society, God. Loneliness, as dependency on the other, is built into man. Isolation is unbearable because one is unbearable to oneself. One is a puzzle, feels unworthy, full of contradictions, strange desires, inchoate yearnings, and boundless ambitions. The isolated person has no resources to be able to stand up to the world and to justify himself. This is almost wholly true in childhood and adolescence.

Added Complications to the Problem of Loneliness

Now, this task of finding the meaning of one's life is compounded in several ways. In the first place, by natural narcissism. Each is in his own skin, on his own mission to justify his life. . . . Each strives to make his own distinctive talents unfold. As [Ralph Waldo] Emerson put it, each person has to be ready to create the whole world anew out of himself, if necessary. This brings up a nagging paradox, namely, that all those on whom one is dependent for validation are to some degree strangers to one's deep inner narcissism, and therefore expendable, not capable of imparting solid, unambiguous meaning to one's life.

The second compounding fact about loneliness is that each child has a unique bringing up, a unique family and setting. Thus, he has unique insides, a way of looking at the world that is not quite like anyone else's. This raises the paradox that no one can really understand him or thoroughly validate him because he is completely separate from others in some basic ways most of the time.

A third compounding fact, which is related to the above, is that each person's anxieties and needs are peculiar; he has to solve them in his own way. We are always shocked when we learn how individually others perceive and react to experience: "Is *that* what is troubling you???" As [William] James put it, there is no advice to be given. Or, put another way, there is no really adequate solution to being alone with one's problems.

Finally, the problem of loneliness is compounded by a paradox that results from what we must call *the basic ontological motives of the human condition*. These motives are the familiar ones of Agape vs. Eros, the strivings of man in two different directions. Otto Rank summed them up for psychology by designating them as the universal problem of *sameness vs. difference*. Wilhelm Reich saw them as the intensive longing for, and fear of, freedom. Under the impulsion of Agape, or sameness, man wants to merge with the larger human group, come under its sway entirely, be exactly like everyone else. The person feels lonely when he is different or apart, feels guilty for sticking out. We may remember that as children we often tried to infect others with our contagious disease because we could not stand the stigma of difference and separateness. Under the impulsion of Eros, or difference, on the other hand, the person wants to affirm his own uniqueness, his particular identity, his special talent. He wants to stick out of nature as much as possible, be as unlike others as he can. He then becomes lonely when he is merged in the group, feels estranged from his own true self. This is the cause of the guilt that results from failing to develop oneself. Hence, the paradox which cannot be straightforwardly resolved. To fulfill the Agape motive plunges one into the loneliness of non-individuation. To fulfill the Eros motive plunges one into the loneliness of separation.

We can sum this section up, then, by saying that loneliness is built into the human condition in several ways. By dependency on the other, on a beyond for validating who one is. By natural narcissism and organismic separateness. By the uniqueness of each socialization and the peculiar needs and anxieties it engenders. And finally, by the paradox of Eros vs. Agape strivings, the urge toward both sameness and difference. In sum, there can be no cure for a problem that goes this deep into the human condition.

The Varieties of Loneliness

Having thus reviewed the background of the problem of loneliness, it will be easy to understand the many forms it can take. (I'm sure I haven't covered all of them.)

1. **Developmental loneliness.** This is the simple loneliness of the baby who needs a succoring object and the experience it gives to him. At first it is purely physical, probably related directly to the primate need for succoring and the anxiety of annihilation that results from maternal deprivation. As time goes on and the self is being developed, the loneliness of the child comes to be one of using the object to find out who he is, how 'good' he is, how he qualifies for love and protection, how special he is. Gradually the child comes to discover his place in the world, how he is

supposed to perform, how to be safe, how to get others to respond to him and approve of him according to what he does.

2. **Neurotic (and often clinical) loneliness.** This is related to the above and would characterize the adult who is completely bound to the object for self-validation. He needs a beyond in which to validate himself, but the object becomes his all, so that he has little capacity to tolerate himself unless he is continually immersed in others. He fears losing others as he fears losing his whole world, as he is so dependent on them for validating or otherwise fulfilling his needs. This would probably apply to sadistic types as well as masochistic ones. Otto Rank wrote about this problem with breathtaking insight and breadth.

3. **Maturational loneliness.** This is really a cultural-developmental loneliness in our society, the loneliness of the adolescent who doesn't know what his unique identity is, what his special talents are that qualify him as a cultural and cosmic hero. He wants desperately to know that he has a distinctive contribution to make to world-life, but he hasn't yet found it, and so he can be plunged into an abyss of feelings of unworthiness and futility. Other societies, especially 'primitive' ones, handle this type of loneliness beautifully by the puberty rituals, which automatically launch the adolescent on the road to becoming a performing cultural hero in the particular plot of that society. We leave him floundering in limbo for many years, not knowing the conditions of nor the role for his manhood. Ruth Benedict and others have written perceptively about this problem of negotiating the stages of life so as always to know who one is.

4. **Social-environmental loneliness.** This is the loneliness caused by ways of life which separate people from one another. Modern life is particularly characterized by it, due largely to the automobile, which has abolished neighborhood and village life and substituted instead freeways and life on the move. It is also a characteristic of modern rampant, development-mad urbanism, which has produced cities of incredible ugliness and desolation. There is little public life, few social festivals or markets and such, which were so characteristic of smaller-scale traditional society and which bound people together in identifiable places at regular intervals. Many critics have been at work on this aspect of loneliness and alienation.

5. **The loneliness of psychosis.** Here we must harken back to our discussion of the Eros vs. Agape paradox, which I think is very apt for summing up the problem in a simple and direct way. In schizophrenic psychosis we find an individual who, by accidents of birth and development, feels particularly vulnerable to life, death, and others. When we talk about a normal socialization, we mean one which takes the anxieties of life and death and transmutes them under the protective cover of culture. Culture provides a world-picture that denies human vulnerability, and we call a child 'socialized' precisely when he covers over his natural anxieties with the cultural superego. The schizophrenic is unable to share the agreed cultural version of the denial of vulnerability and death, and so he is isolated from others. He experiences others, and even his own body, as a great threat, and is plunged into the loneliness of

Eros, which takes the form of an acute 'sticking-outness' and difference.

In depressive psychosis, we have a person who feels vulnerable and lonely at the threat of being separated from the objects, or at the failure of his habitual social role to reflect adequate meaning to his life. His socialization into dependency on others and on the cultural world-picture has been only too complete, and he feels the acute guilt of the lack of individuation, of the complete submersion in the Agape dimension of existence.

Each of these two forms of psychosis, then, represents a debt to life that has not been paid, to Agape by the schizophrenic, to Eros by the depressive. It takes a certain organismic solidity and strength to merge with the group in trust and hope. It takes a certain confidence and venturesomeness to pull away from the embeddedness in the objects and affirm one's independence and uniqueness. H. F. Searles and Ernest Schachtel have written outstanding studies on these problems.

6. **Historical-political loneliness.** I am referring here to the self-isolation of the political leader—the type of Hitler or Stalin especially, but every leader to a certain extent. If the schizophrenic suffers the loneliness of his failure to share an agreed world-picture or cultural-action map, then this type of leader suffers from the opposite extreme. He becomes completely part of a stereotyped action map. He uses others to attest to his invulnerability, affirm his greatness, carry out his grandiose and megalomaniac projects. He has before him at all times a performance audience that carries out his wishes, [who] even adjusts reality to suit his wishes by lying to him, withholding information from him, or even killing off large segments of the people who would contradict him and undermine his fabricated reality. The result is that the leader becomes very dependent on his minions and suffers a type of loneliness and isolation akin to that of the depressive, the loneliness of Agape, of being unable to move out of the merger that monopolizes one's whole sense of self, or that fails to express and support convincingly one's deepest personality. The leader no longer knows exactly who he is, can only see his reflection in those around him, a reflection which he himself has programmed, and so must have deep doubts about. He knows at some level of his personality that his beyond is his own creation, and he its creation, and therefore he cannot get really objective or true self-evaluation from it.

7. **The loneliness of individuation.** Finally, we come to the loneliness that is achieved, that is the fruit of a full life, the mark of a mature personality. It is the loneliness of the man who has found his talents, realized his identity, pushed his ambition to the fullest, and achieved something of a success in his life, a recognition of his talents. He is then often put in a position to realize that the superlative achievement of cultural heroism somehow rings hollow. He has, so to speak, achieved himself right out of the agreed cultural world-picture. Its rewards don't deeply satisfy, and his life seems for some reason to have fallen short of his aims and hopes. The reason is, of course, that he developed his talents so well and has been so rewarded for this that he is now in a position to be something of a philosopher of the human condition. He is no longer blindly driven to make his mark on the world, and so the cultural world has

lost its hold over him. It only holds those who run uncritically for its rewards, are still dazzled by its promise. The individuated man is in a position akin to that of Lear after his mental breakdown: he sees the transparency of cultural ambition. And, very much like Lear, he risks madness himself if he continues to run on the treadmill of cultural achievement. There is no sense to it anymore. This is why so many of the great individuated figures of history—Goethe, Plato, Rousseau—at the end of their lives preached a philosophy of renunciation: it was the only way to keep their sanity after the expectations of life have been betrayed.

This is probably a wisdom that not a few achieve in old age, but it is a wisdom that has its disadvantages. The person has lost the support of the agreed cultural world-picture, and he must now himself question the meaning of life. Tolstoy came to this position in his middle life, and was nearly undone by it. He turned to God and to the religious answer to the problem of life as the only way of finding a meaning to it that transcended the now-defunct cultural one. It is the only logical step to take. Unfortunately for the person in this position, there is a great difference between reaching for God and finding him. This is the gulf between belief and faith that Kierkegaard was caught in. One wants to believe that there is a God, even sincerely does. But he cannot take the step to faith, that is, feeling and trusting that God really cares about man, can or will do anything to save man. The individuated person is usually left with the problem of the absent God. This is a distinctive historical achievement, a luxury of civilized man, this loneliness of the extra-cultural personality yearning for an *absent God*. It began in the melee of cultures in the Mediterranean basin a couple of thousand years ago, where men could so easily compare the obsessiveness of competing cultural ambitions and see into their fictional nature. It has reached its pinnacle in the modern world, where the last comforting religious myth has gone into eclipse.

Conclusion: The Great Problem That Emerges from the Study of Loneliness

Even in such a brief and sketchy overview of a deep-going and broad human problem, we have been able to see, I think, two major things about loneliness. One, that it is rooted in the constitution and nature of man and so is an inseparable companion to everyone at some time and in some way. And two, that it is also something that man has achieved, a level of awareness that emerged in evolution and history that gives man a peculiar burden and also a special dignity. He is the only animal who senses that he might have been abandoned on this planet. If I may be permitted a personal opinion, I think this level of awareness might have something in it of a destiny for man, that at his highest point of personal liberation from the constraints of others and of culture, he comes face to face with the problem of the meaning of all of life. And, having come to this, that he can find no secure answer or hope, but only a yearning that has in it elements of both love and despair. Perhaps it is only at this point that one can speak of an authentic religious consciousness for our time, much as the Psalms represented such a consciousness for an earlier time.

I think this is why the great Max Horkheimer, after a lifetime of development of the best sociological thought in the Frankfurt School, now talks about *communities of the abandoned* as the proper level of social-historical consciousness for modern man. This is a powerful, seminal idea that is thrown down as a challenge to students of man and society, and it is one that we must now begin to ponder and discuss. That is, if we can ever begin to agree that the house of science is one in which ideal types of human nature and social arrangements are to be envisaged. What kind of social forms can we begin to imagine, in which the loneliness of individuation could be considered a desirable developmental goal in one's personal life, in place of the frantic drivenness of cultural and national achievement that now characterizes society, along with the goal of continued mental oblivion of old age? What kind of *quality of perception of the absence of God* can we cultivate, so that men may come together without the smugness and righteousness that drives them today, the rigidity of secure and true believers in the idols of money, nationalism, materialistic science? We know that something immense is needed to shock man out of the pathetic yet deadly heroisms to which he has been accustomed. And the first step in this kind of shock is a new openness of perception about the human condition, what it means to have been created on a planet in the sun, why we seem to have been left here to murder and poison ourselves, to wheel and deal in such an idiotic frenzy. With the right intensity and scope of shock, we might even ask ourselves what are we to do with our lives. We might then begin to think of how again to give to people a secure feeling that their lives count, that there is a heroic human contribution to be made to cosmic life in a dialogue with a community of one's fellows. These are gigantic problems, to be sure, and I am not claiming they are answerable in today's world. But they seem to me to be the authentic problems of a fully critical and introspective modern consciousness.

Ernest Becker's Writings

Articles

(1960). Psychotherapeutic observations on the Zen discipline: One point of view. *Psychologia,* 3, 100–112.

(1961). The psychotherapeutic meaning of East and West. *American Imago,* 18, 3–20.

(1961). A note on Freud's primal horde theory. *Psychoanalytic Quarterly,* 30, 413–419

(1961). Private versus public logic: Some anthropological notes on the problem of mental health. *American Journal of Psychiatry,* 118, 205–211.

(1962). Anthropological notes on the concept of aggression. *Psychiatry,* 25, 327–338.

(1962). Toward a comprehensive theory of depression: A cross-disciplinary appraisal of objects, games and meaning. *Journal of Nervous and Mental Disease,* 135, 26–35.

(1962). Toward a theory of schizophrenia: External objects and the creation of meaning. *Archives of General Psychiatry,* 7, 170–181.

(1962). Socialization, command of performance, and mental illness. *American Journal of Sociology,* 67, 494–501.

(1962). The relevance to psychiatry of recent research in anthropology. *American Journal of Psychotherapy,* 16, 660–617.

(1963). Personality development in the modern world: Beyond Freud and Marx. In ed. H. W. Burns (ed.), *Education and the development of nations,* pp. 83–105. Syracuse, NY: Syracuse University Press.

(1963). Social science and psychiatry: The coming challenge. *The Antioch Review,* 23, 353–366.

(1963). The significance of Freudian psychology. *Main Currents,* 19, 45–50 and 61–66.

(1964). Mills' social psychology and the great historical convergence on the problem of alienation. In I. Horowitz (ed.), *The new sociology: Essays on social theory and social values,* pp. 108–133. New York: Oxford University Press.

(1964). The validity of 'Oedipus Complex' as an abstract scientific construct. In E.
W. Count and G. T. Bowles (eds.), *Fact and theory in social science,* pp.
165–179. Syracuse, NY: Syracuse University Press.

(1964). The social psychology of indecent exposure. *Noetics,* 1, 26–31.

(1968). The second great step in human evolution. *Christian Century,* January 31,
135–139.

(1972). The spirit and the ghosts of sociology. *Indian Journal of Sociology,* 3, 79–82.

(1972). Letter from Ernest Becker to Virginia Robinson. *The Journal of the Otto
Rank Association,* 7, 100–101.

(1972). Biological Imperialism. *Transaction: Social Science and Modern Society,* 9
#5, March, 40–43.

(1974). A conversation with Ernest Becker. *Psychology Today,* April, 71–80.

(1974). An anti-idealist statement on communication. *Communication,* 1, 121–127.

(1974). The spectrum of loneliness. *Humanitas,* 10, 237–246.

(1974). Toward the merger of animal and human studies. *Philosophy of the Social
Sciences,* 4, 235–254.

(1977). Letters from Ernest. *Christian Century,* March 9, 217–227.

(1982). Growing up rugged: Fritz Perls and gestalt therapy. *ReVision,* 5, 6–14.

Books

(1961). *Zen: A rational critique.* New York: W.W. Norton.

(1962). *The birth and death of meaning: A perspective in psychiatry and anthropology.*
New York: The Free Press.

(1964). *The revolution in psychiatry: The new understanding of man.* New York: The
Free Press.

(1967). *Beyond alienation: A philosophy of education for the crisis of democracy.*
New York: George Braziller.

(1968). *The structure of evil: An essay on the unification of the science of man.* New
York: George Braziller.

(1969). *Angel in armor: A post-Freudian perspective on the nature of man.* New
York: George Braziller.

(1971). *The lost science of man.* New York: George Braziller.

(1971). *The birth and death of meaning: An interdisciplinary perspective on the
problem of man.* New York: The Free Press.

(1973). *The denial of death.* New York: The Free Press.

(1975). *Escape from evil.* New York: The Free Press.

Important Secondary Works

Articles

Aden, L. (1984). The challenge of Becker: A new approach to pastoral care. *Journal of Psychology and Christianity*, 3, 74–79.

Aho, J. (2002). The transcendent dimension in social science. In D. Liechty (ed.), *Death and denial: Interdisciplinary perspectives on the legacy of Ernest Becker*, pp. 117–124. Westport, CT: Praeger Publishers.

Arcaro, T. and Cox, T. (1988). Human existence as a waltz of Eros and Thanatos. *Humanity and Society*, 12, 75–94.

Barbre, C. (2002). Death anxiety in the treatment of children in poverty. In D. Liechty (ed.), *Death and denial: Interdisciplinary perspectives on the legacy of Ernest Becker*, pp. 105–166. Westport, CT: Praeger Publishers.

Bianchi, E. (1977). Death and transcendence in Ernest Becker. *Religion in Life*, 46, 460–475.

Bregman, L. (1984). Three psycho-mythologies of death: Becker, Hillman and Lifton. *Journal of the American Academy of Religion*, 52, 461–479.

Duncanson, W. T. (2002) Ernest Becker's anti-idealist theory of communication: Death, drama, and purgation. In D. Liechty (ed.), *Death and denial: Interdisciplinary perspectives on the legacy of Ernest Becker*, pp. 149–160. Westport, CT: Praeger Publishers.

Elgee, N. (2002). Mortality anxiety: An existential understanding for medical education and practice. In D. Liechty (ed.), *Death and denial: Interdisciplinary perspectives on the legacy of Ernest Becker*, pp. 137–148. Westport, CT: Praeger Publishers.

Greenberg, J., Pyszczynski, T., and Solomon, S. (2002). A perilous leap from Becker's theorizing to empirical science: Terror management theory and research. In D. Liechty (ed.), *Death and denial: Interdisciplinary perspectives on the legacy of Ernest Becker*, pp. 3–16. Westport, CT: Praeger Publishers.

Hartz, G. (1980). The denial of death: Foundations for an integration of psychological and theological views of personality. *Journal of Psychology and Theology*, 8, 53–63.

Kauffman, J. (2002). The hero and the addict: Reflections on the apprehension of death. In D. Liechty (ed.), *Death and denial: Interdisciplinary perspectives on the legacy of Ernest Becker*, pp. 93–104. Westport, CT: Praeger Publishers.

Kenel, S. A. (1998). A heroic vision. *Zygon: Journal of Religion & Science,* 33, 59–70.

Kopas, J. (1982). Becker's anthropology: The shape of finitude. *Horizons,* 9, 23–36.

Liechty, D. (1998). Reading Ernest Becker: His contribution to spiritual, pastoral and psychological counseling. *American Journal of Pastoral Counseling,* 1, 49–69.

Liechty, D. (1998). Reaction to mortality: An interdisciplinary organizing principle for the human sciences. *Zygon: Journal of Religion & Science,* 33, 45–58.

Liechty, D. (2003). Fascination with violence as a response to mortality awareness. In A. Roland, B. Ulanov, and C. Barbre (eds.), *Creative dissent: Psychoanalysis in evolution,* pp. 161–172. Westport, CT: Greenwood Publishing.

Lipman-Blumen, J. (2002). Our existential vulnerability to toxic leaders. In D. Liechty (ed.), *Death and denial: Interdisciplinary perspectives on the legacy of Ernest Becker,* pp. 161–174. Westport, CT: Praeger Publishers.

Loy, D. R. (2002). The denial of No-Self: a Buddhist appreciation (appropriation) of Becker. In D. Liechty (ed.), *Death and denial: Interdisciplinary perspectives on the legacy of Ernest Becker,* pp. 217–230. Westport, CT: Praeger Publishers.

McCarthy, E. (1981). The sources of human destructiveness: Ernest Becker's theory of human nature. *Thought,* 56, 44–57.

Mowrey, M. (2002). The religious hero and the escape from evil: A feminist challenge to Ernest Becker's religious mystification. In D. Liechty (ed.), *Death and denial: Interdisciplinary perspectives on the legacy of Ernest Becker,* pp. 269–280. Westport, CT: Praeger Publishers.

Piven, J. S. (2002). Transference as religious solution to the terror of death. In D. Liechty (ed.), *Death and denial: Interdisciplinary perspectives on the legacy of Ernest Becker,* pp. 237–246. Westport, CT: Praeger Publishers.

Solomon, S., Greenberg, J. and Pyszczynski, T. (1998). Tales from the crypt: On the role of death in life. *Zygon: Journal of Religion & Science,* 33, 9–44.

Books

Evans, R. (1992). *The creative myth and the cosmic hero: Text and context in Ernest Becker's The Denial of Death.* New York: Peter Lang.

Farrell, K. (1989). *Play, death and heroism in Shakespeare.* Chapel Hill, NC: University of North Carolina Press.

Firestone, R. and Catlett, J. (1989). *Psychological defenses in everyday life.* New York: Human Sciences Press.

Forde, G. (1982). *Justification by faith: A matter of life and death*. Philadelphia, PA: Fortress Press.

Harvey, V. A. (1995). *Feuerbach and the interpretation of religion*. New York: Cambridge University Press.

Kagan, M. A. (1994). *Educating heroes: The implications of Ernest Becker's depth psychology of heroism for philosophy of education*. Durango, CO: Hollowbrook Publishing.

Kenel, S. A. (1988). *Mortal gods: Ernest Becker and fundamental theology*. Lanham, MD: University Press of America.

Leifer, R. (1997). *The happiness project*. Ithaca, NY: Snow Lion Publishers.

Liechty, D. (1990). *Theology in postliberal perspective*. Philadelphia, PA: Trinity Press International.

Liechty, D. (1995). *Transference and transcendence: Ernest Becker's contribution to psychotherapy*. Northvale, NJ: Jason Aronson, Inc.

Liechty, D. (2003). *Reflecting on faith in a post-Christian time*. Telford, PA: Cascadia Publishing House.

Lifton, R. J. (1979). *The broken connection: On death and the continuity of life*. New York: Simon & Schuster.

Loy, D. R. (2003). *Lack and transcendence: The problem of death and life in psychotherapy, existentialism, and Buddhism*. Amherst, NY: Humanity Books.

Martin, S. (1997). *Decomposing modernity: Ernest Becker's images of humanity at the end of an age*. Lanham, MD: University Press of America.

Piven, J. S. (2004). *The psychology of death in fantasy and history*. Westport, CT: Praeger Publishers.

Pyszczynski, T., Solomon, S., and Greenberg, J. (2003). *In the wake of 9/11: The psychology of terror*. Washington, DC: American Psychological Association Press.

Schneider, K. (1999). *The paradoxical self: Toward an understanding of our contradictory nature*. Amherst, NY: Humanity Books.

Sontag, F. (1989). *The return of the gods: A philosophical/theological reappraisal of the writings of Ernest Becker*. New York: Peter Lang Publishing.

Westphal, M. (1984). *God, guilt, and death: An existential phenomenology of religion*. Bloomington, IN: Indiana University Press.

Yalom, I. (1980). *Existential psychotherapy*. New York: Basic Books.

NAME INDEX